Psychotic States in Children

Reprinted 2002 by Karnac Books
6 Pembroke Buildings
London NW10 6 RE
Tel.(0)20 8969 4454
Fax. (0)20 8969 5585

First published in 1997 by
Gerald Duckworth & Co. Ltd.

Reprinted 2003

Library of Congress Cataloguing-in-Publication Data
Psychotic States in Children / edited by Margaret Rustin & al.
1. Psychoses in childen 2. Psychoses in adolescence
3. Developmental disabilities 4. Child Psychotherapy I. Rustin, Margaret. II. Series
[DNLM:1. Psychotic Disorders--in infancy & childhood. WS 350 P9707 1997a]
RJ506.P69P795 1998
618.92'89--dc21   97-44057
DNLM/DLC
for Library of Congress   CIP
ISBN: 185575 901 2

Typeset by Ray Davies

www.karnacbooks.com

Printed and bound in Great Britain by Biddles Ltd., Guildford and King's Lynn

Contents

Contents

Preface

Since it was founded in 1920, the Tavistock Clinic has developed a wide range of psychotherapeutic approaches to community mental-health which have always been strongly influenced by psychoanalysis. In the last thirty years it has also developed systemic family therapy as a new theoretical model and clinical approach to family problems. The Clinic has become the largest training institution in Britain for work of this kind, providing post-graduate and qualifying courses in social work, psychology, psychiatry, child, adolescent and adult psychotherapy and, latterly, in nursing. It trains about 1200 student each year in over 45 courses.

The Clinic's philosophy has been one of influencing mental health work toward therapeutic and humane methods and has, as an aim, the dissemination of training, clinical expertise and research throughout Britain and the rest of the world. This major new book series is designed to make available the extensive experience that the work of the Clinic represents, covering all its departments, specialist workshops and research seminars. The series seeks to be accessible to a wide audience by presenting new approaches and developments in a clear, readable style and at reasonable prices. It will enable the Clinic to describe many aspects both of its established clinical work and of current growing points and innovations in the practice, theory and research of experts in the field.

Psychotic States in Children is one of the first two books of the series. It offers a detailed study of clinical work with psychotic children and adolescents and discusses the recent developments in psychoanalytic theory which have enabled this work to take place. The writers are child psychotherapists with leading expertise in the field and the book is an accessible study of an extremely challenging area of clinical work. It is edited by Margaret Rustin, Maria Rhode, Alex Dubinsky and Hélène Dubinsky.

Nicholas Temple and Margot Waddell
Series Editors

vii

Acknowledgements

The work on this book has been supported by the generosity of many colleagues. It was an honour for us that our book was one of the books chosen to launch the Duckworth/Tavistock Clinic Book Service, and we thank Nick Temple and Margot Waddell at the Tavistock and Robin Baird-Smith at Duckworth for bringing this project to fruition.

Secretaries at the Tavistock have been most patient in typing early drafts and we should like to thank in particular Eleanor Morgan and Michèle and Marcos de Lima for presiding calmly over the production of the final text. Margaret Walker, the Tavistock librarian, has also been most helpful to us.

Other individuals who deserve special thanks are Daphne Briggs for translation of Geneviève Haag's chapter, Richard Graham for help with the formulation of some entries in the Glossary, Bill Young and Wendel Caplan for drawing Maria Rhode's attention to papers by Kilchenstein and Schuerholz, and Robertson.

As editors we have benefited enormously from the thoughtful and attentive discussion of each other's writing, and have learnt a great deal from the theoretical and clinical debates the work has generated among us. This mutual support and encouragement has been a great pleasure.

Families always deserve a mention for their forbearance during the writing of books. We should like to add a special thank you to Michael Rustin for his original suggestion that such a volume would be a worthwhile contribution to child psychotherapy theory and practice. Finally, we wish to acknowledge the courage of our patients and the devotion of their parents. Their commitment to the psychotherapeutic process has been an inspiration to us. All names and personal details have, of course, been changed to protect confidentiality.

The Editors

Introduction

Margaret Rustin

This book is intended to represent the psychotherapeutic approach to psychotic children and adolescents which has been found helpful by child psychotherapists trained at the Tavistock Clinic.

These children are often deeply cut off and immersed in their private delusory world. The extreme psychological pain which characterises their experience can easily overwhelm them – terror, confusion, panic, and madness take over. In attempting to gain relief from their mental tortures, they sometimes find it through inflicting their distress on others, and sometimes through bizarre behaviour whose purpose is to protect them from unbearable states of tension. When these defensive measures shut out or confuse the adults attempting to care for and educate them, the consequences can be devastating. Families, teachers and others in close contact become baffled, upset and acutely anxious. Below the surface of their conscious emotions, those affected by the children's disturbance are likely to be enraged, terrified and disturbed in turn by their own emotional response, since these children do not respond in comprehensible ways to the ordinary demands of life, and they bewilder those around them. Having a psychotic child as part of a family usually means that the family home to some degree becomes like a hospital, providing special care for a distressingly fragile member, and making it hard for the rest of the family to recognise themselves as part of the ordinary world. To find ways to treat these children and help them to rejoin the human community, so that their appalling isolation and their family's suffering can be ameliorated, is the aim of the work described in these pages.

Psychoanalysis has developed theories which make it possible to think about the primitive emotional experiences at the core of psychosis. The understanding of the absence of symbolic capacities, of concrete thinking, of states of extreme withdrawal and mania, of massive confu-

1

sion and disorders of thinking has been revolutionised by the work of Klein, Bion, Segal, Rosenfeld, Joseph and others working in the British psychoanalytic tradition. While their ideas have had an impact on thinking about the broad range of adult mental illness, the literature on psychosis in children and young people has tended to focus rather more on autism. The contributions of Meltzer, Tustin and Alvarez in elucidating the phenomena of the failure of development in autistic children has opened up new approaches to psychotherapy for this group. Perhaps there is something particularly poignant about the often rather frozen state of being in autistic children – they seem so helplessly trapped in their private worlds, and Alvarez's concept of reclamation and the more active therapeutic techniques now practised seem to fit this aspect of autism.

Where does this leave the theorisation of non-autistic psychosis in children? The difficulty in facing the even more actively and openly destructive schizophrenic-type illnesses is only too understandable. It is profoundly disturbing to encounter the active turning away from life, the degree of perversity and hatred and the destruction of reality inherent in madness, and to see this in children is doubly difficult. Nonetheless, it is clear that meaningful communication can be achieved with such children in psychoanalytic psychotherapy. A space for this approach to treatment does not involve giving priority to particular theories of aetiology, but rests on a commitment to the relief of psychic suffering, and the conviction that a richer description of the phenomenology of the children's inner worlds is one useful component in an overall understanding of childhood psychosis. Children have a life ahead of them, and the forces of growth and development provide a potential ally for therapeutic interventions. The child's family, too, can supply crucial support, when parents are offered appropriate help for themselves.

The clinical work reported in this book relies on a broadly classical psychoanalytic technique. The maintenance of a consistent setting, the patient observation of all that takes place within the therapy, the systematic attention to the unfolding of the transference and the countertransference, and interpretation at the moment and in the mode in which the child can comprehend are the central features. While reassurance is not part of this approach, containment of distress is the therapist's initial aim.

We hope to add to the as yet small body of published work about psychoanalytic approaches to such ill children. The range of contributors demonstrates that there is interest in work of this kind and a

2

gradually growing range of experience available for reflection. Quality of clinical description has been a prime aim of the editors: the fine detail of the observation of the children and their relationship with their therapists is what permits theoretical conjecture. A fuller understanding of psychotic levels of disturbance in young children and adolescents has the potential to contribute something fresh to psychoanalytic thinking about the complexities of human development and about adult mental illness, and it is our hope that the book will be read with these wider considerations in mind.

The book is organised as follows: there are two introductory chapters, one to lay out the psychoanalytic theories which underlie the clinical approach described, and one to provide an example of work-in-progress, through the description of one session with a child emerging from a psychotic state of mind. The core of the book consists of clinical description, and the cases discussed have been organised in three sections. In the first, we consider children and adolescents whose psychotic breakdowns have followed massive sexual abuse, and for whom the abuse has clearly been a major precipitating cause. In the second, we discuss children who manifest severe developmental delay in conjunction with their psychotic illness. In some instances, there is clear evidence of non-specific brain damage, and in others this is more uncertain. In the third section we present cases where there is a complex mixture of aetiology and of symptomatology, an entwining of factors intrinsic to the child with traumatic impingements of various kinds, and a complicated balance of forces within the children's nature. Each section is followed by an editorial commentary on the clinical cases, drawing out some of the clinical and theoretical implications. A postscript indicates some lines of further research and places the provision of child psychotherapy in its national context.

It is essential to keep in mind that the difficulty in comprehending the nature of childhood psychosis is profound, and that the understanding of its multiple causes is only just beginning. All workers in this field depend on a multi-disciplinary approach in which the contributions of different specialists can be appreciated. Care for the children, adolescents and their families depends on good working relationships between a wide variety of health, education and social service professionals. Indeed, skilled work in support of the parents is a fundamental requirement for any effective intervention. At the same time, the nature of the illness tends to impact on professional networks in damaging ways, causing splitting and confusion, intensifying rivalries and undermining co-operativeness. We hope that this book will contribute to

3

de-mystifying the particular contribution child psychotherapists can make. The special setting and techniques of their work can offer containment for the extreme anxieties of the children and support the development of shared meaning, thus enabling them to make better use of school and family life. The organic element in psychotic illness is a matter of intense current research effort. We see this as going alongside the psychoanalytically-based exploration of the strange inner worlds of these children. The evidence we have from 25 years of work is that feeling understood and coming to understand themselves a bit more is a great source of relief to the children, and opens up the possibility of more fruitful relationships.

Theoretical Overview

The Apprehension of Emotional Experience

Alex Dubinsky

... Better I were distract:
So should my thoughts be sever'd from my griefs
And woes by wrong imaginations lose
The knowledge of themselves. (King Lear, IV. vi. 278-281)

Psychotic states of mind are characterised by a profound disturbance in the sufferer's relationship to reality, internal and external. At the level of description associated with the practice of psychoanalytic psychotherapy, these mental states can be explicated in terms of a severe disruption in the apprehension of emotional experience.

The view taken in this chapter is that psychotic states occur in response to mental pain beyond the endurance of the ego. This can be due to the nature of the emotional experience or to the immaturity of the personality. When these states become the habitual way of coping with mental pain, the development of the personality is profoundly affected and mental illness sets in.

The failure of the capability to comprehend emotional experience will be discussed first. This failure leaves emotional experience in a form suitable only for manipulation and projection, but not for symbolic thinking. Mental pain is then not amenable to modification, while recourse to concrete thinking causes confusion.

The other kind of psychotic disruption in the apprehension of emotional experience discussed in this chapter is caused by ordinary defence mechanisms *when they are used to excess*. Instead of seeking to modify mental pain through understanding, the self resorts to these defences in an effort to avoid suffering. Splitting, for instance, destroys the cohesion of the self, and of mental experience. The self is then prevented from apprehending part, or the whole, of the experience.

5

When projection and the identificatory aspects of projective identification are in operation, the emotional experience becomes confused with that of another person. Vulnerable parts of the self are ignored and dependence on parental figures is denied because of omnipotent narcissism. When associated with concrete thinking, which occurs as a result of the failure of the capability to comprehend emotional experience, the phantasy of intruding into the internalised mother induces a confusion between phantasy and reality.

These issues, together with the role of helplessness and omnipotence, will be discussed in the light of clinical experience with children and adolescents, within the theoretical framework provided by the Kleinian tradition. The present considerations make no pretence of being exhaustive. Only passing reference is made to autism (see Part III of this book), and manic depressive psychotic states are not discussed. The role of extremely dangerous internal objects (Klein 1958, pp. 240–1) is examined in Part I, Discussion.

The Capacity to Comprehend Emotional Experience

By emotional experience will be meant the conjunction of emotions, sense impressions and thoughts, including unconscious phantasies, present to the mind at a given moment. In this definition, Bion's concept of emotional experience is extended to include thoughts (as distinct from the process of thinking), and, in particular, unconscious phantasy. This broadening of the concept corresponds to the presupposition that emotions and sense impressions are embedded in a matrix of thoughts and fantasies, however primitive. It makes possible descriptions such as: 'the child's emotional experience in entering the room was such that he wanted to soil it; part of the experience was his association of the room with his mother's mental space which, in his phantasy, had been taken over by his younger brother.'

The capacity to comprehend sense data and emotions was called alpha function by Bion (Bion 1962, pp. 5-6). The Alpha function transforms sense impressions and emotions into a form appropriate for symbolic thinking. In this chapter we will make use of the broader notion of *emotional comprehension*, the particular form of thinking which, when applied to emotional experience, understood as a conjunction of emotions, sense impressions and thoughts,[1] transforms it in a form suitable for symbolic thinking. In the absence of emotional comprehension, the emotional experience remains indistinguishable from the presence of a concrete object, the 'thing-in-itself': that which, in the

6

external world is assumed to be the occasion of the emotional experience (cf. Bion 1962, p. 6).

This conceptual framework, quite simple in its outline, has profound implications since it makes explicit the intimate link between thinking and emotionality. Without the transformation which emotional comprehension provides, emotional experience remains in a form only usable for evacuation by projection or for retention as 'undigested' memory. Untransformed emotional experience leads to acting out, as when the boy who wanted to dirty the room proceeded to soil it with debris of food taken from his school bag and with spit.

Emotional comprehension may be severely affected by certain aspects of the emotional experience, such as over-intense emotion, and in particular mental pain, or a powerful sense of omnipotence, or the thoughts and unconscious fantasies (and thus the relationship with internal objects) present to the mind. Clinical evidence shows that the therapist's role is often that of supplementing the patient's emotional comprehension. The chapters by Lynda Miller and Deborah Sussman demonstrate how psychotic children project into the therapist 'undigested pain' until it can be made tolerable by thinking. When it is not fully evacuated by projection, persecutory experience can be felt as a concrete presence fixed in the mind. It then torments the patient until it is transformed by thinking.

The name of containment is usually given to the relationship described by Bion as that between 'container' and 'contained'. This concept is an abstraction based on the model of a mother (the container) who, through her comprehension, transforms the painful projections (the contained) from her baby in such a way that the baby can then introject them back into a tolerable form. Bion suggested that part of alpha function results from the introjection of the relationship between container and contained (Bion, 1962, pp. 90-1): part of alpha function is provided by internalised parents who are capable of understanding emotional experience. We will assume the same is true for emotional comprehension. The personality may be lacking in its capacity for containment because this introjection has not taken place or because, in phantasy, the internal parents are being denied their role.

Concrete Thinking and Terror

Failure of emotional comprehension gives rise to a confusion between emotional experience and the presence of the 'thing-in-itself'. This confusion often results in the non-differentiation between thoughts,

7

sense impressions, emotion and the 'thing-in-itself' (see the description in Bion, 1962, pp. 57-8). As a consequence the object of the thought is assumed to exist in external reality (this may not be true) and is not distinguished from the representation of the thought by words, mental images or situations in external reality (for instance children's play, films, stage representations or traumatic situations). This latter confusion corresponds to the thought disorder known as concrete thinking (or symbolic equation Segal 1957).

A play session[2] will illustrate the difference between symbolic thinking and concrete thinking. A young patient, Anna, who was five years old, had some autistic traits. Her capacity to symbolise was at first in evidence, as she said: 'This is Anna' while pointing, in a familiar book about a group of children, to a drawing of a little girl sitting in the mud (Anna, who often looked unkempt, always identified with her). Anna was then read the story of the Ugly Duckling. She was upset when the other animals mocked him and was now identified with him. Anna was then told a fairy tale where larger and larger animals get inside a tower. She chose to play with some new toys used to illustrate this story and she tried to get a red cockerel in between the crossed beams at the top of the tower. A bear was supposed to be the next to get inside, but Anna now lifted her foot and tried to climb on the minuscule ladder leading to the tower.

Anna was in projective identification with the girl in the mud and the ugly duckling, and with the animals entering the tower, but in the first two instances, she knew these were characters in a story and not in external reality (the pictures in the books and the corresponding stories were thus functioning as symbols). With the new toys, the excitement became too intense and became confused with her thoughts about the story, with her perception of the toys and with the 'thing-in-itself'. The imaginary world of the fairy tale became confused with the reality of the toys used to represent it.

Concrete thinking was also in evidence in the therapy of Juliet, an adolescent with a severely schizoid pathology, who was finding the interruption between sessions very difficult, although she denied it. This isolated girl tried to foster the sense that I belonged to the family circle by telling me of all the people they knew. One of these acquaintances had the same surname as a statesman who had died some years before. The patient's speech became confused as she attempted to explain that these were two different people. She had been trying to give herself the illusion that she could muster the immediate presence of people by naming them. This imaginary presence had become confused not only with the name of the man she knew, but also with the thought of the politician. She could no longer understand that two different people could have the same family name.

Concrete thinking can be due to a lack of containment (Segal 1979). It can also be due to the very nature of the emotional experience. Omnipotence causes intense emotion to be confused with thought. The intensity of the emotion is then taken to be evidence of the presence of the 'thing-in-itself', as in the case of Anna and the new toys. Sometimes just the thought of a ghost can terrify a child. An unsettling coincidence between fantasy and external reality can also suggest the presence of the 'thing-in-itself'. For instance, some children believe they hear ghosts if someone walks past the door of the therapy room or the wind blows outside at a moment when, in phantasy, they are at the mercy of their persecutors. When the persecutors in a phantasy are perceived as being actually present, concrete thinking gives rise to feelings of terror since the omnipotence pertaining to the phantasy is attributed to the persecutors.

Failure of emotional comprehension can lead to murderousness (cf. Bion 1962, pp. 5-6) or self-destructive impulses. This is illustrated by a session with Jim, a meek ten-year-old patient, who had a delusional fear of another boy. As he talked of his resentment of this boy's teasing, it became clear that he was driven to distraction by his fear of this boy. The omnipotent persecuting brother in the patient's murderous phantasies, the boy at school, and the fear he had of them, were becoming confused in his mind. Jim was desperately upset and, as he felt the need to concretely suppress this unbearable experience, he announced that he would harm either the other boy or himself.

Mental Pain, Helplessness and Omnipotence

Like pleasure, mental pain is a quality of emotional experience. It is attached to feelings such as jealousy, envy or humiliation. Anxiety, depressive or persecutory, is a particular form of mental pain.

Children and adolescents susceptible to psychotic states show a profound helplessness, often hidden by omnipotence. This helplessness corresponds to an inability to comprehend certain experiences of mental pain. Clinical work shows that these experiences reflect earlier situations where the mental pain was not matched by the capacity of the self, often still very immature, for comprehension. Besides instances of actual trauma, such as abuse or physical illness, the history may show that the child was deprived of emotional attention by a mother distracted by preoccupation or depression. The child may have felt displaced by the birth of a sibling, or experienced the pain of being abandoned, possibly for other children, as the parents separated. The pain of the Oedipal conflict may have been left unattended by a divided parental couple. The adolescent may have felt unequal to the new demands made by examinations and the peer group. The severity of the disturbance is not proportionate to the gravity of the early situation. Other significant factors include the internalised capacity for containment and, more generally, the quality of the internalised parental figures. Determinant too is the choice of defence mechanisms and the extent to which they were used in the course of development. Constitutional factors seem also to play an important role.

The sense of helplessness and, more generally, mental pain can be obviated through recourse to omnipotence. However, omnipotence is not 'a defence in itself but only ... an adjunct, a potentiator, of defensive operations such as omnipotent control over objects ... this excited state of mind would contain the attitude, "I can do it", whatever the "it" at issue may be, not "I can do everything". It is a transient state whipped up in relation to a task at hand' (Meltzer 1967, pp. 100-1).

The role of omnipotence is obvious in the pathology of the boy I called Jim. This timid child was obsessed with make-believe and with attempts at building impossibly over-ambitious large-scale models (cars, a show-jumping course, a snooker table . . .). It became apparent that when he thought about these models and became breathless with excitement, he was trying to evade some frightening emotional experience. The import of the models was that in his eyes they confirmed his delusion that he could instantly become grown-up and thereby, he believed, avoid the pain of helplessness.

As Klein indicated, omnipotence is intimately linked with the phantasies characteristic of such defence mechanisms as splitting, projective identification and phantasies of intrusion which we will consider below. Although the function of these defences is the avoidance of mental pain they generate additional psychic suffering. The resulting deterioration of the personality and of the capacity to think, and the consequent social isolation, are the source of new torments. The confusions induced by projective identification and phantasies of intrusion elicit the fear of madness and, in conjunction with concrete thinking, they evoke terror.

Theoretical Overview

Splitting

Klein described splitting as the process whereby 'feelings and relations (and ... thought processes) [are] cut off from one another' (Klein 1946, p. 6). Emotional experience is thus profoundly altered and painful aspects of reality may be obliterated. Splitting often obtrudes in clinical experience as a splitting of the self or as a splitting of the object (that is, a splitting apart of some aspects of another person), but the two appear to be indissolubly linked, as Klein suggested (1946, p. 6).

Splitting can result from an active attack performed in phantasy on the cohesion of the self (Klein, 1946). Splitting can also be a passive response of the self to mental pain beyond endurance. This corresponds to the passive splitting described by Klein as a 'falling to pieces' of the ego (and of the self) (1946, p. 5). Bick (1968) described the early means (the second skin processes) by which such disintegration can be prevented. The dismantling (Meltzer, Bremner, Hoxter, Weddell, Wittenberg 1975) which is characteristic of autism corresponds to such passive splitting.

Splitting divides the self into separate parts. This can be recognised in everyday life as, according to circumstances, people often present distinct facets of their personality equipped with different attributes. Some splitting of the self seems necessary: even in a child a responsible, adult and courageous part of the self becomes differentiated from a more vulnerable but also more demanding infantile part (this is the horizontal splitting of the self described by Meltzer (1967, p. 37 and p. 103). Such splitting allows for some of the inherently conflicting demands originating from the self to remain unresolved. As Klein showed, a central form of splitting is that which keeps apart love and hatred when confusion threatens. It keeps apart good and bad objects, loving and hating aspects of the self. Often, the adult part of the self can also be distinguished from omnipotent or destructive or delinquent parts. Different lines of partition are possible and contribute to the determination of character. While some parts of the self are more apparent, some others may remain in the background while still wielding influence, beneficial (for instance the sane part of the personality of the psychotic, Bion 1957), or noxious (for instance a hidden destructive or omnipotent part of the personality, as we will see when we consider omnipotent narcissism). The division of the self into parts appears clearly in dreams as these different facets of the personality are often incarnated in different people. Further evidence of the existence of

11

recognisable parts of the self is provided by their projection into others, which we will consider when we discuss projective identification.

Splitting belongs to ordinary mental life. However, a rigid or wide splitting apart of the self leads to severe deterioration, as the self is rendered unable to tolerate mental pain. The splitting is then maintained with desperation and ever greater rigidity as a protection against psychic suffering.

Rigid splitting consistently prevents different parts of the personality from co-operating in facing emotional experience, which is correspondingly divided. The isolated parts of the self cannot support the modification of mental pain by bringing together both their own resources and those of their respective internal objects. Learning from experience is impaired, and emotional and intellectual immaturity ensue. A common pathological instance is that of a personality systematically dominated by parts of the self concerned with promoting a sense of omnipotence, while vulnerability is cut off: the dominant parts of the self avoid reality through recourse to omnipotence, while the vulnerable part is mostly isolated from reality and cannot grow up. This was the case for Jim and also for Paul, a boy with severe developmental delay (Part II, Chapter 4).

A great width in the splitting leads to instability, as markedly distinct parts of the self alternate in their dominance of the personality. Again learning from experience is impaired as the apprehension of reality is parcelled out in apparently disparate episodes. In the case of splitting and idealisation, this is the familiar oscillation as the part of the self concerned with the appreciation of the good and beautiful and reassuring, alternates in its dominance with a part which experiences the bad and ugly and painful. For Jim and Paul, the width of the split led to moments of collapse, sometimes followed by outbursts of desperate violence, when the experience of helplessness displaced the omnipotent part of the self: the part of the self which came to the fore was so vulnerable and defenceless that it could not deal with feelings of persecution. It was replaced by a destructive part of the self which incited these boys to violence in the cause of survival.

The case of Juliet further illustrates the effects of a wide and rigid splitting of the self. Her condition had markedly deteriorated in adolescence when she had to sit for school examinations and suffered from paranoid delusions. She wanted to stay at home and limit to the utmost her social contacts. This was the view proposed by the apparently reasonable part of her personality, which could be engaged in talking but explicitly denied the very existence of feelings, and of an infantile self. In the first months of therapy, Juliet's face was mostly expressionless. Often, however, while she talked in a reasonable manner her face became contorted with rage and she would briefly interrupt what she was saying and shout abuse or scream in a high-pitched voice or laugh loudly. There seemed to be two different patients in the room, as an angry and crazy part of her abruptly interrupted the saner, apparently grown-up part. It became clear that the angry part was enraged at the pain involved with feeling. Most of Juliet's capacity for hatred seemed to be located in this angry part. The more reasonable part of her disapproved of any form of violence, but showed in this real fanaticism, probably under the influence of the angrier crazy part. The more reasonable part seemed however to keep the crazy part mostly in check and at a distance in order to preserve her sanity. Both parts were over-critical, arrogant and contemptuous, and thus omnipotent. A third part of her personality, vulnerable and hurt, seemed out of reach, except that remnants of pain informed what Juliet was saying. The pain was that of feeling worthless. In her phantasy, she was abandoned for rival siblings.

Mental pain can be avoided by isolating thinking from feeling. The blinded Gloucester exclaims, when he meets Lear who has become insane:

So should my thoughts be sever'd from my griefs

The rigid avoidance of emotional experience is associated with the schizoid end of the spectrum of mental disturbances.

Splitting may cause some specific intellectual function, such as memory, or the capacity to think symbolically and to understand metaphor, to be cut off in order to prevent the making of painful emotional links between certain thoughts (Bion 1959). An even more thorough fragmentation leads to the minute splitting of the self described by Bion, or the disintegration described by Rosenfeld (1947, pp. 26-29) and thus cause the cessation of thinking and feeling. Such fragmentation is in evidence with traumatised children (see Part I, Chapter 3) or adolescents (see Part I, Chapter 2).

Fragmentation also affects adolescents suffering from schizoid disorders. Juliet was often in a stupor at the beginning of her session. She would emerge from this state of disintegration to give a factual account of some social network: family, friends of the family, friends at school in the past. Passages which conveyed the emotional meaning of the session and thus the transference were inserted in this enumeration of relationships. These significant passages concerned events in the life of these people: the loss of a close relation, humiliating disappointments in their attachments, their capacity or incapacity to care ... By the second year of therapy, Juliet could briefly show emotion as she related these events which minute fragmentation was still isolating in her narrative.

Turning to Idealised Parts of the Self: omnipotent narcissism

Narcissism, the state of mind which denies dependence on parental figures, contributes to the withdrawal from reality, external and internal. Rosenfeld (1971) introduced the concept of destructive narcissism and distinguished it from the libidinal narcissism which he had described earlier (Rosenfeld 1964).

> In considering narcissism from the libidinal aspect one can see that the over-valuation of the self plays a central role, based mainly on the idealisation of the self. Self-idealisation is maintained by omnipotent introjective and projective identifications with good objects and their qualities. In this way the narcissist feels that everything which is valuable relating to external objects and the outside world is part of him or is omnipotently controlled by him.
>
> Similarly, when considering narcissism from the destructive aspect, we find again that self-idealisation plays a central role, but now it is the idealisation of the omnipotent destructive parts of the self. They are directed both against any positive libidinal object relationship and any libidinal part which experiences need for an object and the desire to depend on it. The destructive omnipotent parts of the self often remain disguised or they may be silent and split off, which obscures their existence and gives the impression that they have no relationship to the external world. In fact they have a very powerful effect in preventing dependent object relations and in keeping external objects permanently devalued, which accounts for the apparent indifference of the narcissistic individual towards external objects and the world.
>
> (Rosenfeld, 1971, p. 246)

Omnipotent narcissism is defined in this chapter as a possibly transient state of mind where the need to depend on parental figures is denied as the self, or some grouping of one or more parts of the self, is idealised and endowed in phantasy with omnipotence. Instances of omnipotent narcissism include libidinal and destructive narcissism as well as narcissistic states of mind where the idealised parts of the self do not comprise a well-defined destructive part. In terms of the organisation of the personality, the corresponding notion is that of an *omnipotent structure*

14

where, in phantasy, parts of the self are idealised and endowed with omnipotence while other parts are cut off. In this definition there need not be a well-defined destructive part among the idealised parts of the self. The function of such structures is to replace mental pain (including feelings of helplessness) by a sense of omnipotence.

The organisation of the self can vary from moment to moment. This was very clear in the case of Jim. He often presented himself as a gently spoken pseudo-adult, as he was trying to establish an illusory competence. He dressed like a little man and told me that he shaved although there was no trace of facial hair. He was obsessed with make-believe situations and with the design of mostly unrealisable models. In this omnipotent structure, vulnerability and destructiveness were cut off while an omnipotent part of him was identifying with an omnipotent internal father. Jim had enough sense, however, to know that he was in serious psychological trouble. When he first tried to tell me of his fears and terrors, he could only groan, in contrast to his excited eloquence when he described his models. The mental pain he tried to avoid could be that of extreme anxiety (fear of flying, fear of lifts) or a difficult experience he was unable to deal with, such as the memory of a bullying incident or the fear of being told off. The undeveloped vulnerable part was then cut off and the personality was dominated by an omnipotent part of the self, in projective identification with an omnipotent father. This particular omnipotent structure was itself sometimes replaced by another omnipotent structure where a destructive part of the self dominated. Indeed, when he felt threatened, this gentle boy remorselessly attacked other children or the school staff. He insisted that no limit should be placed upon his retaliatory attacks, and for a while there was anxiety that he would cause serious injury. The destructive part of the self, identified with a bad object, could be recognised when he recounted a desperate fight in which he had been provoked: he said that he had felt there was 'something' standing by and telling him 'Go on!' With a coy but 'naughty' smile he continued to tell me his aggressive thoughts.

In the case of Paul, a boy with severe developmental delay who staged endlessly repeated football matches between his toy cars (see Part II, Chapter 4) it was the physical aspect of his personality, the 'champion footballer' part of him, which was idealised. Apart from a period when he idealised brutality and identified with wrestlers, destructiveness only appeared when he felt threatened, or jealous. As with other children who indulge in repetitive play, at times control seemed to be an end in itself. Paul's control aimed at the avoidance of mental pain by

15

asserting the power of an omnipotent part of the self (the 'champion footballer').

The omnipotent structure of the personality was well in evidence in a session with Juliet when the angry, destructive and crazy part of the self allied itself with the more grown up part of the self and Juliet asserted: 'I have no feelings ... People have no feelings ...' The crazy, destructive part could erupt, or hide, but it could also enter into a quiet coalition with the apparently grown-up part of her. Both parts shared a hatred of feelings, which they hoped to confine to the split-off vulnerable, deprived and somewhat envious infantile part of her personality. At other moments the more grown-up part of her instead co-operated with the therapy.

Each particular omnipotent structure of the self corresponds to a form of omnipotent narcissism characterised by a specific attitude. It can be arrogant superiority and contempt, and an explicit refusal to suffer any pain (Juliet). It can be the assertion of competence in a limited field (Paul, Jim), the search for safety through self-righteous violence (Jim), or the sadistic projection into others of feelings of humiliation which one encounters with some ill-treated children. It can be the blurring of the distinction between reality and phantasy which Jim was trying to achieve when he was building his models.

These different attitudes are underpinned by a desperate avoidance of mental pain which can lead to the promotion of psychotic states by an omnipotent part of the self. Jim kept drawing sketches on my blackboard demonstrating any incident he was involved in, or displaying his latest design. Part of it was, undoubtedly, linked to his wish to be in a position of superiority as he was giving me explanations. But there also was a wish to promote concrete thinking and a sense of omnipotent excitement by making the scene, or the design 'real'. As for Juliet, she started a session by announcing she needed to stop treatment because it made her mother ill. Juliet's mother had to bring her to therapy, since Juliet refused to come on her own. 'It's your fault!' Juliet told me. 'What are you going to do about it?' She told me of her mother's physical frailty, but also that she was making her mother's task very arduous by always being late when they had to leave home. Juliet returned to accusing me. I suggested that she was making it harder for her mother. Juliet pointed out she was now thinking in German and said: 'Ich heisse Juliet.' A few minutes later Juliet worried about this episode and wondered why she had then been thinking in German: 'Nein, nein'! She quietened down when I suggested that she had found it difficult when I had said that she was causing hardship to her mother.

16

I explained that she had pushed away this kind of thought by saying 'No, no!' in German and that speaking in German had allowed her to feel more assertive, more aggressive. I now think that the split-off, mad, attacking part of her, which had manifested itself at the start of treatment by its incongruous interruptions, but had then become silent for a few months, had spoken again after fostering the projection of guilt and destructiveness into me. 'Nein, nein!' expressed its categorical refusal to experience guilt for the suffering Juliet imposed on her mother.

When omnipotent narcissism becomes habitual, a systematic and aberrant limitation of experience also takes place. For instance, in order to avoid pain, Juliet wanted to spend her life at home and was sure she knew what was good for her, while Jim and Paul were perpetually asserting an illusory competence. As a consequence of this limitation of experience the self is weakened, and the dependence on omnipotent parts increases. Disturbance and psychotic states become entrenched. Attempts at making the child or adolescent abandon, even momentarily, behaviour which props up their sense of omnipotence are experienced as an attack on essential safety.

Progress in the therapy of psychotic or borderline psychotic patients with well established omnipotent structures of the personality frequently appears to take place at moments when they become aware that their sanity and development are at risk. This often occurs as they reach adolescence. It should be noted, however, that during the periods of apparent stagnation in their treatment these patients have slowly internalised better parental figures and can thus turn to the therapist in their moment of need.

Narcissistic Withdrawal

Narcissistic withdrawal is a form of omnipotent narcissism characterised by the turning away from parental figures and by the phantasy that essential needs can be satisfied by the individual alone, in autarchy. Klein used this term as she quoted a beautifully observed account of a baby making use of her thumb to deny her need of her mother (Klein 1952, pp. 102-3). The concept of narcissistic withdrawal can be used to describe the withdrawal effected by autistic children. Mindlessness is a particular form of narcissistic withdrawal. Another form is based on the phantasy of having appropriated a part of the mother, or of possessing a substitute for her (a doll can be a symbol of the mother, a dummy a symbol of the nipple; but they can also be a narcissistic substitute for

17

them, depending on the meaning they are given by the child). A particular instance is the phantasy of being inside the mother's body when it is used as a shelter or an exciting refuge. This phantasy is common among psychotic children, as we will see further below in the section on the claustrum.

In the case of Paul, narcissistic withdrawal was pervasive. One day, although I commented as gently as I could on his fear that he would not make good use of new pencils I had provided, he joined two armchairs, lay down on them and fell asleep for the rest on the session. In Paul's phantasy the armchairs seemed to represent the inside of Mother's body which he was appropriating and where he was seeking refuge. Furthermore, his falling asleep constituted a mindless avoidance of mental pain. Another child, who spent most of his sessions staging repetitive, mindless fights for the possession of the doll's house, kept his tongue rolled up in his mouth in a manner which suggested that he was supporting his sense of omnipotence with the illusion that he had appropriated the mother's nipple.

Projection and Projective Identification

Projection and projective identification are common, and essential defence mechanisms. As there is an abundant literature on the subject (see Spillius 1988, pp. 81-6), we will only consider some essential points. The projection of mental pain into others is a primitive method for avoiding emotional experience. It causes the explosions of aggression and disparagement which mark the therapy of seriously disturbed children.

Klein (1946) introduced the further concept of projective identification whereby, in phantasy, parts of the self are projected into another person. As pointed out by Meltzer and by Rosenfeld (1952, p. 72) this projection can be effected into an internal object. Projective identification can lead to the patient's characteristics being attributed to others (Klein 1946). This could be seen when Juliet attributed to me her destructiveness, and her guilt. Projective identification at times caused her paranoid anxieties as she was frightened of an aggressive part of her which had been projected into other people. Projective identification can also result in the patient taking the others' attributes to be his or hers (Klein 1955), as in the case of Juliet when she identified with her physically frail mother, or in the case of Jim when he was identified with an omnipotent internal father.

Projective identification belongs to ordinary mental life, but can lead

18

to a confusion of identity (Rosenfeld 1949, p. 48; and Rosenfeld 1954, p. 121), or result in hallucinations (Rosenfeld 1952, p. 81).

The phantasy of intruding into the mother's body, which is at the centre of the claustrum phantasy (see below), is a form of projective identification. Material reported by Rosenfeld makes it clear that projective identification can shift between a form where identification prevails and a fantasy of intrusion, with the attendant claustrophobic anxieties (Rosenfeld 1954, p. 121).

Being Inside the Mother: life in the claustrum

Meltzer has made an extensive study of the phantasy of being inside the internalised mother and shown its implications as it informs the whole of the apprehension of reality (Meltzer 1967, 1982, 1992). The import of the mother's inside can be understood if one remembers that for the infant the mother is the Alpha and the Omega, the object of passion. The imaginative wonder at what the mother has inside her which enables her to love, understand, interest and delight the baby suffers, however, a radical impoverishment when, in phantasy, intrusion takes place: admiration of the world is replaced by the indolence or extreme persecutory anxiety attendant upon possession (Meltzer 1992, pp 62-67).

Meltzer has pointed out that in phantasy the inside of the mother's body, which he calls the claustrum, is divided into three compartments: the head, as the seat of omniscience, or alternatively, the breast with its promise of ease and satiation, the genitals where erotic activity constantly takes place, the bottom compartment where relationships are degraded to an unmitigated striving for power. Claustrophobia expresses the anxiety, often extreme, of being trapped in a dangerous place and of being exposed to the attacks of those which, in phantasy, are the legitimate occupants: the father, or his penis, and other children.

Claustrum fantasies are marked by a sense of place: the setting of the story determines what sort of things may happen. Children in psychotherapy often enact the story of Jack and the Beanstalk: invited by the Giant's wife (the therapist in a maternal aspect) the child is taking over the Giant Ogre's house (the therapy room) and becomes very worried lest the Giant (the therapist's paternal aspect) returns to his house (any noise might announce him) and discovers the intruder.

The claustrum phantasy often overlaps with a phantasy of Oedipal and sibling rivalry, as the child perceives that by intruding into the mother's body he is stepping into the father's and siblings' preserve.

These phantasies also overlap with the sadomasochistic phantasy where a child is being beaten, hurt or murdered.

This overlap is clearly recognisable in a session with Jim at a time when he was terrified at the prospect of a stay in hospital for a small medical intervention. He told me that some people had bent the aerial on his Dad's car. He made a drawing to show how the aerial was caught under the wipers, and said that he had helped his Dad to fix this. Jim now said that on the next day his Dad had run to the window as there was some noise outside. I pointed out that Jim was talking of his street as if it was dangerous, although I thought it was a quiet area. With a fleeting, coy smile he drew the scene of an accident in his street where a friend's Mum had driven a moped into a car. When I pointed out that again he was presenting me with a picture of a dangerous neighbourhood Jim said there was a dangerous man living in his street. He drew the houses along the street, and told me the man would saw cars into two halves and would join the front of a Mini with the back of a large Mercedes. He told me of an occasion when the man was 'stretching' a Mini, which caught fire. I had no doubt that Jim felt identified with the Mini and I pointed out that little ones were getting hurt. Jim drew the man's dirty back yard and told me this man had scared him by booing him from behind his fence. With another fleeting, coy smile he told me his mother had had an argument with that man. I then interpreted that the hospital seemed so dangerous because in his mind it was a place were the doctors would want to hurt children, in the same way that he thought that his street was a place where grown-ups would hurt children. During the sessions which followed, his terror of the stay in hospital had dissipated.

As we just saw, the phantasy of being in the claustrum can be evoked through its congruence with external circumstances. A common instance is the experience of entering the therapy room. Alternatively there may be a congruence between a situation where the child or adolescent feels threatened and the phantasy of being at the mercy of persecutors inside the mother's body. This can arise on the occasion of actual conflicts with parents and siblings, or threatening situations at school. The occasion may also be the pain and dangers of physical illness (Dubinsky 1986) or the experience of trauma. The claustrum phantasy can also be evoked by an essentially internal situation when the patient feels abandoned by good parental figures and exposed to persecution.

The phantasy of intruding in the claustrum may be induced by difficulties in the early relationship, as the child may want to intrude omnipotently inside a mother experienced as inaccessible. The child may indeed feel that there is no place in the mother's mind or heart, because the mother is depressed or preoccupied, or because the child's jealousy portrays the mother as wholly absorbed with his father and siblings.

The claustrum may be felt to offer shelter from external or internal reality in the form of an alternative world. In the therapy room children may then retire under a desk or inside a cupboard, or curl up on a piece of furniture representing the breast. However, as the story of Hansel and Gretel reminds us, the quest for a substitute home inside the mother eventually leads to terror as the phantasy of intrusion exposes the patient to feeling entrapped with the resident persecutors. The claustrum can also be a refuge where the omnipotence inherent in the phantasy of having succeeded in penetrating the mysterious inside of the mother masks the patient's infantile helplessness and provides a rather innocent intoxication. It can be, however, a place where a perverse sense of power is attained. An example of the latter alternative is that of children who excitedly foul the therapy room, session after session. It is clinically useful to distinguish between the search for shelter, the seeking of a sense of safety through omnipotence and the addiction to perverse aspects of the life in the claustrum, although these motivations can coexist.[3]

The material which follows shows how these motivations were intertwined in the mind of William, a very intelligent, essentially friendly but very insecure ten year old boy with a borderline pathology. He was capable of genuine depressive concern but drove his family to distraction with his perpetual arguing. He started his therapy by re-counting vivid dreams and by telling of his terrors when he was three. He had then believed that at night on his way to his parents bedroom (his mother was pregnant with his sister) he encountered wild animals in the staircase. After a few sessions, however, he turned to setting up mindless but excited fights between the toy animals. There was now barely any communication with me, but I established that he also played like this at home to assuage his night fears. My efforts to interpret were rejected as groundless: he insisted these fights were fun and that this was all there was to it.

He was obviously interested in the code which controlled entry in the clinic. In his play some of the protagonists began to speak with the voice of a little child. A colleague who was seeing his parents reported that William was very frightened of his imminent change of school and that at home he wanted to be a small child again. One day he brought to his therapy a book about a fantasy world where animals were

21

engaged in constant fighting and where a fox was wearing the skull and skin of a wolf. He told me that his very 'hard' friend had beaten up boys who had snatched his (William's) money at the amusement arcades. I linked this to his fear of being beaten up by the older boys at the new school. He told me he wished he could stay at his old school, but this was not possible. If only he could spend his time eating … or at the amusement arcades. By now he was 'training' with a soft ball. I talked of all he had been doing in this session (and all the recent sessions) as his way of trying to make himself feel safe. In a sad tone William replied that one was never safe. I realised that he was looking for safety in these imaginary fights in the therapy room, at home, in his book, and at the amusement arcades under the protection of his 'hard' friend (where the latter corresponded to an aggressive part of William). These places represented for him the bottom compartment of the claustrum (as distinct from the longed for constant eating inside the breast). The fights were the defence of a very insecure little boy, who cried all the time when he was a baby.

The phantasy of having succeeded in penetrating inside the mother generates a sense of omnipotence. In the fairy tale, Jack gets to the Giant's house by climbing up a giant Beanstalk (the appropriated adult penis) which sprouted from a magic bean. Some of this omnipotence also derives from the phantasy of appropriating creative parental capabilities. In the fairy tale Jack steals from the Giant the harp which sings by itself and the hen which lays golden eggs. In therapy children use water to prepare elaborate mixtures in order to manufacture milk and babies. The price paid for the intrusion is that of being at the mercy of the occupants of the mother's inside, especially in the bottom compartment: the father and jealous siblings, who are endowed with powers commensurate with the omnipotence mustered for the intrusion. These figures are part objects: they are reduced to embody only the brutal striving for dominance.

The compelling character of the conscious thoughts, feelings, daydreams or play which express the claustrum phantasies derives, in part, from the sense of being in a place which defines the course of events. But it is also the sense of omnipotence and the resulting concrete thinking associated with the claustrum phantasy, and with the phantasies of rivalry, and of sado-masochism, which provides the claustrum with its fascination. The distinction between phantasy and reality becomes blurred. The child or adolescent is exposed to claustrophobia, the fear of ghosts, night terrors … Feelings of persecution may lead to desperate upsets and, if terror sets in, to panic attacks or to frightening

22

outbursts of violence as the patient feels immediately threatened. The clinical illustration which follows shows the upset and sense of persecution.

Jim had recounted with delight how well he had got on with the girls at a school disco. There was a distinctly erotic quality to his pleasure. But as he had left the disco (the genital compartment) an old man had provoked his fury by coming out of his back garden and protesting against the noise from the disco. On the next day he was beside himself, feeling persecuted and crying desperately with impotent rage because he had to spend the time of his session with me, instead of being at home (in the breast) 'drinking his favourite drink.' He calmed down only after I pointed out that I had become for him the old man (in the bottom compartment, the place of persecution). This material also illustrates what Meltzer calls the helter skelter characteristic of the claustrum: the tendency to move from one compartment to another located lower down inside the mother.

The sense of immersion in the claustrum is reinforced by concrete thinking resulting from the associated omnipotent and excited play, daydreams and thoughts. The resulting enhanced omnipotence is felt to be protective and the claustrum is experienced as a refuge. Patients then cling to it despite the terrors of the bottom compartment. Again there is a considerable danger of confusion between the claustrum phantasy and reality (which accounts for the sense of the 'uncanny' so famously described by E.T.A. Hoffmann in the short story The Sandman). Indeed, if the claustrum phantasy comes to dominate mental life, there is a serious risk of psychosis.

As life in the claustrum arouses new anxieties, the conscious representations of this phantasy as confrontations in play or daydreams serve further defensive purposes. The concrete thinking associated with these representations provide the patient with a sense of being in control, since the imaginary fights are thought to dispose of the resident persecutors. The child or adolescent holds on to the phantasy of being inside the mother, while in the outside world relationships are restricted. Daydreaming or play is endlessly repeated to the detriment of genuine mental activity. Development may then stop (as in the case of Paul).

The protection and influence based on the sense of reality which good parents provide does not extend inside the claustrum. Life in the claustrum is a form of omnipotent narcissism, and in its violent and perverse aspects, a form of destructive narcissism. Good internal objects need to develop somewhat through the experience of the therapist's caring attention before the patient can relinquish this narcissism and emerge from the claustrum.

Interpreting the debris of rivalry with father and siblings can be a step towards restoring these figures to their whole object status and widening the patient's contact with experience. Meaning will then be restored to play previously reduced to mindlessness by continual repetition. Precautions must be taken, however, in order to avoid suggesting that the therapist has joined the patient in the claustrum, as this would evoke unbearable feelings of persecution.

The Psychotic and the Non-psychotic Personality

Bion (1957) noted: 'I do not think, at least as touches those patients likely to be met with in analytic practice, that the ego is ever wholly withdrawn from reality. I would say that its contact with reality is masked by the dominance, in the patient's mind and behaviour, of an omnipotent phantasy that is intended to destroy either reality or the awareness of it, and thus to achieve a state that is neither life or death'. Bion was considering patients suffering from schizophrenic illness and making massive use of splitting and projective identification, but the distinction he introduces between what he calls the 'psychotic personality' and the 'non-psychotic personality' seems to be applicable to the whole range of psychotic children and adolescents. The patient appears to be equipped with two separate personalities. The psychotic personality, under the dominance of omnipotent phantasy, is destroying contact with reality through the massive use of some defence mechanism. The non-psychotic personality, which has retained contact with reality, ensures that, on the whole, the patient attends for therapy, and often ensures the patient's functioning outside sessions (soon after starting treatment many children function better in ordinary life while still showing serious disturbance in the therapy). It can sometimes be glimpsed when it ensures that in the therapy room the attacks against the therapist and the setting remain within the bounds of safety. Or when there is suddenly evidence that a patient has been internalising good objects and that there actually exists a positive transference. This suggests that some split-off parts of the self were actually in contact with the emotional experience of a dependent relationship to the therapist all along. Up to then, the dominance of the omnipotent phantasy had however only allowed debris of the experience to reach consciousness and be expressed in the material.

The psychotic personality corresponds to the dominance of omnipotent parts of the self interacting with each other. The non-psychotic personality corresponds to a different grouping, where the vulnerable

24

part of the self is accepted, and where the influence of omnipotent parts is restrained.

Conclusion

The view proposed in this chapter is that psychosis corresponds to a profound and complex distortion of mental functioning caused by the inability of the personality to tolerate emotional experience. This inability is sometimes accompanied by a perverse choice, made under the aegis of a destructive part of the self, to persevere in seeking the illusion of omnipotence. However radical the distortion of mental functioning, however frightening the departure from ordinary mental life, it can be understood in terms of the patient's (and the therapist's) emotional experience. It is this essential continuity provided by emotional meaning which makes psychoanalytic psychotherapy possible.

Therapeutic work thus depends on the containment of mental pain. It relies in part on the therapist's ability to bear and transform emotional experience by giving it meaning. Mental pain is further reduced when the sometimes terrifying confusions which ensue from psychotic state are resolved. Development of the weakened personality needs to be promoted through a greater integration of the split asunder aspects of emotional experience, and of the corresponding parts of the self. This corresponds to a reorganisation of the personality as omnipotent or destructive parts of the self need to be both acknowledged and restrained. This requires the internalisation of dependable good objects.

Notes

1 In the presence of emotions and sense impressions, thoughts may need to be restored to a form suitable for symbolic thinking. There is no circularity involved in this description since thoughts, which result from thinking, can be the object of further thinking, alone or in conjunction with emotions and sense impressions.

2 Reported by Marina Bardishevsky, from Moscow State University.

3 The claustrum is a particular instance of the psychic retreats discussed by Steiner (1993, p. 8).

The Technique of Child Psychotherapy

Between Sanity and Madness: an example of a child psychotherapy session

Susan Reid

In this chapter I attempt to describe the experience of being with Joshua, a psychotic boy who, when I first saw him for assessment, reminded me of some medieval painting of madness. His speech was unintelligible. He pulled at, and contorted his face and tried to stand on his head as if he genuinely did not know which way up he should be. His movements were compulsive and frenetic. The session to be presented is from the beginning of his third year of therapy, and shows work with a child emerging from psychosis.

Background to the Session

Two weeks prior to the session, Joshua who had been upset by my haircut, told me with anger, fury and outrage that I was a 'pasny plonker' and later that I looked like 'a dead flower'. In common with many psychotic patients, there was some accuracy in his description, but it was magnified by his anxieties about change. My hair is curly and had been cut short and cap-like. The curls could indeed make my head to him seem like a flower (pansy-pasny) but also my new haircut showed the white in my hair more clearly (dead flower). The change of hairstyle propelled Joshua into a psychotic state that we had not seen for some time. It became possible during the session to take up his fear that I was not myself and indeed his sense that I might be tricking him. I acknowledged his real fear but also noted that he was 'winding himself up', something with which we were both familiar. I interpreted in particular how his way of looking distorted my familiar, friendly face, making the change in me much worse than it really was, and how he was in fact giving himself over to a crazy way of thinking without calling up the thinking boy associated with his reading of 'The Lion, the Witch and the Wardrobe'. By the end of the session he was peaceful and calm.

The following week he missed the first of the week's sessions due to illness and in the second session of that week (his sessions had been increased to two per week six months earlier) he was silent throughout the whole session for the first time ever. The atmosphere was charged with aggression but also a sense of boldness and courage on Joshua's part in taking such a risk. I suggested that the previous week he had felt tricked by me when I had changed my hair style, but that now I was wondering about his session earlier in the week. Was he really not well enough to come or had he tricked his mother? He looked slyly at me, turned away, smiled and hid his smile behind his hand. By the end of that session his own trickery had been acknowledged, albeit non-verbally.

The following material is from Joshua's next session and is presented in order to share with the reader the development, as illustrated within one session, from a psychotic state of mind, to one in which there is some real contact with reality. The material is taken from the detailed notes I recorded after the session, and is kept in the present tense in the way it was recorded at the time in order to keep the immediacy of the experience of being with Joshua.

Session

In the waiting room Joshua gives an awkward but friendly smile and says 'Hello'. As we walk along to my room he turns to look at me from time to time, smiling in a friendly way, but also obviously checking on me. As we walk he hunches his shoulders and says 'Hello' again (I am aware of his anxiety in relation to his silence in the previous session and his concern that we should be friends).

Inside the room he sits on the couch, arms folded across his chest, looks at me for a second or two, smiles rather falsely and repeats 'HELLO', again, with awkward emphasis and then folds in his lips. I am very aware of the previous Thursday session, his first ever silent session and that for him this had felt very bold and openly aggressive. For this reason I am aware that he will listen very carefully to my first words and that these will be used by Joshua as evidence of my state of mind. Discarding a number of possibilities tried out in my head, I finally say 'You are showing me that you want to be friendly and that you hope I will still be friendly too' (I decided not to refer to the Thursday session too soon).

He then smiles naturally at me, lets out pent up air and his arms move

28

up and down in his lap. He then lifts his hand, and brushes it over the top of his hair. I say 'You want to be friendly but you haven't finished yet with feelings about my hair. Still not quite used to it.' He responds quickly and, in an overly bright voice says 'It's alright really.' He pauses and then adds in a reassuring voice 'It's grown a bit.' In my own mind I feel that he is telling me that he has grown a bit used to it, my hair has settled down so that it really does look as if it has grown a little and is perhaps less severe. Joshua always notices things about me and is now reassuring me, he doesn't want to hurt my feelings. He also doesn't want all that anger to start up again. I feel the usual difficulty with words and that I am on a knife edge; if I say too little, he will take this as being unable to tolerate his madness; too much and he will hear me as underlining it. So I say 'You want me to feel that it will be alright, that my hair will soon grow again and I shall be the familiar, curly-hair woman, not a too-short hair man.' I am careful to keep eye contact with him as I speak.

He is quiet for a minute and then moves to his box to remove two dolls with which we are both now familiar. These he has called Mr Sullivan and Rockon. As he does this I feel a sinking of heart; this is old material from the beginning of therapy and was very hard to shift. He stands the two figures together on top of the box holding the Mr Sullivan figure by the waist with two fingers – the pipe-cleaner doll is actually unravelling at the middle. Joshua begins a conversation between them. He makes the Mr Sullivan doll say to Rockon 'Where have you been you naughty boy, get out!' with this he kicks Rockon off the box. As he slides over the edge he is offered a helping hand by the Mr Sullivan doll and, in a familiar, sickeningly ingratiating voice he says 'Let me help you up.' As he does so Rockon is flung over the other side of the room and onto the table. This is accompanied by 'Biff-bang-bash-ow-ouch' (monster comic dialogue). The two figures in the play become increasingly confused and indistinguishable from one another. As I watch, his confusion between the two of us is revealed as he constantly touches his own hair.

I begin to speak, but as I do so Joshua talks louder and I realise that I have come in too soon and so wait a little longer. Mr Sullivan and Rockon continue their fight. Joshua begins sentences several times over; he loses his thread, sentences unravel and themes disintegrate. 'You, mister (frown) – I … Rockon, what do you? What did you …?' Gradually his speech melts into such non-sense that I am quite unable to recall it myself only seconds after he has spoken. A familiar oppressive fog begins to descend on me. It becomes increasingly hard to think. I try to clarify once or twice. He has sometimes found this helpful evidence that I have not got as confused as he is, but today he ignores me. I struggle to hold on to my confusion as meaningful – linking it in my mind to the loss of a theme in his play and of differentiation between the figures. I reflect upon the insincerity and trickery evident in the game and the violence perpetrated indiscriminately by each upon the other. It is difficult to describe the heavy, leaden quality of my own state of mind; it feels something like coming around after an anaesthetic; links come and go and I feel an

29

increasing panic. After a while I become more able to relax as I process my countertransference response and then feel less drawn to 'follow all the material'.

A small boy figure is taken from the box. He begins to battle with the Rockon figure and the previous scene is then repeated. This time the little boy begins to 'bash up' the Rockon figure. He whirls him around his head to the accompaniment of 'Take that – Biff – Bash.' Vague and mumbled insults are hurled between the figures. I manage to catch 'You silly poska plonker.' The small figure reminds me of Daniel facing Goliath. Joshua begins sentences and does not finish them; other sentences are finished but not begun; my head starts to reel with feverish activity as I try to complete his unfinished sentences in my mind, struggling to put in meaning, wondering how long this will go on for this time.

I start to speak but he looks up anxiously and says, very clearly, 'Can I just finish the story?' I nod agreement. In response Joshua gives me a sane, straight look as he seems to perceive me as myself and as agreeing to wait. He gives me a steady look before continuing. I had started to say something about a baby and am now corrected 'It wasn't a baby, it's a boy.' Joshua then removes a baby doll from his box and a McDonalds paper napkin. (The napkin had figured in an earlier session when he had arrived, as he often did, with a McDonalds hamburger wrapped in a napkin claiming 'I'm starving'. He had, however, not eaten his hamburger. I had taken up his puzzlement that he had not been able to notice that he was not hungry, but had merely got into the habit of bringing a McDonalds hamburger to his second session of the week. He seemed relieved by this observation and decided to keep the napkin.)

The earlier scenario is repeated with very small variations. After watching for some time, I interpret the game as a way of controlling me when he fears that I have turned into a bad daddy, the 'silly poska plonker' (plonker is a slang word he uses for penis). Again Joshua says anxiously 'I have not finished the story', in a slightly pleading voice. I am uncertain; the theme is now repetitive and previous experience with him tells me that these games or stories can go on interminably and that in the past I have sometimes allowed the story to go on for too long.

Joshua is meanwhile continuing and I now feel more convinced that the 'story' that he is telling me is no longer working anything out that is useful; instead I become convinced as I watch him that its repetitiveness is beginning to 'wind him up' so that he is becoming more and more mad, and that this is in fact an important aspect of what is happening. It is his own incapacity to stop himself from going on and on in a useless way that is actually driving him mad.

I therefore say that I think it would be a good idea now to do some thinking about the story. From previous experience I feel it is unwise in Joshua's present state of mind to take the story immediately into the transference. Rather it seems to help if I can just tell him the story as I have understood it, as a way of giving him another perspective on it so that he in turn might become interested; it is then sometimes possible to

30

take it into the transference. I say that each of the three stories had been about a battle – that the people in his stories fight and then get muddled up together. Rockon and Mr Sullivan become a muddled up character, Rockon-Mr Sullivan. They both feel muddled up and can't think; they can't think because they feel tricked, but no one knows who did the tricking – they feel you can't trust anyone – how do you know whom to trust? You can't trust a friendly voice; it may be a tricky cover for some bad-hearted falseness.

Joshua begins to listen whilst continuing his game in a low key way: it changes to become an accompaniment to my words, rather than as previously, a drowning out of my voice. I try to pace my comments to take account of his accompaniment. In turn Joshua becomes able to adapt his rhythm to mine. Now we are in tune, and when I refer back to something that is not actually going on in his current game, he looks at me and re-enacts it with the toys, and I nod. I say 'In each game someone is being punished, but he then punishes someone else; someone is angry and someone gets thrown out. I notice that there is no difference between children and grown ups or at least not for long.' He is still listening so I add 'On Thursday you didn't want to talk to me.' He throws a quick, anxious look at me, but then checking my expression he says 'I didn't say a word all session, did I?' I agree that he hadn't, and add that I thought this had made him worried that I would want to punish him for it. He begins to look uncomfortable, so I say 'You aren't sure today if Mrs Reid can stay Mrs Reid or whether she will turn into a spiteful little-boy-Mrs Reid and punish Joshua because you punished me on Thursday.'

'Last Monday you missed your session, do you remember?' 'Yes', he responds, 'Was that a punishment?' I say 'Your story was about you feeling that I would stop being myself and not be a reliable grown up. My short hair made you worried that I had become like a boy or a bad daddy, and that I would punish you and then you would punish me and we would get stuck forever in a terrible fight that would just go on and on with no one to say 'Stop it, that's enough'.

In response Joshua says 'You know what I like best about you?' I look inquiringly. 'You know – not the hard bit.' This sends my thoughts reeling – what does he mean? I think he is telling me something about thinking but I do not understand his reference to 'Not the hard bit' which he seems to feel I will understand. He then adds in an over-bright voice 'You know, Narnia?' (The imaginary world of 'The Lion, the Witch and the Wardrobe'). I wonder then if he is telling me that I have still not left him for long enough; did he feel I hadn't sufficient tolerance of the hard bit – that is, feeling mad. So I say 'Although you seem able to listen and be interested in what I was saying, perhaps you feel that talking then was my way of saying that I didn't like the hard bit of listening and trying to understand, that I just like the Joshua-Narnia-boy, the boy who is interested in thinking, and not the boy whose brain sometimes melts' (an image from an earlier session taken from a horror comic).

Joshua goes to his box and takes out the bull who then squares up opposite Mr Sullivan. The bull charges Mr Sullivan saying 'Take that, take that.' In response the Mr Sullivan doll is made to say 'Can I fight the bull?' The McDonalds napkin is again taken from the box to become the bull fighter's cape. Joshua stands the Mr Sullivan doll together with the bull on top of the box; the bull charges the cape and falls over the edge of the box. The bull returns, this time to charge Mr Sullivan who is knocked flying, first onto the floor, then onto the couch, and so on. The scene is repeated over and over, together with a comic book commentary as follows, 'Take that – this is a trick – good trick – trick – watch this – take that.' I say 'More trickery, no one is to be trusted. Maybe Mrs Reid is like a bull – she rushed in too quickly – I didn't wait long enough – that makes you feel that you must protect yourself like the bull fighter with the cape – but also you want to attack.' Mr Sullivan is then made to say 'You can't fight your ... (pause) you can't fight your way ... (another pause) out of a ... you can't fight in your own bag ... paper bag.' Joshua struggles and struggles to say coherently what must originally have been intended to be 'You couldn't fight your way out of a paper bag' (a familiar insult, meaning 'you're too weak': this seems to be a reference to the pasny-plonker, weak father who cannot protect the babies). As I wonder how to tackle all this, I notice that Joshua rolls the Mr Sullivan figure up in the paper napkin and off the table. I become aware that my mind has now become unable to take anything in. The observations I am making roll over the surface of Joshua's activities, but I am quite unable to make meaning from them. Gradually I realise the link between my counter transference and the figure whom Joshua says, cannot fight his way out of a paper bag. This enables me to say 'I think you are saying that when things go wrong like last Monday, and the one before when you missed your session, and I had my hair cut, then you don't want to talk to me. You feel helpless and hopeless – it feels all too much – more than can be thought about by you and by me. In your imagination we get muddled up inside your head, so that you can no longer see or feel a difference between us and now feel that we are both trapped and helpless together.'

Joshua flashes a look at me. I begin to describe what I have understood of the session, but he quickly looks anxious again and goes to the table on which I keep a doll's house. I therefore say 'Too soon again, Mrs Reid. You must listen first – for a long while, till Joshua is sure that Mrs Reid has a head and mind different from Joshua's – a mind that can hold onto muddles, and wait and work it out. If you talk, Joshua feels it is because you are in a muddle and that you will push it back into Joshua.' Joshua sighs. He takes the mother doll from his box. She is made to pick up the Mr Sullivan doll and tell him 'You've been a naughty boy.' The Mr Sullivan doll begins to cry in mock fashion. 'Boo hoo, boo hoo, boo hoo.' The mother doll is then made to say 'I've heard about you, and I'm very cross, very cross indeed.' I say 'Someone's been telling tales.' Joshua looks at me (a clear look) and says 'Rockon wanted to get him into trouble so he has tricked him and told a story about him.' This is said quite coherently, but the story then begins to go on and on; the Mr Sullivan figure is made to slide off the roof to the ground, is bumped into a wall, bashed into the doll's house, and kicked through the air. I feel invaded by a sense of timelessness; memories of long passed sessions with this same theme.

I say 'When things go wrong, it's hard for you to think, to notice, to remember. I think Joshua got cross when he missed a session, crosser still when I had my hair cut and by Thursday you were very angry, and anger frightens you. You thought I would be too weak, a pasny plonker, a dead flower, or just a little boy-spiteful daddy and that your anger would kill me. When you get angry you kill the Mrs Reid in your mind with this anger, the good-hearted Mrs Reid, and feel stuck instead with pooey, black, tricky, witch Reid who can't help you, but instead you feel wants to hurt you.' Joshua began biting one of the pieces of wooden furniture as he listened to me. I said 'Yes, an anger that starts in your mouth – with a baby Joshua who wants to bite the hard bit, the daddy nipple ...' I do not get to finish my interpretation as Joshua has picked up the mummy doll again. The doll's arm has become unravelled and is hanging loosely by a thread from the shoulder. Joshua looks terrified and begins to make hissing sounds, his eyes widening. I have no doubt that the mother doll's broken arm has frightened him but his hissing also has a theatrical quality and I begin to wonder if he has started to 'wind himself up'. He might not know whether he is frightened or pretending to be frightened.

Joshua makes Rockon and Mr Sullivan rush over to the other side of the table, shouting 'Help, help, get away, her arm is broken!' I say 'In your game, when the mummy has a broken arm, Rockon and Mr Sullivan are frightened *of* her and not worried *about* her. They don't go for help *for* the mummy. They feel *they* need help, protection from the broken mummy. Did you notice that?' Joshua says 'Yes, they are frightened of her, they have to get away, she's broken her arm.' He then seems transfixed, hypnotised by the doll's dangling arm. He seems unable to put it down, or put it away. I say that he has got frightened of the mummy doll in his hand – the doll no longer feels like a doll, but like a real broken mummy in his mind. He is obviously so frightened that I say to him 'Would you like me to take it for a minute?' He nods. I put out my hands, cupping them and he tips the doll into them. He then pulls his chair up close to me and looks at me; it is a look he gives me when he is able to listen. I say that just as he needs me to hold the mummy doll in my hands for now, because she is broken, he has also wanted me to hold onto his stories. The stories are about how his thinking mind gets broken up into pieces and about what attacks his ability to think.

Joshua nods. I therefore continue 'Because it is broken you need me to hold onto it and listen, but not talk – talking too soon makes you frightened that I have become a broken mummy – my speaking then makes you feel I am punishing you for breaking me with you anger.' I add that the broken mummy Mrs Reid is felt by Joshua to be full up with Joshua's anger and trickery and he then fears that I will push it into him and get muddled up with him. Joshua is watching me carefully as I talk.

33

I emphasise that *for a while* he hadn't noticed any more that it was just a doll and that is why he had got so frightened and, when the doll's arm had come off, this had made him feel that what he feared most must be true – that his anger had broken not only the helpful, friendly Mrs Reid inside his imagination, but also the real Mrs Reid, me, who lives outside his mind. I ask Joshua if he remembers that in his game Rockon and Mr Sullivan had called for help when the mother doll's arm was broken, not for the mother, but for themselves. He nods. I say that I think this is because when the mother doll was broken, when he felt that I had been broken by his anger, then I turned into the frightening bad, witchy Mrs Reid full of anger, his anger.

I feel very clumsy as I say this, my thoughts like treacle. Joshua asks me if I will put the doll in the box and I agree but he then takes it from me and puts it into the box himself. He then pulls his chair close up against mine. I say 'You can sit close to me like this with a friendly face because you feel the mummy doll in the box is now the bad Mrs Reid and I am the good-hearted Mrs Reid who can be trusted.' Joshua looks at me thoughtfully and then looks into my eyes and says 'Mrs Reid, I have been having very bad nightmares. I dreamt I was in a dark street and I was all alone and there was an owl – you know (he frowns in concentration) – owls (he continues) they've got their big (there is another pause, looking at my eyes again, he finally continues) those big eyes, and it was saying something to me, and then I'd got nowhere to hide and there were the trees and I couldn't hide in there.' He looks puzzled and pauses, so I ask simply 'Why?', but in response Joshua says 'No, it wasn't a white owl, it was one of them … (he hesitates) – sort of browny-gingerale (sic). Do you know gingerale (sic)?' I had expected him to say browny-ginger *owl*. My own thoughts start to ramble, brown ale, brown owl, fuzzy drinks … Joshua continues 'This big face came – a big monster face – and it did like this (he contorts his face, reminding me of my first meeting with him) – it was a monster and I was really frightened and then I woke up.' Rambling takes over – something about daydreams, and I feel that dreams and waking life are getting blurred. He then begins to talk about 'Nightmare on Elm Street'. 'Do you know it? Have you seen it? It's really frightening. Lightning comes out of the monster's eyes and hits me here (he points to his chest) and I turn to dust'.

It is very close to the end of the session and I wonder what I can take up from the dream in the time remaining. I decide to focus on what was evoked in me by his dream. I therefore say that I think the dream is about how lonely he feels when he gets frightened – that he feels surrounded by unfriendly monsters. Sometimes when I look at him nowadays, he can feel it's a friendly way of looking and it's something he has called 'looking into my heart, wise-owl-Reid', but sometimes he calls my way of looking 'reading my mind' and then I feel to him, like a bad, poky, Freddie-witch. (The bad figure in Nightmare in Elm street he has told me is called Freddie.) I then find my mind full of the expression 'can't see the wood for the trees'. I therefore say that sometimes he looks at me with his eyes narrowed and tells me I look funny – nasty. I suggest that the dream shows how easily a friendly white owl's eyes can turn into bad, brown, poo eyes.

In response he mumbles something about 'zigzag thunder'. I say he is telling me that he has always been worried about eyes. In his dream his monster had bolts of lightning coming from his eyes – flashes of hate that struck at his heart. This was a way of saying that they struck at the warm, friendly feelings, turning them to dust. Joshua says something about monsters in comics and books but adds that he has stopped reading these now and has stopped watching monster films. (He has been chronically addicted to monster comics, monster films, anything he could lay his hands on about monsters.) I say that sometimes still, like in his dream and in the session today, he could feel surrounded by monsters. The monsters are the unfriendly feelings – anger, trickery and jealousy. It is hard to remember to call up his memory of feeling friendly towards me and his memory of my showing I was friendly towards him. The friendly bits of himself and the friendly bits of me were what helped him think and struggle with bad feelings. I add that he is, as we know, very frightened of his anger and that his anger makes him feel very powerful. Joshua interrupts me to say 'I don't want to feel that powerful, Mrs Reid, as powerful as a monster.' I nod and say that his dream was about how his anger makes him feel that he has turned into a powerful big monster that can turn the world inside his mind, into a nightmare world where he can't call up a friendly or encouraging voice.

I ask him if he remembers how last week I had talked to him about how sometimes he seems to 'wind himself up' – feeds himself on nasty stories and pictures. Joshua nods. I say that in the dream it then makes it difficult to see the trees as friendly and sheltering. Somewhere here I remind him of his 'daggers eyes' (something with which we are very familiar). He uses these to explode the friendly me away. I say how hard it is when he feels angry to keep alive his friendly feelings too.

Joshua crosses to his box, seemingly absent-mindedly and lifts out the mother doll figure. His body posture has changed and is quite relaxed. He stands staring at the doll figure which he is holding in the palm of his hand. He says 'Poor thing – poor little thing.' He touches her tenderly and in a completely genuine way and then asks me 'Can you bring a needle and thread and mend it?' I say 'You can look at the mother doll now because you no longer feel frightened of her broken arm but instead feel sorry for her and about her arm. You want it to be mended but you need my help. This feels alright because you now also feel friendly to me and feel that I, too, am friendly toward you, and that you can trust in this.'

As he stands holding the doll, Joshua winds the thread back around the doll's arm. This has the effect of gradually reeling in the arm so that it is restored to its proper position. I describe his actions but then have to tell him that it is now time to finish for the day. Joshua, very carefully, lays the mother doll inside a plastic box lid, inside his box. He stands looking at her and then carefully closes his box. It is time to leave the room. On our way back to the waiting room he whispers 'I don't like it when I can't think.' He then adds 'Some of the bad stuff came out today, didn't it?' As we reach the waiting room he says thoughtfully, and very much in his own voice, 'There is still a long way to go.'

Conclusion

I felt touched by the way Joshua had managed to finish his session and his comments on the way back to the waiting room. However, it seems important to note that far from feeling hopeful by the end of that session, I felt both exhausted and anxious. My despairing thoughts reflected, I believe, Joshua's own fragile belief that he could, in any sustained way be sane and his fear that the familiar world of mindless addiction to horror comics would overwhelm his wish to conquer his demons.

When therapy ended, Joshua had managed to join the ordinary world, his capacity to learn developed in school and he became increasingly confident about his future.

Acknowledgement

This session was presented for discussion at a peer supervision group chaired by Betty Joseph. I would like to thank Betty Joseph who first suggested that this material be published and my colleagues for their support.

Part I

Psychosis and Sexual Abuse

1

Finding a Safe Place

A Four-Year-Old Child's Recovery from Sexual Abuse

Deborah Sussman

Introduction

This chapter looks at material from a period of intensive psychotherapy with a four-year-old girl who had been sexually abused and severely neglected.

The therapist links Jennifer's earliest experience of sexual abuse, neglect and deprivation with the development of a psychotic part of herself, at first terrified, later attracted and at times addicted to perversion.

In the first year of her treatment, Jennifer was terrified of being destroyed, of being abused, or of falling apart. She perceived her therapist as a persecutor and abuser and would retreat into fantasies of violence and perversion that seemed to be her means of defence against feelings of helplessness. Her fantasies reflected her past experience but also served to 'hold her together' in the face of chaos and terror.

Later in the treatment Jennifer would allow more and more glimpses of a fragile, infantile, dependent part of herself but would suddenly swing to being in projective identification with a narcissistic, perverse object that enabled her to avoid feelings of closeness, vulnerability and dependency. She would either become the abuser, trying to seduce the therapist into her world of dirt and brutality, or the neglectful mother who allows moments of closeness only to cast the baby away.

Through containment of these states of mind, Jennifer was able to introject a caring, thinking therapist who could help her work through her feelings of ambivalence towards her attachment figures.

Early History

Jennifer's family of origin consisted of her mother and of Susan, her older half-sister. Susan's father had left the family a few months after his daughter's birth, though he continued to visit them off and on. Meanwhile the mother had a number of other boy-friends, one of whom had fathered Jennifer.

In the period before Jennifer's birth, frequent allegations of neglect of Susan were made by neighbours. Within a few months of Jennifer's birth, Susan disclosed that their mother's latest cohabitee, Mr X, had sexually abused her. At the same time, accusations were made against the mother that she neglected her daughters and involved them in sexual activities with other men. Mr X pleaded guilty to abuse of Susan and was imprisoned. Susan later described his oral abuse of Jennifer. Both girls were placed on the At Risk Register but stayed with their mother. However, when Jennifer was 18 months old they were finally removed on a Place of Safety order and placed in local authority care due to long periods of abandonment and neglect.

Jennifer had long periods of crying. Her motor skills and language were underdeveloped for her age. She was a 'finicky eater' and would often only accept food from her sister. It appears that Susan propelled herself into the primary maternal role for Jennifer in the children's home. She was said to be over-protective of Jennifer and unable to tolerate care staff functioning in a maternal capacity to her or Jennifer. A year later both children were fostered with a view to adoption by a professional couple who had been unable to conceive.

After two years of psychotherapy Jennifer said one day in treatment, 'Would you like to know the story of my life? Once upon a time I was born. I had a mummy who died. I actually had four mummies ... (holds up four fingers). The first one died. Then she gave me to another one who left me in a Children's Home (she holds up three fingers). Then my sister Susan became my next mummy (she holds up two fingers). She was my mother until (holds up one finger) the mummy I have now, Barbara.'

Referral for Psychotherapy

When the foster parents visited the children's home they found a deprived, depressed ten year old Susan and a non-verbal, 'pathetic', inactive two-and-a-half-year-old Jennifer.

Over the first year the foster mother became increasingly concerned about Jennifer. She was retaining her faeces, screaming endlessly for long periods of time, and biting, scratching and destroying toys. Her foster mother expressed anxiety that a very disturbed little girl had been placed with her: although she had had professional training that helped her empathise, contain and survive she felt unprepared and wanting support.

Jennifer would retain faeces for long periods of time, sometimes one to two weeks. Repeated hospitalisations for observation and behavioural approaches to toilet training had taken place. Jennifer had been placed on daily medication for bowel retention as well as receiving repeated enemas. She would constantly bite her foster mother and children in the nursery. Because Jennifer's retention had placed her medically at risk, and behavioural treatment had failed, her paediatrician had recommended surgery to widen the anal tissue walls at the same time that I had begun to assess Jennifer for psychotherapy. With careful liaison between myself and Jennifer's child psychiatrist and paediatrician it was agreed to postpone the surgery to give psychotherapy time to begin.

The Assessment

In the first session with Jennifer and her foster mother, her foster mother described Jennifer's history and behavioural difficulties, and spoke about her possible sexual abuse. While her mother spoke, Jennifer began to draw a shape on a piece of paper which was black and phallic with sharp points. She later told me it was a monster. In her play, she took all the family figures and put them on the roof, 'because the monster was in the house.' She showed me how children were being cut up 'by the monster' and then threw them all into my waste bin. When I commented that Jennifer had lots of things to tell me about, and asked if she would mind if mummy waited in the waiting room, she agreed.

When I asked Jennifer why she thought she had come to see me, she replied, 'Because I have lots of monsters inside, ... in here' pointing to the doll's house. She also told me, 'I don't do poos, I save them up inside and keep them.' I asked her why. She replied, 'I don't want to let it come out. I might empty it all out.' She pointed her finger at me accusingly and said, 'You will have to wait. I have my legs crossed ... I will never, never do a plop'.

I decided to see Jennifer initially once a week.

The Psychotherapy

In the second session, she cut up everything in her box along with additional paper I provided. She talked about her fear of having an operation. She told me doctors and nurses want to see her cut up. She said, 'Nurses like to stick things in my bottom.' She cut long thin strips of paper and told me they were sharp and would hurt if I touched them. 'I will cut them up. They think they will cut me. I'll cut them.' She continued cutting as she spoke, describing sadistic nurses who take pleasure in poking, shoving, cutting and giving enemas. Nurses were 'stupid, mean and don't like me and know I don't like them.' She described battles with them over taking pills, enemas, food, injections, or going to the potty. She told me she spat pills out and showed where she used to hide the chewable pills and sweets in her pocket or sock. She told me that she felt the pills were to 'kill and poison' her. In a later session she used her navel in a similar way; she had placed a sweet her mother gave her there. She unwrapped it, examined it, tasted it and announced it was poison.

For many sessions she continued to cut up things from her box into minute pieces that seemed like dust. Scissors went around dolls' necks, fingers, plasticine, string and crayons. She was not satisfied until everything in her box was destroyed. She spent an entire session trying to cut up a plastic farm animal, and became enraged with a 'slippery pig' which kept escaping her scissors. The hardest decision for me at that time was deciding whether to return dust and bits of her toys to her box or to throw them away. In one session I talked with her about all the bits in the box and all these bits of feeling. I started with 'angry and hurtful'; she added 'hard, sharp ... mean.' She left the room announcing to her mother that Debbie had 'put my bits in the box and they are safe away until the next time.' She then reprimanded her mother, pointing her finger and saying 'the Doctor with the doll's house has told you not to force me.'

The next few months were filled with chaotic stories, memories and fragments of fantasy. Her thoughts were difficult to understand or follow. She repeatedly rhymed words with 'pimp' as she cut up drawings after having attempted to make something creative. She tried to make a butterfly in one session, yet was interrupted by a destructive part of herself who whistled and swore at me and then scribbled over it. The butterfly was destroyed and turned into a 'curly wurly mummy.' This mummy then became an 'insect with red eyes' and tried to 'prick' her. She became frightened of her own drawing, then attacked me, and bit herself. Once she tried to scratch the wall, then turned away from the wall to cut her skin and mine, gritting her teeth with frustration and rage.

Jennifer's treatment of her internal objects and of me are similar to

1. Finding a Safe Place

what Shirley Hoxter describes in her chapter in *Psychotherapy with Severely Deprived Children* (Hoxter, 1983).

> What needs to be understood in such situations (when the worker is treated violently) is not just that the child is perceiving the worker as the insufficiently caring parent of his past experience and revenging himself. Beyond this the child is also reversing the original situation. He is behaving towards the adult as he perceives himself to have been treated and is forcing the adult to suffer his insufferable feelings. This time the child feels himself to be the powerful persecutor and it is the adult who is the helpless victim.

When she was in these destructive states she would try to destroy everything in the room, run to the window, stick her finger in electric sockets or roam behind me trying to attack me from behind. Then she fled from me in terror, calling me a 'butcher willy bum'. Initially, I felt she seemed to feel more upset about my surviving her attacks rather than feel made secure and safe by my strength and endurance. I spent the early months having to hold her to prevent her from biting while she screamed at high pitch. Once she screamed in such a way that it so alarmed staff that they began walking up and down outside my door. At times her scream was as if she was tormented, possessed, and trying to expel something out of her body, and at other times as if she was being tortured physically.

At the end of each session she would refuse to clear up or leave the room and cling to furniture or the box. It was as if she felt torn from her mother to come into sessions and, again, severed from me at the end.

Eventually, I made the room child proof, with covers over the plugs, window locks and drawer locks. Scissors were removed after she attempted to cut her clothes. She seemed relieved with my firmness in setting boundaries, and by the sixth month announced that the room was 'finally safe today.'

Intensive Psychotherapy – Contrasting States of Mind

In the sixth month I increased her sessions to three per week. I found that with the increase in sessions, her fantasies poured out and made more sense. She began to use the sink and waterplay. She talked about 'poos and plops', how 'lovely' they were. Faeces became idealised. She began to confide in me her fears of going to the toilet. She told me 'butchers and willy bums' would get her. 'Men with cigarettes are in

43

there waiting for me.' In one session she said 'My insides will fall out, my heart and bones. I might die if I do a plop.'

At this point in the treatment, Jennifer oscillated between two roles. Part of the time she was the victim, overwhelmed by feelings of terror, persecuted by monsters, penises and 'butchers'. When she was not the victim, running from these persecutors, she propelled herself into projective identification with an abuser. When using this defence mechanism to escape the chaos and terror, she sometimes enacted wolf-whistles or made herself into a narcissistic prostitute.

The contrast between these states of mind appeared vividly when one moment she would try to attack me, and the next minute would appear as a made up lady who painted her nails, looked at herself in the mirror and masturbated. She would parade on my desk, lifting her skirt up, showing me her knickers. She would lie on the desk against the window sill and tell me how crowds of men were looking at her, kissing her, giving her cigarettes. If I opened my mouth to talk I was screamed at and called 'willy bum'. On these occasions she would pick at her bottom, masturbate vaginally, lick herself and smell her finger. She encouraged me to admire her. I felt repelled and filled with frustration and hopelessness.

One day she left a baby doll abandoned in the sink with a running tap, forgotten while she sat on my desk telling me all about the boyfriends she had. The baby was left to drown, unless I intervened and turned the taps off. Another day she tried to bite my buttons and earrings, and to look under my blouse. She became excited and hysterical, telling me I was a very sexy lady. As the sexualised, perverse play continued, I felt helpless and wondered if I could ever effect any change in her perception of me. I often felt that I became for her an exciting, titillating breast that over-stimulated her, filling her with wild envy, making the baby too disturbed to listen.

One afternoon, after Jennifer went to the car with her mother, her father described how upset he felt about some of her sexualised behaviour. He had difficulty telling me and was relieved when I empathised.

Jennifer's terror of me, and confusion about what type of therapist/mother I might be made her turn inwardly towards perverted excitement. The excitement of the sadism kept her from feeling the confused fragmented feelings which she found so terrifying.

While I was filled with feelings of hopelessness, in the external world she was making progress. The GP reduced her medication. Jennifer no longer needed to retain physically for such long periods of time. Initially, she had withheld her faeces for weeks; now her foster mother reported it was only days. Her teachers reported a decrease in her aggressive physical outbursts, including biting and scratching. She still remained unable to socialise on her own with other children, yet was able to use a teacher to act as a diplomat to negotiate relationships with her peers. The teacher also reported that Jennifer was extremely bright and was the first child to learn the alphabet, begin to write and attempt to learn to read. At home, Jennifer's mood was volatile – sometimes she asked to be bottle fed and held, and would suck her thumb. At other times she kicked and screamed at her parents.

A Glimpse of Hope

After over a year of treatment, Jennifer began to be able to listen and allow me to complete an interpretation. One day she noticed baby ducklings outside my window in the courtyard. She watched them for most of the session and invited me to watch with her. She began to create stories about the mummy duck and her relationship to all these baby ducks. She would count them each day, become anxious and threatened if she didn't see the mother duck, or if she couldn't count eleven ducklings. The ducks became a shared interest for us to begin to watch and think about together.

Stories were created about where the mummy duck was if she couldn't be seen. 'All mummy ducks come and go. They disappear and fly away, but this one is different, she's back. She's watching them. She is teaching them to eat with her.' 'The mother duck is teaching them to swim.' Jennifer began to show an ability to acknowledge and internalise a mother who could keep her babies safe, but these glimpses of hope would only last a few minutes before she destroyed them, turning away from me and the ducks to her projective identification with a masturbating prostitute. I was allowed to feel hopeful, have a taste of closeness with baby Jennifer, only to have her kidnapped abruptly by the psychotic part of herself organised like a gang. I wondered if her constant re-enactment of this reflected her earlier experience of one moment being with a loving maternal object and then suddenly alone, neglected, and open to sexual abuse.

Following a holiday, Jennifer returned to attacking, biting and pinching me, absolutely wild with jealousy. Any indication of my having other children to look after would send her into a rage. She began to tell me, 'I would like to kill you, get inside your bottom, go up to your heart and rip it out.' She told me she would take out everything from

45

inside me so I would bleed to death. She would like to see the blood and my tears. She would tell me 'it it will really hurt you.'

Then primitive fantasies of wanting to get right inside and destroy any part of me that had the capacity to care for her were evoked by the abandonment she felt during holidays. She told me the ducks were all dead and the mother had flown away.

'The Potty's the Place'

By the thirteenth month of therapy, Jennifer began to write letters on paper. Sometimes the letters were used as ways of learning to write, to sound out her name or mine. She was now five years old and proud of this. She told me about a teacher at Infant School who was kind to her, and was teaching Jennifer how to write her name. She imitated this teacher, making me be the child learning to write, to read and even to cut my meat at table. She began to ask in each session if she could go to the toilet and would narrate to me how she was doing while on the potty. Sometimes she would arrive with a round full tummy telling me she hadn't been able to go poo for a week. 'My mind is full', she said rubbing her tummy and telling me how it hurt.

It seemed for several months that we spent most of our sessions in the toilet. Jennifer's recurrent terror was that everything inside her would fall out and into the toilet. I was needed to collect the 'falling bits', to take the anxiety and provide a place to put it. Sometimes she would play tricks in the toilet such as locking herself in and giggling. Other times she would leave the door open and tell me how she was terrified she would fall in. She would hold onto the walls, talking, singing and whistling to overcome her fears as she tried to let go of her faeces.

At about this time, I bought her a book called 'I want my Potty.' It was about a Queen who was teaching her little princess how to use the toilet. The Queen, the King, the butler and all the servants say to the little princess 'The Potty's the Place.' Jennifer kept this in her locker and asked me to read it to her each session. While I read this book, she could allow herself to feel close to me. The book was something we could do together, just as we had watched the ducklings. The minute the book was over she would mimic a mummy who was interested only in herself, sometimes returning to masturbation or picking her bottom or her nose, telling me how delicious the tastes and smells were.

The 'Potty' book gave a visible example to Jennifer of a benign version of 'potty training'. The process of toilet training is a sorting out and differentiation of clean from dirty. Using the toilet is learning to use an appropriate container. The book offered Jennifer and me some shelter from the chaos, perversion and powerful intensity of her paranoid projections. It seemed to be a 'place' where she and I could safely meet to experience a different kind of closeness.

Starting to Think

The following excerpt shows how Jennifer began to be able to talk about how ill she felt and to tolerate the emotional pain of separation.

Jennifer is eager to come into the room. She shows me a Koala Bear and says hello to the secretary. She chats with me happily about her holiday activities. Today she is going to see her biological mother. It will be the last time because Jennifer and her family are moving.

She lays down on the sofa, rubs her stomach and groans, 'My tummy hurts today'. I speak about her feeling hurt by me in the holiday. She groans and tells me that she thought I was ill during the holiday. 'I'm glad I didn't see you, I'm bored. I don't want to come and see you any more.' She gets up from the sofa and goes directly to her locker and takes out some crayons and a piece of paper. 'Honest, honest Debbie ... I really don't want to come and see you. I really don't like coming. It's boring in here.' I say she is telling me how much she hates coming back to see me after a holiday. I also wonder what bored means. She then says 'I'm angry, not bored.' She then tells me again that she is going to see her biological mother for the last time today. She sits next to me and groans that her tummy hurts. I say that Jennifer's mind is filled with lots of thoughts, having had to keep them all inside her until our session together. I say 'Waiting made you feel sick. A part of you wanted to say goodbye to me so that I would feel like you feel today, have the feelings you have. You want me to know what it feels like to be left wondering why someone is going away'. She sits with me and strokes my head. She wants to hold my hand. I say that Jennifer wants to look after me, be the caring mummy, and for me to have the baby feelings. I say she is showing me how difficult it is for her to be here today, and to think about saying goodbye to her mummy.

She says, 'I have lots of feelings inside today. Sometimes I feel sad and then I feel angry.' She goes to the tap, turns it on, grits her teeth and shakes her body. She turns and kicks me. I say she is trying to show me the angry feelings that make her tummy hurt so much. When she tries to think of them, she wants to hurt me. She then flops down onto the sofa and says, 'Actually Susan said I don't feel so sad. I don't feel anything, I don't care.' She then tells me that her biological mother is sick. 'That is why we don't live with her. She is sick and can't look after us, she is in hospital.' I say it seems that Jennifer is trying to piece together what happens to people she cannot see. Because I did not see her over the holiday, she thought I was sick or in hospital. I talk about how confusing it is trying to make sense of having two mummies, keeping one and saying goodbye to another. She lies down on the sofa and says, 'I feel sad with one, and angry with the other. I'm too tired today. I want to waste the rest of my time.' She turns on her side away from me and begins to pick her nose and eat her mucus.

I say how hard it is to stay here and be looked after and think with a Debbie who can bear painful feelings. Saying goodbye to this other mummy is too hard to think about, so she turns to her own nasty bits. She nods and says, 'Yes, I know I'm doing this.' She then stops and lies on her hands and says, 'I feel so sick. I'm trying to go to sleep. I'm trying to feel better.' Suddenly she begins to cry, scream and kick her feet. She bangs her head over and over on the sofa, then holds her knees up to her chest and begins to rock back and forth. After some time she stops and stares up at the ceiling. She lies on the sofa until the end of the session with her thumb in her mouth, sometimes looking at me, sometimes half asleep.

At the door she says to me, holding her stomach, 'It's a little better now. It doesn't hurt so much.' She sees her mother in the waiting room, hugs her and climbs into her lap and sobs.

Choosing to Waste Time – A Jealous, Defiant Jennifer

In the second year of therapy Jennifer became preoccupied with other children's lockers. She had previously not been curious or interested. She began to kick them, stick things on them and try to hide things in them. She would climb on them, shake them, peer into them. She noticed another boy in the waiting room after her session who she fantasised was coming to see me. She was wildly jealous of him and spent time planning ways of attacking him and setting up things in the room to hurt him.

The session which follows illustrates how Jennifer is beginning to differentiate between 'using' or 'wasting' her sessions with me. She has become rebellious and defiant. She is less confused and is testing out her relationship with me.

Jennifer stands looking out of the window; twelve minutes have passed during which she has ignored me. She says, 'How much time is left?' She then turns away again. 'Today I want to waste all my time, you are a willy bum and a black bogey.' She begins to pick her nose and eats the mucus. She lies on the sofa, pulls her pants down and begins to masturbate.

I talk about her feeling unsettled today. I say to her, 'When you feel like this you are telling me you would rather choose to be in that nasty hole, with willy bums and black bogeys than stay with me as a thinking Debbie. You would rather feed yourself on anger, bogey and poo.' She comes over to me, looks at my nails and tries to get one of my fingers up to her face. She says, 'I would like you to scratch me then I could see the blood.' I say her anger and rage is so great today that she is worried that it is too much for me.

She tells me she saw a boy in the waiting room and says, 'He sees you too.' I ask why she thinks this and she replies, 'Everybody comes to see you. I hate these lockers. I am going to pee in them.' She peeks inside. 'What's inside here? What kind of toys does he get? Does he have the same as me? I'm going to kill him. If I hurt him he will not come here to see you.' I talk of her rage, wanting to be the special one, the only one I see. She cannot bear to think of me with anyone else. 'That's right', she says, 'I told you I will waste my time today.' After several minutes of lying on her back on the sofa she gets up and sits next to me, looks at me closely, pulls my arm and leg, as if trying to see if I'm still there and am all right. She picks up the paint blocks and asks, 'Do you know the difference between white and black?' She tells me white is for me to hold today while she paints with black and yellow. I say 'Have I to hold on to the hope of the idea of a Jennifer that can use her time and remember a good Debbie, while you play with your black poo?' She says, 'Tomorrow I will come in and use my time; today I can't.' I say that when Jennifer thinks of me with other children she is wild with anger and cannot bear to use her time. Maybe she will be able to tomorrow. There is a silence. I ask 'why will tomorrow be different' she replies 'I don't know, but I hope it will be.'

Some time later, Jennifer says, 'I want to take your earrings, ring, shoes, clothes, shirt, hair, make-up, lips, fingers, knees and I'll have them all.' She tries to take my keys, and struggles to get my ring and watch. I talk to her about wanting everything I have and can give her, to eat up everything and have it all. I talk about the Debbie who she thinks has all these goodies, about how hard it is to be with me for a while and then leave and wait to come back. She says, 'I want to have everything, your room, your desk, the whole place, the whole world.' There is a moment's silence. She then screams with anxiety and terror that she wants her daddy. He can carry her. She tells me how big and strong he is; she needs to see him. I say 'When you realise you can't be me and have all that I have, you feel scared and terrified and small.' She nods, wipes her tears. I add, 'When you feel frightened you want a strong daddy's arms around you. When you feel you have a strong daddy inside your mind you feel safer.'

In her state of extreme emotional deprivation, Jennifer wants all that I possess, all the 'goodies' she thinks I have. Yet her scream also expresses terror that she has damaged me, robbed me of my vitality; that her envy may have emptied me.

Separation and Scratching

Jennifer's need for things to remain unchanged in the room was heightened following any gap. She would examine and re-examine the room, walls, windows, desk; she would press switches and taps to see if they all worked. She would run her fingers, and toy cars, around the wall, floor, ledges and desktops. All surfaces needed to be inspected. I thought that her anxiety about change after separation was linked to her terror of losing bits of herself, just as earlier she could not release her faeces.

In *Further Considerations of the Function of the Skin in Early Objects Relations* (Bick 1984), Bick describes how a child clings to surfaces in fear of separation:

> Defects in this early containment of the personality may be devastating ... the catastrophic anxiety of falling into space. The dead end haunts every demand for change and engenders a deep conservatism and demand for sameness, stability and support from the outside world.
>
> Being separated meant being turned away and torn to pieces by persecutory hands ... that destroyed the play material and had earlier scratched her [the child's] skin to bleeding. The desperate clinging for survival was mounted in the face of an experience of lacerating separation which would let her life leak away like a liquid substance ... It, therefore, seemed likely that the identification and consequent mimicry of my phrases was due to her stroking on to my surface. I came to think of it as an adhesive identification rather than a projection.

The experience of lacerating separation was apparent in Jennifer's material, for instance in this session:

> I notice Jennifer comes in with scratch marks on her arms, legs and fingers. She tells me she has started at 'a big girls school' now. I link starting school with starting back in therapy, and talk about how she feels she needs to be a big girl here. She asks me to read 'I want my Potty' to her. She continues to scratch while bringing me the book. I notice she is scratching and wonder how she is feeling about being here with me today. She puts her thumb in her mouth and cuddles against my chest, as far into my lap as she can get without actually being in it. She screams, 'I want my potty' every time the words are on the page. When I finish she whines immediately, beginning to pick her nose and scratch. We talk together about how hard it is to feel safe here, how uncertain she is of me since the holiday.
>
> I begin to read to her again, saying she needs space between us today, the 'safety' of the book. She nods. At some point in the book I notice she

is no longer listening to my words or looking at the book. She is picking her nose and eating mucus. She pulls the scab off a healing cut and puts it into her mouth. I wince with pain.

I talk to her about her need to turn away from me, and our time together, to her own 'nasty bits', rather than enjoying the good feeling of sitting here with me. She stops and sits on her hands. Later in the session she tries to cut her clothes and mine. She tells me that she wants to die so that she won't have to see me any more. I say she wants to kill any good feelings she has left for me. It is easier than the anger she feels when I leave her during the holidays. She begins to sing loudly and tell me how she is going 'back inside'. She sits on the floor telling me 'butchers are here and curly wurly willy bums.'

I say aloud that although Jennifer talks over my words, I think she can still hear me. She wants to punish me for leaving her. She interrupts me and says, 'I can't help it.' She continues to masturbate while talking to me. She says 'I hate you. You will die.' I say, 'You hate me for leaving you and when you feel alone you turn to your willy bum world rather than miss me, feel alone, separate and angry.' 'It's better than you', she yells, as she masturbates. I ask how. She says, 'It feels good, I can touch it when I want. I have it all to myself.' I say I think Jennifer is angry with me because she knows the difference between bad stuff and good stuff, being with a thinking person who cares about her. When she is angry with me for leaving her and thinks I don't care about her, she says to herself, 'I'll show Debbie, I'll go back to my nasty old world.'

Terror and Dread

A holiday in the second year of treatment again triggered the deep anxiety and memories of terror, darkness, pain and abuse.

Session

She immediately talks about crocodiles and jumps onto the sofa and then up onto the desk. She tells me there are sharks and crocodiles; they are swimming around and her feet get caught in the crocodile's mouth. She says, 'Ouch.' From my desk she describes these crocodiles attacking her. I remind her about the sharks and whales attacking her in the last session and about her still feeling unsafe in the room. I say that she feels that the room is filled up with scary, attacking objects. She is still not sure that I am a therapist who can deal with all these shark and crocodile feelings inside her.

She tells me that she is on a big ship and that she can watch people being killed from it. She then says, 'I want to kill', and kicks her chair at me and tells me that she wants to kill me. I say, 'A part of you wants to kill off the Debbie that's sitting here with you now, a Debbie that's been away from you and hasn't been here to help you with your dangerous feelings.' Jennifer assumes the role of a laughing witch 'I'm going to stay on this island and you are going to stay in the shark's mouth. Ha Ha Ha.' I tell Jennifer that she is so angry that I went away on holiday that she's going to throw me to the sharks. That means that I, the therapist, cannot help her; I am to become the victim in the shark's mouth, like Jennifer felt when I was on holiday. She stands up and points at the lamp and tells me how she's going to put me in it and burn me. I comment about how much easier it is to be the mean, dangerous witch, attacking me, than to be the Jennifer who feels safe with the thinking Debbie.

She comes over and touches my face and lip and delicately squeezes it, then rubs her face and smells her hands as if inhaling me. She says, 'Umm. I smell sweet. Lipstick.' She puts it on her lips. She stands and looks at me and continues to smell her hand then tells me she's got a great big box of sweets and that I haven't. I say that there's something nice about touching my face and smelling my lipstick and my scent that makes Jennifer feel close to me, but it also makes Jennifer feel like she has taken something from me. She turns to the window and says, 'There's fire outside and there's real people killing other people and they're going to kill us.' She hides under the desk. I say maybe she feels I will be angry at her for stealing some of my goodness. At that moment we hear a loud noise outside the window and she says, 'There's lots of planes and noises outside', and she gets up and she looks out of the window. She tells me that there is a fire and that two birds are dead because of this loud noise, saying 'Ssh, the Concorde is killing people and they'll kill us.'

I say that she doesn't think that I can protect her from anything today. She holds onto my foot and tells me 'they're dropping bombs on us and people's houses ... the plane is only getting children not adults.' Then she compares my lips to hers and touches her own. She touches her cheeks while staring at mine. She compares her lips, her hair colour, her eyes and her skin to mine. I say that when Jennifer feels that she has the same things as me, she feels safer.

Jennifer was here using projective identification with a terrifying object (the witch) to avoid falling apart and feeling torn to bits. However, she was able to regain contact with goodness, and feel safe again, by touching her therapist's face.

How to Prevent Fighting

In the third year of treatment, both Jennifer and Susan were coming to the Clinic for psychotherapy. Susan had requested 'someone to talk to about my mothers.' They were both seen on the same day at the same time. In the following material, Susan's therapist was ill and Jennifer offered to 'share' her session with her sister. This session shows how Jennifer has become capable of thinking about other people's distress and wanting, albeit omnipotently, to care for them. She worries about her sister and also about the soldiers in the Gulf War:

> 'Why can't Susan come in with me? I hate you. Mummy said it's important to share. You never share!' I responded by talking about how angry she was with me, that I hadn't allowed Susan to come into the session. 'Mum says there might be a war. Who are we fighting? Kuwait? Why? ... I'm worried about fighting; why do we have to fight, people will get hurt.' After we talk about how terrifying she thinks all this is, she says 'Why can't they just play a game with plastic soldiers so no-one gets hurt? Or a board game? Then the one who loses has to lose the war.' I ask what happens if one side cheats or throws a tantrum? She giggles and replies 'Well, you have a problem. I remember I used to do that; I tried to break this car, and your watch.' Talking further about how she used to destroy the toys, she adds 'You stopped me. You wouldn't let me break them. Why can't someone stop the fighting?' I ask who should stop them? She replies 'If there's going to be fighting, all of the animals, babies and old people and the sick should be moved. I want to become a giant. You can become a giant with me and we can get the babies out. This war makes me nervous.' She lies on the sofa and says 'I had this nightmare about the house on fire. Where will the bombs drop? Will we all die? Will there be bombs dropped here?' I say she is worried that she and I will be separated if the war continues. She says 'What will you do if there's a war? Will you go back to America? (Jennifer knows that I come from America.) Please stay away from the windows.' She spends the rest of the session taping paper over the window 'in case the war comes to Portsmouth.'

Coping with Adoption

As Jennifer grew more secure, she began to internalise a therapist who had the capacity to think about her. She was able to use me to think about the differences between her foster mother and her biological mother and her own conflicting loyalties. Just as she had me at the clinic and her foster mother at home, she also had two mothers. Her foster parents were in the midst of adoption proceedings for both girls, and the biological mother's access visits had decreased, though she was contesting the adoption.

During this period, Jennifer stole jewellery from her sister and foster mother. She appeared in therapy with pockets filled with her mother's ear-rings and rings, lipstick and money ... 'I'm rich!' One day she arrived with a bow she had taken from a friend at school. She was frustrated and annoyed that her mother had insisted she return it. 'I took this bow because I need it. I wanted it so I took it – it looks prettier on me. She can have my old one. It's not stealing because I left her my old one.' She told me she would like to steal her biological mother's new baby 'or you could take her away, and then I could go and live with my Mum.' We talked about how feeling deprived and wanting more made her steal and how she also felt deprived of her biological mother. She asked me what adoption meant and then said 'Never mind – I don't want to know.'

Step by step we unravelled her fears about why she was abandoned and placed in care. She invented stories about why her foster parents wanted to adopt her. 'Today I'll tell you another story. This one's different. It didn't really happen. It's not the truth – it's my imagination.' In some stories, her biological mother was ill, or gave Jennifer to Mr and Mrs J because they could not have a child of their own. She wished her foster mother would have a baby so that she could return to her birth mother. 'You see, my other mum can always have more babies but mummy can't have any.'

When faced with the sadness of her lost birth mother and the envy of a new baby who replaced her, Jennifer's interest turned to her foster mother's insides. 'I wish my mother could have a baby. She has a scab inside, that's why she can't have one. Maybe if she goes to the doctor he can give her some medicine. If she has a baby, then Susan and I can go and live with my other mum, then mummy wouldn't be sad if we left. This desire to repair things was very different from her earlier wish to get inside and kill her mother's capacity to have children.

Many months later Jennifer became preoccupied with what happens after adoption. She was aware that I would write a court report in support of the foster parents' wish to adopt her. We had spent a great deal of time discussing how she felt about my involvement in the legal proceedings; she was understandably ambivalent about my position. Her feelings about the adoption oscillated between disinterest and deep anxiety. It could merely be a continuation of how she was living, or it could become a prison that would keep her from her biological mother. 'If the judge asks me what I think, I'll say 'I'm not interested, I don't care.'

Conclusion

Jennifer's emotional disintegration manifested itself with painful clarity in her terror of separation and of falling apart. Her early experiences left her without an internal object capable of holding her together.

Initially, Jennifer saw me as either an attacking, life-threatening, sadistic therapist, or a sick, weak, damaged one. She distrusted my capacity to provide a continuous safe environment for her. She reacted by retreating into a state of highly sexualised confusion, where her primitive anxieties became perverse and sadistic as a defence against terror. She would 'jump' into projective identification with a narcissistic mother who was cruel, unprotecting and concerned only with her own needs, leaving me to feel the hopelessness of a messy unattended baby.

Although the material explored in the treatment was full of persecutory projections and anxieties, I also felt that there was an extraordinary vitality in Jennifer, a desperation to survive the madness and escape the terror. Her language was articulate, vivid, unusually so for a four year old. With time, she slowly became able to internalise the containment of a thinking, caring parental couple, who could pull her away from her dark internal world of sadism and violent fantasies of abusing and being abused.

Postscript

Jennifer now seems a very different girl. She is toilet-trained and her violent outbursts are gone. I continued to see her for intensive psychotherapy for another year. The family then moved away and it was only possible to see her once a week. She adjusted well to her new school and became deeply attached to her adoptive parents, her 'official Mum and Dad'.

Acknowledgement

I would like to thank Hélène Dubinsky for her help in thinking about this case.

2

The Difficulty of Establishing a Space for Thinking

The Therapy of a Seven-Year-Old Girl

Lynda Miller

In this chapter the interweaving of internal and external factors in one year of therapy of a very damaged, sexually abused child is described. In particular I want to focus upon the unbearable states of confusion experienced by this little girl when her external situation too closely replicated her internal world, and the effects of this on her therapy.

Her state of mind for much of the time during therapy could be described as psychotic. I would suggest that this was engendered by traumatic past events and further exacerbated by contemporary environmental factors.

Rosenfeld (1950), developing Melanie Klein's concept of paranoid-schizoid functioning, describes infantile states of confusion as states of disintegration associated with extreme anxiety. He suggests that '... under certain external and internal conditions when aggressive impulses temporarily predominate, states may arise in which love and hate impulses and good and bad objects cannot be kept apart and are thus felt to be mixed up or confused.' In such states of mind the destructive impulses seem to threaten to destroy the libidinal impulses and the whole self is felt to be in danger of being destroyed. If the capacity to differentiate between love and hate cannot be regained, splitting mechanisms become reinforced.

In thinking about this little girl, whom I will call Yvonne, I have found Rosenfeld's description of confusional states and their relation to splitting very relevant. For much of the time in her sessions with me Yvonne seemed quite unable to differentiate good from bad, food from urine and faeces, cleaning up from making mess. At other times she resorted to violent splitting, which reverberated in her support network.

56

2. The Difficulty of Establishing a Space for Thinking

I will now briefly outline her history and then describe some aspects of the therapy, bearing in mind an external and an internal perspective, as both revealed relationships characterised by splitting and confusion.

Yvonne, a mixed race child with an Irish mother and Algerian father (he left to go back to Algeria following Yvonne's birth and did not return), was taken into care at the age of three when sexual abuse by friends of her mother was discovered by a social worker. Yvonne's mother was known to social services as she kept company with heroin addicts and was thought to use drugs herself. Investigations revealed that Yvonne and her younger half-brother were severely neglected and had been witness to, and included in, violence and sexual activities. They were described as dirty and unkempt when taken into care, and apparently had at times slept in the streets with 'down and outs'.

The children were placed together with Mr and Mrs B, experienced foster parents who had no children of their own. They seemed quickly to become attached and committed to the children, but Yvonne's provocative, demanding and overtly sexual behaviour caused such distress that the placement seemed likely to collapse. However, they decided to foster Yvonne on a long-term basis, and the little boy, aged just two, was moved to another family who planned to adopt him. Contact between the children was virtually severed at the request of the prospective adopting parents.

These children must have provided for each other some sense of continuity of identity in their early years together and with their natural mother. Yvonne as the older child perhaps provided a source of containment for her baby brother's unwanted projections, thereby exacerbating her degree of disturbance. Presumably, the actual loss of continuing contact gave rise in both children to further confusion and a fractured sense of identity.

The question whether the B family could manage to keep Yvonne with them on a long-term basis continued to erupt both prior to and during the period of therapy. Within the Social Services team there was a marked division of opinion over this matter. Yvonne's social worker voiced repeatedly her serious doubts concerning the B's very stretched capacities for caring for the child. The B's social worker supported the foster parents' wish to keep Yvonne despite their obvious difficulties in managing her extreme behaviour, and endeavoured to set up additional support systems: respite care, outreach workers and an escort, to relieve some of the burden on the B's.

In meeting with the B's myself, to set up the therapy and for termly reviews, I became aware of their very powerful loving feelings towards

Yvonne, but also their inability to sustain their commitment to her when the strain of coping with such a disturbed child wore them down. Mrs B in particular seemed to need Yvonne's liveliness to bring vitality to her own life, and found it upsetting to contemplate separation from Yvonne, either brief, as in weekend respite, or long-term when a move to another family was suggested. However on numerous occasions the B's would convey that they could no longer cope with Yvonne's sexualised behaviour and prolonged tantrums, and several times requested that she be temporarily removed to another family whilst they went away on holiday for a rest and to try to make a decision about whether or not they could foster Yvonne.

The B's variant and incompatible communications were taken up separately within the support network, continuing splitting amongst those involved with the placement. Consequently, Yvonne's external world was precarious and unstable, providing a very shaky basis for the exploration of her internal world in psychotherapy.

An extract from the nineteenth therapy sessions follows, to illustrate Yvonne's state of confusion and her excessive use of projective identification to rid herself of unbearable experiences which threatened her from without and from within. At this point in time I had been seeing Yvonne for three times weekly therapy in a Child Guidance Clinic close to the B's home, for two months. Most sessions began with Yvonne clinging adhesively to Mrs B in the waiting room. With a struggle, and Mrs B's assistance, I would eventually manage to keep Yvonne in the therapy room for her session. Yvonne had been expelled from the local primary school after a few weeks, because of uncontrollable sexualised behaviour. She was waiting for a place in a day school for children with serious behavioural difficulties. I had agreed to transfer the setting of my work with Yvonne to a therapy room on the school premises. In agreeing to this, I was unavoidably contributing further to the instability facing Yvonne in other aspects of her external world.

19th Session

Yvonne said slyly 'I feel hot', took off her shoes and socks and the rest of her clothes, then grabbed the bin, filled it with water and did a wee in it. She very quickly threw the bin across the room, trying to splash me, then slid up and down the room on her stomach shrieking 'you fuck, you shit.' I said that in Yvonne's mind I change into the sexy Mrs Miller lady ... Yvonne can't trust me to hold the little, left-out Yvonne in my mind – she feels that I throw the baby Yvonne in the bin. She shrieked 'You've got a boyfriend, you fuck, lick my arse' and was still sliding up and down the room on her stomach, interspersed with imitations of a brutal sexual act (Yvonne on top) with abusive swearing. She shouted 'lovely swimming' and I talked about Yvonne filling herself up with sexy, exciting feelings, while showing me the little Yvonne left by herself, all cold and wet, covered in wee, with no-one to look after her.

She came close to me for a few seconds and showed me her stomach, saying she had a 'rash'. I said Yvonne wants me to know this sexy stuff isn't good for children but she feels that it goes on and on inside her and comes out on her skin – it fills the room, spills out in floods – all over me (she was splashing me). Yvonne said to me 'are you crying?' I said Yvonne knows that she has just splashed me but she is saying that the very hurt feelings, the wanting to cry, get all mixed up with the excited sexy feelings and Yvonne wants to get them into me – wants me to feel them too, to know how she feels inside … (A struggle followed because I prevented further flooding of the room) … Yvonne was very angry when I held the taps; she threw the bin across the room, climbed on the sink and did another wee, then slyly asked for a drink. She 'sucked' the water from the tap and spat it out repeatedly, laughing. I said there is a little Yvonne who wants to have milk from a therapy-mummy Mrs Miller, but she shows me that it changes into wee in her mouth and I become the sexy lady who tricks her and she is the little tricky Yvonne who tells me she wants a drink but wants to make more and more wee-mess everywhere. She isn't going to let me be a therapy-mummy who can feed the baby Yvonne.

I think this session illustrates a primitive part-object level of confusion in this child; a confusion between good and bad breast, between breast and penis/bottom (the tap), between self and object, inside and outside.

Meltzer (1967) describes the 'geographical confusions' which can arise when the infantile tendency towards massive projective identification with external and internal objects is in the ascendancy. This can be the case when 'the differentiation between good and bad is poorly defined due to inadequate or faulty splitting-and-idealisation of self and objects' and the motive for massive projective identification is omnipotent control. Aspects of geographical confusion cited by Meltzer include utilisation of the therapy room as the inside of an object with the therapist equated with the room, as well as representing the persecutory internal part object. Intense erotisation adds to the consequent claustrophobic anxiety, and I think that Yvonne's persistent attempts to escape from the therapy room, refusals to enter the room, on some occasions barricading me out, at other times spending all the session time racing around the building or hiding from me, can be understood both as a terror of being trapped inside a bad object and as attempts to escape from internal persecutors. The difficulty of keeping the therapy inside the therapy room often dominated the sessions.

Interpretations on some occasions seemed to be experienced by Yvonne very concretely and she would scream full-force over my words as a means, I think, of preventing their entry, or of evacuation. Hanna Segal (1957) describes the primitive projective and identificatory processes by which 'disturbances in differentiation between ego and object lead to disturbances in differentiation between the symbol and the object symbolised and therefore to concrete thinking characteristic of psychoses.' Words may thus be experienced as concrete non-symbolic, objects and in this state of mind verbal interpretations are misunderstood and can be frightening in effect.

The technical problem of how to talk to this little girl when her state of mind was one of primitive infantile confusion necessitated much reflection and changes in interpretative technique. I gradually learned to keep interpretations in a projected form, locating Yvonne's unwanted and intolerably painful experiences in myself, without explaining that these feelings really belonged to her. This helped to diminish persecutory anxiety in that it lessened Yvonne's sense of my using words to push unbearable evacuated experiences back into her. However, at times it seemed that she could not allow herself to tolerate my words at all and would scream, shout or run away so as not to hear.

As an illustration of this point, close to the end of a session (the 36th) immediately preceding a holiday break, Yvonne was shredding up soggy paper towels, saying to me 'go on, eat your dinner, it's mashed potato.' I interpreted that Yvonne was being the Mrs Miller mummy feeding the little Yvonne/me before the holiday so that we can be close together. I then felt that I had to point out that we had 'five minutes left', feeling acutely aware of her denial of the impending separation. At these words, 'Yvonne let out a great yell, a wild expression in her eyes. She grabbed all the soggy paper towels and threw them at me, trying to stuff them into my mouth, then threw them on the floor ...'

I felt that she had experienced my words 'five minutes left' as a violent act of reversal; my forcing back into her the projected feelings of desperate hunger and need. On reflection, it would have been preferable to continue to locate the hungry-baby feelings in myself, perhaps to interpret that the Mrs Miller baby was going to be feeling very hungry and lonely without her therapy food in the holiday ahead.

Anne Alvarez (1992) makes this point in her thinking about the process of recovery from child sexual abuse. She says: 'In the past, I think the psychoanalytical therapist might have felt it necessary to

60

remind the child that it was his own outrage he was projecting. Now there is greater understanding that the child may need that experience contained by someone else who can stand it better than he can.'

From her early history it will be apparent that Yvonne suffered a very deprived childhood, perhaps the most confusing element being the experience of having a mother who in some manner looked after and fed her baby, yet failed to protect her from harm, allowing her baby to be a highly vulnerable recipient of emotional and physical intrusions. Bion's (1959) model of containment allows understanding of the way in which an infant would be driven to intensify phantasies of projective identification when deprived of maternal containment, thereby exacerbating a malign cycle of mother-baby interaction. Presumably the scenario of sexual abuse, and in particular an unprotecting mother, would have played into the baby Yvonne's confusional state of mind, fuelling the tendency to erotisation, and the violence of her uncontained infantile fantasies. Consideration of the qualities of Yvonne's internal objects may also contribute towards an understanding of her psychotic confusional state of mind.

The trauma of sexual abuse as a violent intrusion of a child's body and mind can readily be linked with a rupture in cognitive and emotional development, giving rise to severe disturbance, and in more extreme cases, psychotic states. Where the abuser was an adult man (or men) as in Yvonne's case, subsequent fear of men, and in the internal world, a frightening, sexual internal father would be expected.

It seemed that Yvonne's mother was unprotective or even collusive in the sexual abuse, and it could be conjectured that Yvonne internalised a maternal object suffused with confusion, incapable of differentiating erotisation from affection, and felt to be lethally treacherous. Yvonne's mistrust of me was extreme, and any interpretation seemed often to be experienced by her as dangerous, regardless of content and meaning.

A place soon became available for Yvonne at a school which was felt to be appropriate for her special needs, and after a few weeks of settling in and re-establishing therapy in this new setting, there was a brief period in which the therapeutic process could develop. Yvonne began to be able to differentiate her very needy and deprived baby self from the cruel, abandoning mother of her internal world, mainly by putting me in the role of the neglected and unwanted baby, herself as the narcissistic uncaring mother. This seemed an important step, the beginning of the emergence from chaos and confusion, as prior to this her identifications in sessions would seem to switch in a rapid and incomprehensible manner, with very little possibility of differentiation.

Then the B's went away on holiday without Yvonne as Mr B was in poor health and the couple were again in doubt as to whether they could continue with the placement. Yvonne was placed temporarily with another foster family and was waking at night in terror with nightmares. During the day she experienced frightening delusions of creatures getting in and under the skin of her arm. This sudden predominance of psychotic functioning seemed to have been precipitated by a sudden and unexpected loss in Yvonne's external world of that which was safe and familiar to her, and an equally sudden and unprepared-for move into a strange and unknown place. This could be understood psychically as an experience of something horrible and frightening being suddenly pushed into her mind, perhaps linked in Yvonne's internal world with earlier experiences of being the vulnerable recipient of horrible and frightening projections; in phantasy the intrusive creatures against whom she felt defenceless. The predominant sensation in Yvonne's sessions during this period was one of sickening, senseless chaos. Yvonne was in a panic about where she belonged, which was very distressing to behold.

In the B's absence a decision had been made between the Social Services and the new school that a place at a therapeutic boarding school should be sought for Yvonne as soon as possible, the present situation being clearly unviable. The B's were told of this on return from their holiday, and also told that Yvonne might be permanently moved to another family. In this emotional climate Yvonne was returned to the B's who had been advised not to discuss any of these matters in the child's presence. The B's always returned from their holidays with renewed resolve to keep Yvonne, so they were upset and angry.

An extract follows from the 47th session, in the midst of this period. I think it is clear that Yvonne was desperately trying to control the sense of chaos and helplessness that threatened to overwhelm her. For this child, her lack of good, firm internal objects was being replicated externally and this made it very difficult for her to make use of my help.

47th Session

Yvonne raced to the bathroom and filled her mouth with water from the taps, spitting at me repeatedly. She punched me when I held the taps, then smeared her hands with dirty water from the floor and tried to wipe them on me, shouting 'are you going to send me back to the classroom?' She ran down the corridor shrieking and I blocked her exit, saying that I thought Yvonne was determined to turn me into a dirtied messed-up Mrs Miller who feels hopeless, who can't look after Yvonne. She ran back to the toilet saying 'I wanna wee', laughing and racing ahead of me. When I got to the door she was sitting on the toilet. She got up and said 'do you know what I've done?' and put her hand into the toilet bowl, pulling out a full roll of soaking wet toilet paper. She pulled off handfuls in lumps and threw them at me, aiming at my face. I felt very angry and held her, telling her to stop. Yvonne struggled, saying 'are you sending me back to the classroom now?' I said I thought that Yvonne was trying to make me all messed up, useless and unwanted – to get rid of me.

Yvonne had a very powerful capacity to fill me with feelings which she could not tolerate in herself; in this session feelings of rage, of helplessness, of being dirty and rejected. I felt at this point that she was unable to make any use of interpretations intended to facilitate re-introjection of these feelings, or even interpretations referring to her intention to provoke a rejecting response in me. If I did so, she would become quite frenzied and extremely difficult to manage. Indeed, her behaviour in the classroom was becoming increasingly disruptive and at times beyond the limit manageable even in a specialised setting with small groups of severely disturbed children.

It remained unclear when the transfer to a boarding school would take place, but the aim was to effect the move as soon as a place became available. The implication of this with regard to my work with Yvonne was that I knew the therapy would be curtailed and perhaps at quite short notice. However, intensive therapy continued with a climate of instability and uncertainty pervading Yvonne's life.

Then a playground incident involving sexual behaviour between two boys and Yvonne precipitated her suspension from school for two weeks, during which time she could not attend her school-based therapy sessions. She was then allowed to return on a part-time basis only, and it became clear that in this setting, intensive psychotherapy could not continue. There were no extra staff members to support the task of taking Yvonne between classroom and therapy room (quite a distance). Her attacks on the boundaries I tried to maintain became increasingly relentless, as she no longer felt contained within the overall school structure.

At the beginning of the therapy, in a clinic setting, Mrs B had been available in the waiting room during Yvonne's sessions, should she be needed, and to help with the transition between therapy and waiting room on difficult days. It seemed particularly unfortunate that the absence in the school of the resources needed to support Yvonne's therapy, replicated in a painful way her continuing deprivation of a holding structure such as would normally be provided by a family.

I decided to offer to see Yvonne once a week from this point onwards, planning to continue until she would leave to attend boarding school at some date in the near future. I felt that it was preferable to continue with the therapy in a way that might be manageable, rather than attempting to continue with intensive therapy with little support and a possible breakdown.

In writing about children who have been deprived of the opportunity to develop within a family, Britton (1983) considers how this situation might best be remedied. He begins with the recognition that a child needs to be contained within a bounded space, and that in attempting to reconstitute a family for a child there must be clarity of thinking with regard to provision of the qualities essential to a meaningful family life, in particular predictability and continuity.

Britton emphasises that 'The strength and viability of the context for the care or psychotherapy of disturbed children needs to be carefully considered at the outset and as far as possible the children protected from suffering the experience of their supporting framework once again breaking down under the strain of their own destructiveness or the anxieties they provoke in others.'

Clear decisions had not been made when Yvonne and her brother first came into care. An assessment recommendation of therapeutic boarding school for Yvonne, based on the view that a foster placement probably would not be adequate to contain her degree of disturbance, was not heeded. The extreme anxiety, sudden aggressive outbursts, sexualisation and violent splitting associated with this little girl's confusional state of mind engendered the perpetual threat of breakdown in the supportive framework. For Yvonne, her external world replicated in quality the attributes of her internal objects; unprotecting, unpredictable and discontinuous.

At the same time, despite their enormous difficulties in caring for this child, the B's had provided Yvonne with what one would imagine was her first experience of loving parenting. She had been with them for three years and Yvonne clung to them desperately, deteriorating in a very distressing way in their absence.

After eight months of intensive therapy I was now seeing Yvonne only once a week. I felt that initially my task was to attempt to differentiate for Yvonne the sort of work we might now be able to do together. At this point in time the B's were again 'on holiday' without Yvonne and breakdown of the placement seemed imminent. This followed an incident where Yvonne had been discovered initiating sexual play with the small children of the B's neighbour, who proceeded to sever friendship with Mrs B. Yvonne was due to return to the B's after their holiday as a final decision about the placement had not been reached.

In the first few weeks of once weekly therapy, Yvonne attempted to initiate situations that were very familiar to both of us, of highly sexualised confusion, followed by violent attacks and usually desperate attempts to get out of the therapy room. In this, the 78th session, Yvonne tried to cover me with glue, expressing both her wish to stick to me, and her rage at feeling that I was rejecting her by reducing the number of her sessions:

> ... I eventually retrieved the glue and Yvonne kicked and punched with full force, shrieking excitedly, grabbing then pinching my left breast as hard as she could – I had to prise her hand away. She then lay on the floor trying to kick between my legs.

I talked to Yvonne about her anger with me about the lost sessions, and her worries about returning to her foster parents the following weekend. I felt that Yvonne first had to be helped to make some sense of her very confused external world, and that until circumstances were such that she felt she knew where she belonged, it would only serve to add to her confusion to talk to her in terms of the internal/transference relationship to a cruel, sexual abandoning mother whom she wished both to invade and to attack.

Rosenfeld (1950) points out that where attempts to overcome confusional states fail, splitting mechanisms are reinforced, bringing about further disintegration of the ego. Yvonne clung adhesively to Mrs B as an idealised object, splitting off her awareness of the precariousness of the foster placement. She would insist that the B's had adopted her, and this was colluded with in that she was allowed to use their surname instead of her own.

In offering Yvonne one session a week with more tightly defined boundaries than would be usual in psychotherapy, it did become possible to be very clear with her that we were meeting to try to think together about what was happening in her life, to attempt to sort out some of the external confusion. To some extent Yvonne was able to respond to this and it facilitated a shift from enactment of phantasy based on projective identification, to Yvonne at times being able to see me as a separate person with whom she had a more ambivalent relationship, with the beginnings of a corresponding shift from concrete to symbolic thinking.

In the following extract from the 82nd session Yvonne is able, with difficulty, to find symbolic expression for her primitive anxieties and to be able to use words and to receive words as communications, rather than to experience them concretely as persecutory objects or actions. This development seemed to be associated with a diminution of both excessive splitting and massive projective identification, evidenced in her growing capacity to differentiate between self and object, and internal and external reality.

82nd Session

She began to shout 'fuck my arse', very loudly and aggressively, a bellowing sound, slamming the door shut repeatedly, very hard, then started to throw a chair around the room. I stopped her, with Yvonne trying to punch and kick me. She went into the corner of the room and shouted 'leave the door open', then said 'I've got a boyfriend, he's seven' (not said in a wild, sexualised way). I said 'have you? what's his name?' Yvonne said 'shut-up, don't talk' but looked pleased. She pulled some books out of her drawer and sat in the arm-chair looking through one, saying 'you don't know what this is, you can't see.' I said that Yvonne wants me to be interested, to be curious about her holiday and what's been happening. She said 'I'm not talking to you.' She stood at the desk and opened a book saying 'this is my news book' and began scribbling wildly in circles. I said that Yvonne's news this morning is about muddles … about what is happening in her life at the moment. She might not be talking to me because she is not feeling sure that the grown-ups can sort out the muddles. It's hard to feel safe when there are lots of muddles around (Yvonne was scribbling on all the pages). She suddenly ran to the door saying 'I can't manage', looking frightened. I said I thought she could and to come and sit down. She did, and said 'I want to write "this is a bonfire" – spell it.' I spelt it for her and she wrote "this is a b" then jumped up, upturning the table and shouting and punching. Whilst trying to restrain her I said I thought Yvonne's feelings about what is happening in her life are very hard to manage, but she was managing to write them down, rather than having to leave the room. The bonfire might be like how she feels inside; suddenly all the muddles get too much and it's like having a fire inside you, angry burning feelings. Yvonne climbed on top of the door and shouted 'you can't get me', then asked me to help her down.

Meanwhile numerous meetings to include all professionals involved in the case were convened by the social services team, in an attempt to clarify their thinking and to facilitate making a decision with regard to where Yvonne would be living for weekends and holiday breaks from boarding school, in effect, who would be providing a parental function.

2. The Difficulty of Establishing a Space for Thinking

At the meetings I attended throughout the duration of the therapy, it was necessary to draw attention to the catastrophic effect upon Yvonne of not knowing where she belonged. The unbearable degree of uncertainty and confusion permeating this case, which Yvonne had to contend with, was often overlooked as a significant factor in thinking about this child.

When an offer of a place for Yvonne at a therapeutic boarding school was made, it was finally decided that the B's should continue to be the long-term foster parents. This was a hard-won decision as the social services team remained irreconcilably divided on the question of Yvonne's placement. My view with regard to Yvonne's internal world was that she had not yet achieved normal splitting and the establishment of good parental objects. I felt that rudimentary developmental processes, of introjective as well as projective identification, were under way, although still heavily dependent upon the presence of reliable, consistent and containing external objects. I felt that to remove her from the B's and to expect her to be able to 'transfer' to another set of foster parents would probably be disastrous. Her emotional equilibrium was delicately and precariously poised and readily tipped into disintegration and an infantile confusional state. I hoped that when the immense strain of full-time care of Yvonne was lifted from the B's shoulders in that she would only be with them for weekends and holidays, the placement would be viable.

The last two months of Yvonne's therapy can be considered in the context of a more stable background, although she had to face ending therapy and going away from home to a new residential school. The B's were able to tell me of some very positive changes in Yvonne over recent weeks, and we shared the pleasure of developments we had both seen. They reported that Yvonne was now able to engage in imaginative play with her dolls and toys, playing by herself for periods of time. They also commented upon her developing capacity to differentiate between 'pretend' and 'real'. This paralleled my experience of Yvonne in her sessions, where it had become more possible to talk with her about external events, in particular the difficult changes awaiting her in the near future, without her becoming overwhelmed by panic and confusion; in other words her destructive impulses were more contained. Rosenfeld (1950) describes attempts at recovery from confusional states, in which 'the libidinal impulses can help to modify and control the danger of the aggressive impulses, and feelings of reparation can begin to develop'. He notes that if the aggressive impulses temporarily predominate, they will interfere with the recovery processes. Yvonne's aggressive outbursts continued both at home and in therapy, but with the diminution of excessive splitting, her loving impulses towards her objects could come into play to modify her destructiveness and allow recovery and reparation.

Mrs B described to me another aspect of Yvonne's emergence from a confusional state, in particular a confusion between past and present. She spoke of the way Yvonne still had of staring, as if transfixed, at tramps and down-and-outs. 'She used to go up to them with sexual invitations ... but I told Yvonne not to do it, and she doesn't now, she knows it's wrong, and when I say "come on Yvonne" she comes out of her glazed state.' We talked about Yvonne's developing capacity to distinguish between good and bad, right and wrong, while still relying on others to pull her out of the confusion which filled her early life.

During the course of the therapy Yvonne had put her memory of her abuse into words to her foster mother, utilising her growing capacity to symbolise rather than to enact. Whilst Yvonne needed Mrs B to receive her communications as descriptions of actual past events, to be able to contain them for her as such without being overwhelmed, my concern was rather with Yvonne's tendency to avoid psychic pain by entering into a highly eroticised, excited confusional state fuelled by violent sexual and abusive fantasies.

In writing about massive projective identification Betty Joseph (1984) comments: 'I suspect there is much yet to be teased out about the relation between certain types of massive projective identification of the self and erotisation'. It is perhaps particularly difficult in the case of a child who has been sexually abused to differentiate the elements of remembered experience from the distortions of unconscious phantasy.

On reflection, it seems helpful in sexual abuse cases that the role of the psychotherapist is clearly differentiated from that of other available adults, in that, in therapy, the focus is upon the child's internal world, the meaning of experiences in the present, rather than upon the facts of sexual abuse as memory of past traumatic events. Yvonne seemed to respond to this differentiation; it enabled her to use Mrs B and myself in different and appropriate ways, thereby lessening her confusion. In that I knew that my work with Yvonne would be prematurely curtailed and that we lacked both the time and an adequately supportive framework for intensive psychotherapy, I felt that my main task was to help her to develop and to maintain her as yet very fragile capacity to differentiate between her loving and hating impulses in facing the end of therapy.

2. The Difficulty of Establishing a Space for Thinking

A brief extract from the second to last session with Yvonne follows, when she was very soon to be leaving for boarding school.

86th Session

Yvonne said that she would talk to me if I didn't look at her, and would I make her a house out of cushions? We did this and Yvonne said 'now I won't talk – I can't see you' and sent the cushions flying all over the room. I said Yvonne wants me to know how she feels about leaving me. She can't look at me because that makes her think about not seeing me when she leaves. She wants me to make her a little house, keep her inside so she doesn't have to leave – then she feels it gets all broken up and she is outside, not safe and hidden. Yvonne was throwing cushions around. I said Yvonne wants me to know how hard it is to think about leaving – it feels as if everything is flying around in her mind, not safely held inside ... She then ordered me very bossily to clear up, shouting orders about where the cushions should go. She said 'is it all right?' I said she needs to feel that we can put things together again, we can think about Yvonne leaving me and having a new place to go to ... it's not all in bits.

Hanna Segal describes the process of symbol formation as 'a continuous process of bringing together and integrating the internal with the external, the subject with the object, and the earlier experiences with the later ones'. Towards the end of this very complicated and curtailed piece of therapeutic work there did seem to be moments in which integrative processes had come into play. Yvonne showed, at times, a developing capacity to communicate symbolically, through play and through words. However it seemed to me that our work had come to an end at a very precarious point in her development, and the danger of unmanageable anxiety giving rise to disintegration and primitive infantile confusion felt very present.

Conclusion

This chapter evolved out of my attempt, in retrospect, to make some sense out of the very disturbing and confusing experience of working with a seven-year-old child, who had been severely neglected and sexually abused, before being taken into care.

From a theoretical perspective, I have focused upon the psychotic confusional state which dominated the therapy sessions over the year of work. I have tried to indicate the interplay of the internal and external factors which I feel contributed to the child's confusion, and to suggest

69

the particular difficulties in psychotherapy with children whose external situation is very unstable.

From a technical point of view, I felt that the containing and differentiating functions of interpretations were most useful in helping this child to develop a capacity to think. The therapist's capacity to contain and differentiate could gradually be internalised by the child, facilitating a shift from concrete to symbolic thinking.

Acknowledgement

I would like to thank Margaret Rustin for her support, and supervision of this case.

An earlier version of this chapter appeared in Psychoanalytic Psychotherapy Vol. 6, No. 2, 1992) under the same title.

3

Survival of the Self

A Sixteen-Year-Old Girl's Search for a Good Object

Chriso Andreou

Introduction

This Chapter explores the search of an adolescent girl for a good object and her struggle to preserve her sanity. Her experience of early deprivation and the subsequent trauma of sexual abuse had left her very fragile. As her external circumstances changed she was faced with the threat of psychic disintegration. This paper concentrates on the first two years of therapy when the patient, after beginning to overcome these experiences of disintegration, had to resist the attempt by perverse and psychotic parts of the personality to dominate the self. The clinical material illustrates how her sense of abandonment affected the nature and intensity of the transference relationship.

Background

Information about Mary's background and family history is very sketchy. She was born to a very young adolescent mother. A brother was born two years later. Shortly after this second birth the mother abandoned the children who were then looked after by their grandmother. When Mary was three years old, both children were taken into care due to physical neglect and placed in a residential nursery. Mary reported good memories of this home, but vividly remembered her jealousy of the other children including her brother who was thought of as attractive and loveable and received a lot of attention.

Mary and her brother were then placed in foster care. A series of non-accidental injuries led to the removal of her brother.

When Mary became physically and verbally aggressive at home and at school and began to steal, her foster parents said that they could no longer manage her. She was removed and placed in a children's home. Further attempts at fostering failed as she herself always rejected the prospective foster parents. She liked her school and was very attached to one of her teachers. She refused all contact with her family and expressed hatred towards her mother, who embarrassed her and who she thought of as a prostitute and an alcoholic. This was in fact a true picture.

Referral and Psychotherapy

Mary's social worker referred her for psychotherapy when she was sixteen years old. She now lived in an adolescent home in preparation for leaving care. Her social worker's main anxiety was Mary's depression and preoccupation with suicide. She was also concerned about Mary's violent feelings of hatred towards her mother, saying, for example, that she wanted to kill her. She expressed dislike of the colour of her skin and projected this disgust into a black residential social worker whom she called thick and stupid.

Introduction and Setting for Therapy

Mary was too anxious to meet me on her own and asked her social worker to accompany her to our first meeting. I agreed to this, with the idea that after this consultation she would be able to come on her own for assessment.

What struck me about Mary was her physical appearance. She was very neatly and fashionably dressed, but her attractive face was devoid of all expression and had none of the freshness of youth. It was drawn, dark, and constantly scowling. The best description was her own subsequent comment – 'Although I am young, I am old, an old hag.' She sat very stiffly in her chair, without looking at me and allowed her social worker to talk for her. She told me that Mary was unhappy and felt she needed help. Mary nodded in agreement but did not ask any questions or say anything. I did not put any questions to her. Her demeanour and posture stopped me. The silent message that shrieked at me was, 'Don't ask me anything.' She agreed to a trial meeting one week later on the understanding that it would simply be to see whether we could work together. She did not keep that appointment or the next that I sent her. A month later she telephoned and asked the secretary for an appointment with me.

3. Survival of the Self

She arrived twenty minutes early. When I went to collect her from the waiting room, my first thought was how ill she looked. My thoughts were of physical illness rather than someone suffering emotionally. She looked exhausted, and slumped in her chair. She followed me without looking at my face and sat opposite me in my room, her body lifeless. I began to feel afraid. I found myself commenting on how tired and depressed she looked. She opened her mouth to say something but no words came out. She started to shudder, her whole body trembled and she began to cry. When I commented again on how unhappy and distraught she looked, her face tightened, she started to tap her forehead, shaking her head as if to free herself from unbearable thoughts. Shivers went through my body. I felt helpless as I sat there watching her disintegrating. My words seemed to hurt her; she would shiver at the very sound of my voice. I stopped talking, covered her in a blanket and held her physically without speaking until she gradually stopped trembling. In a very low voice she started to talk, saying that she wanted to die, she couldn't stand the pain any longer; she kept repeating that she wanted to die. I sat there without saying anything, feeling that any comment would merely be a way of relieving my own feelings of anxiety and pain at being with her. She did not look at me. I was not even sure whether she was aware of me as a person at that time. Gradually between silence, crying and shuddering, she began to tell me that her foster father had sexually abused her. She had never told anyone before. 'No one would listen' she said desperately. They would have thought she was a disgusting black girl. She used to try and tell people that she felt dirty, that she didn't like her skin. They would say 'Shame on you, you should be proud to be black.' It had nothing to do with being black. She wanted to die, to kill herself.

I said I thought that she wanted me to be someone who listened to what she had to say without interrupting her so that she could say how she felt about herself and her very painful experience of being sexually abused. She looked at me briefly with a look that had no life, as if light and life had gone out of her eyes.

I said then that I thought she really did want to die so that she would stop feeling the pain and I believed her when she said she wanted to kill herself. That is why she came to see me today to tell me that she wanted to die, but I also thought that part of her wanted someone to stop her killing herself and to help her. She said no one could stop her. I said that I was going to let her social worker know that she felt very bad and she might want to talk to her. I would see her again tomorrow. She nodded and agreed to come.

73

She was still in a state of deep depression when she left. I phoned her social worker to tell her of my anxiety about her state of mind and the possibility of a suicide attempt and asked for the residential social workers to keep an eye on her. That night she took an overdose and was admitted to the local hospital. I had a phone call from the duty psychiatrist telling me that he was very worried because she was still suicidal. I visited her in hospital, and after discussion it was agreed that with guaranteed supervision from the residential social workers and a commitment from the consultant psychiatrist to admit her to hospital if necessary, I would see her for psychotherapy three times a week and the residential social workers would receive support from one of my colleagues.

When working with vulnerable and disturbed young people it is very important that, before beginning therapy, the therapist assesses the strength of the external containing structure that needs to be available to contain any acting out that may be precipitated by therapy. Although Mary was very difficult and aggressive at times in her home, her stark raw pain and need for help made everyone want to help her rather than attempt to get rid of her and get away from her pain.

The Beginning of Therapy

Mary came to her sessions with frightening regularity – and on time. During the first month of therapy she would come in a very depressed state, would not look at me, was too vulnerable and frightened to use the couch and used the sessions mainly to evacuate her feelings and thoughts. Though not aware of me as a person, she did want a container for her terrifying thoughts and unbearable pain. She would say that her thoughts were in a muddle; her brain was like spaghetti Bolognese. She worried about going mad, that I would be unable to tolerate her, and would have her put away. Then she would remember that I visited her in hospital, and 'got her out of there.' She wanted to talk but often couldn't. Part of her felt dead, everything inside was cracked. She would become listless, lifeless, and want to go to sleep. She continuously talked about wanting to be dead so that the pain would stop. Interpretations were difficult, not only because I seemed to spend a lot of time trying to cope with my own fears and panic about her, but also because she found even the sound of my voice difficult. Her thinking was so concrete that my words seemed to hurt her physically. Segal (1957) has described how words can be experienced as concrete, non-symbolic objects.

74

3. Survival of the Self

Mary expressed murderous rage towards her mother, whom she would call a dirty prostitute, who had no business having her, then throwing her away. 'Everyone knows I am a bastard' she would shout; then she would describe the sexual abuse. 'He called me a blackie, a dirty blackie; that's why he did it.' She washed and washed but could never feel clean. While her mother was so bad she could not bear to see her, her teacher was idealised and she wanted to be fostered by her. She needed to see her every day, otherwise she became very depressed.

I suggested she write or draw if it made it easier for her to communicate with me. I realised that when she was in a state of despair she could not speak. She started to draw pictures of coffins and crosses with her name and her mother's name on them. When I said, 'Better together in death than separated in life' she looked at me, smiled sadly, and said 'You've got it.'

She wrote this poem:

> I am a little girl
> In a tiny world.
> My mother has gone and left me alone.
> I hate myself because I am black.
> I am going away to another world
> Where someone can hold me in their arms
> Surrounded by love, surrounded by charm.

I asked where this other world was. She said 'You go there when you die, there is only peace there.' At this stage in the therapy I would make simple interpretations about feeling dropped, alone, without a mother, how this made her want to die, and about the part of her which needed and hoped for a good mother, perhaps a good therapy mother who could listen and accept that part of herself she called the shitty black baby. When she talked about killing herself I would speak about the hopeful part of her, the part that brings her to therapy and to someone whom she hopes is strong and can tolerate what she has to say and do some thinking for her.

One day she handed me two poems and asked me to read them, saying they were written for her teacher. She smiled sadly and said when she was young she used to go up to women she knew and ask them to take her home. When I finished reading them I looked up and found her looking straight at me without fear for the first time. 'You can keep them for a while if you like.' I found myself thanking her. The pain and the longing for love and her search and belief that there is love and a good object that will heal her pain was very clearly expressed in the

75

poems. She laughed nervously and said she used to tell her teacher that they were held together by a piece of string and she was waiting for her teacher to cut the string. I interpreted that perhaps she was beginning to see her therapy as a piece of string which is joining her and me as a mother therapist together and she is frightened that I will abandon her. Suddenly her expression changed. She looked away from me. A morose look came over her face 'I am not going anywhere' she said scowling and shaking. 'Everyone looks at me outside, something horrible is going to happen.' I had forgotten how concrete her thinking was: my words were felt as a real threat to abandon her.

She took out two photographs, looked at them then showed them to me (she had shown them to me before – they were pictures of herself and her brother and other small children when she was in the first children's home). I said that she was showing me pictures of herself as a three-year-old. She was asking me to remember that there was a three year old part of her that became very frightened. She interrupted me to say 'I am a baby, I hate myself, I took something last night'. I asked her what she had taken but she shook her head. 'You are going to be horrible to me, I don't care. Everyone is horrible to me. I am just a number, no one cares.' She took a piece of paper, shook her head the way she usually did when she tried to get rid of painful thoughts and started to write. She wrote 'If life was full of flowers and my heart a bed of roses, because I am.' Then she drew a coffin. She asked me what I thought.

I suggested that she wrote to get away from the thoughts that were telling her I was going to hurt her; she wished life could be full of beautiful things like flowers and she could feel beautiful feelings in her heart, but all this seemed to disappear and go dead.

With a frightened look she told me she was not leaving, took the two photographs, tore them into pieces and threw them on the floor saying that she was only a shitty black baby. I felt horrified. Her symbolic action of tearing up her child self felt very concrete to me and I found myself collecting the pieces. 'Put them in the dustbin' she demanded. 'No', I said, I will keep them. One day you might want to see them together again.' She smiled and looked away.

Her Sense of Abandonment and Sexual Abuse

Mary became passionately attached to me, expressing very vividly how it felt to be deprived, how much she needed to be close to someone. She would beg me to let her stay just a few minutes longer, turning me into a rejecting, cruel mother figure who was throwing her out. At times, I found the feelings I had to contain unbearable, though I tried very hard to maintain my thinking capacity and to respect the fifty minutes limit of the session. Sometimes I did not succeed and she remained up to fifteen minutes longer.

At that time, the residential social workers began to worry. They felt Mary was becoming too dependent on me, appearing more depressed and threatening suicide, to such an extent that they were frightened to leave her alone. She cried a lot and needed to be cuddled (only by the female social workers: she would not allow men near her). She kept saying that she wanted to see me; nobody else would do. They needed a lot of support to go on feeling that they could help Mary, especially when, at times, she would explode in violent rage against them.

Sometimes she arrived smiling, but immediately reverted to unhappy brooding. She would tell me accusingly that she was not well, that it was all my fault; she had not been able to eat anything, she could only drink a little water. In her mind I became the cruel, depriving and abandoning mother who left her to starve.

At this time she told me about what she called a dream: that I left her and she was crying out to me but I was gone. Then a man came along and sexually abused her. The abandoned baby thus became again the sexually abused baby. She also told me that she still visited her ex-foster parents occasionally; she felt obliged to go back and though she wanted to scream and shout at her foster father, she could not. She began to drink and smoke marijuana, and would arrive drugged, laughing hysterically. I was very firm with her and told her clearly that if she really valued her therapy, which I thought she did, she would have to struggle against the wish to damage herself and her therapy. I explained that I would refuse to see her if she were stoned. I expected resistance but all she said was that nobody had ever told her to stop smoking hash. She would not come to sessions stoned again, if that was what I wanted.

In the following session she told me that she was feeling ill.

'The good feelings don't last very long.' She described the meeting she had with the residential social workers, convened because of her violence. I said that inside she felt bad and guilty and didn't like herself and was worried in case I didn't like her, and would throw her out of my therapy home. She started to laugh, a hysterical uncontrollable laughter that chilled me, the laughter of 'madness'. 'I am thick, I want to kill myself.' She tried to pull herself together. 'No, no', shaking her head, 'I don't, I don't know any more, I don't care if I am sent to hospital.' I interpreted that she felt confused and unable to think and that frightened her. She wanted to kill herself to stop the pain and confusion but another part of her, a more thinking grown-up part, was saying 'No, Mary, you don't want to kill yourself.' 'That's right, I'd like to get drunk or smoke grass tonight. Friday, Saturday, Sunday, Monday, I can't bear it. How can I survive those days . I'll get drunk tonight and tomorrow. I don't know what I'll do on Sunday, at least on Monday I will see you tomorrow.'

She clearly linked her addiction to drink and drugs with anxiety about being abandoned. I interpreted her dread of those days when she felt abandoned and uncared for, like a baby without a good caring mother to look after her, a baby frightened that it will not survive. She started to rub her skin. 'No one likes to be abandoned. My skin is bad, I am getting eczema again. It's bad, it's horrible, if only I could be white.' I said that she felt me to be a very cruel abandoning and abusive mother who didn't take care of her and left her because I thought she was a nasty black baby.

She rubbed her forehead again and again and spoke of how she used to spend a long time in the bath trying to wash her skin white. Sometimes she wants to kill herself. She will phone her teacher tonight, maybe she could go and stay with her. She appeared to be saying her thoughts out loud rather than addressing me as if I was already gone and she was searching for another person who could look after her during the weekend break. Then she appeared to be back again and more aware of me. She looked at me vaguely, and I interpreted that she had gone away from me as if the break had already happened and she was looking for someone like her teacher to be there for her during the weekend so that the separation between us would not be so painful.

She looked away and touched the bars of the electric fire. 'Bars, do you know what they remind me of? Something unpleasant, something horrible.' I asked what the memory was but she said she didn't remember, just that it gave her a funny feeling. 'Where do you find bars? In prison?' I asked. 'Can you read my mind?' She said, and went on to say that she had remembered when she was in the foster home she had put nail varnish on and to punish her, her foster mother had locked her in the room and gone out and left her for hours. 'Did you think they were not coming back?' I asked. 'I wished he wouldn't but I wanted my foster mother to come back.'

Towards the end, she looked at me, frightened, and said 'You are going to throw me out now, aren't you? I am not going, I don't feel well. Go on then, tell me to go. I don't care, no-one cares. My mother, bloody cunt, all she did was to open her legs, and I dropped out, that's all, she did nothing else.' A dazed expression came over her face. I felt she was slipping away from me to protect herself against the terrifying pain of being thrown out. I said that she felt like a baby who needed to be inside mother, just as she wanted to be inside my room. She felt I would open the door and throw her out into the terrifying world outside where she could not survive. 'It's so frightening out there', she said. I waited until she came gradually back to life before ending the session.

78

3. Survival of the Self

This particular session overran by fifteen minutes. I felt that she needed time to come back from her withdrawn regressed state. I invited her to stay in the waiting room until she was ready to go home.

Eroticisation of the Transference and Drawings of Confusion

As the holiday break approached she became more and more anxious and confused. She could not cope with the flood of feelings and thoughts. She would beg me to be careful not to let anything happen to me. The transference became eroticised – she would complain that my room was too hot. 'I know you come from a warm climate, but this is too much.' The couch became dangerous, she thought its brown cover was disgusting. How could I expect her to lie on it?

Rosenfeld (1987) in discussing the origins of the erotic transference of the schizophrenic, differentiated apparently Oedipal phenomena from eroticised links with a part object, breast or penis. This was illustrated vividly in Mary's drawings. She drew breast-like objects with the name of her therapist inside and wrote 'man out', 'danger'. Thus her object was split into good and bad – a 'good' therapist – outside of which lay confusion and danger. Klein (1957) has shown that the confusional state is caused by a failure of the normal splitting between good and bad objects and parts of the self. Mary drew spirals to indicate this sort of confusion. Her drawings bore witness to the torment of her inner world. The monster that was torturing her she called the devil. As Bion (1962) suggested, words are not always suitable vehicles for highly charged emotional states. The psychotic patient may try to find images instead. As Mary felt less overwhelmed, she began to bring me letters. She wrote that she missed me, she loved me, she couldn't stand the pain, she needed me to cuddle her like a baby and I wasn't there. When she could tolerate my absence no longer, her love turned to hate.

> Chriso please don't leave me
> If anything happens to you
> What will I do?
> Sometimes I become so nervous and
> frightened. Please be careful
> Just to see if you can feel what I feel.
> The pain is unbearable, You make me sick
> I hate you, You Hate, You Sick ...

The Battle Between Good and Bad Objects

She came back from the summer break in a good mood telling me that she was surprised that she had enjoyed herself. She had passed her exams and was to continue her education. Her appearance was strikingly different, the scowl had disappeared and she was proud to show me how dark she had become from her exposure to the sun. The good feelings, though, would not last a whole session. She observed this: 'I don't know what happens to me when I come here. I feel very mixed-up inside because all those horrible feelings in me decide to come up.'

She talked a lot about her traumatic experience of being sexually abused and drew pictures to show how trapped and frightened she felt. Her mind, she said, felt as if 'it went to pieces', describing vividly in this way what trauma meant.

Preoccupied with her mother, the 'fucking cunt', she started to go out with boys and sleep with men, then feel disgusted. She asked, 'Why do I do it?' She was in projective identification with a neglectful prostitute mother and I worried that she would get pregnant. It still terrified her if I tried to explore the negative transference evoked by the thought that I was with a man. She was totally possessive in her love for me, like a baby at the breast. I had to remain idealised; her intelligence and thinking was projected on to me. Mary's more adult part was available outside the therapy. She began to be able to struggle with reality, not hating it so much as long as she could remain in touch with her good object At this stage I was able to begin to differentiate between the baby part and the more adult part that she could call upon to pull her out of states of disintegration.

Mary's therapy had become a lifeline which strengthened her although she was still very fragile. She began to contact her mother during the weekends in the hope that she would find some good qualities in her that could help her get rid of the awful image in her mind, but in reality her mother was an alcoholic, immature woman, who disappointed her over and over again. I began to realise that turning to her mother at weekends represented turning to her bad objects during separations, and left her vulnerable to psychotic delusions.

She could hear voices in her head fighting with one another – there was one tiny good voice, but all the others would gang up against it. She knew how this tiny one felt. Sometimes 'they' would tell her not to go to her session and not to go to school either. In fact, in one session 'they' came into the therapy with her, either in her pocket or in her handbag.

80

3. Survival of the Self

She was afraid I would say she was mad, and sometimes she herself felt she was.

The following session illustrates this state of mind.

She arrived looking cheerful and said 'Hi' in a bright voice. As soon as she sat in the chair, her face tightened and she told me accusingly that she had not been well all weekend. She started to giggle uncontrollably. She said, 'My laughing has come back. I can't control it. Oh fuck', holding her forehead tightly and squeezing it as if it ached. She bent her head down and rubbed her forehead as though to ease the pressure that the erupting disturbing thoughts were causing.

She looked up, giggled, and, averting her face, told me that she had gone to her aunt's yesterday. Her aunt was depressed too. She was sitting on the floor eating her dinner, then she went and sat next to the oven. She said that she too did funny things, giving me a sneaky look, but refused to elaborate. She said that it must run in the family. She is depressed, her aunt is depressed, her mother is fucking mad. 'I am going to see my mother today. I phoned her. She is at my Nan's. She hates me you know.' She sounded pained and upset. 'Fucking hell, she racks my brains. She is mad.' She went on to tell me that she had spent the weekend with her friend Janet and how she kept waking up. She is all tensed up, cannot relax these days. She started to rub her forehead. 'I am fed up with being depressed all the time. What's the point. It goes away for a while and then it comes back. I want to kill myself, no, I don't.'

I said that I could see she was in a lot of pain and was in despair that it would go on and on. Over the weekend when I was away, the only adults she had to turn to were her depressed aunt and her mad mother. I seemed to have changed in her mind from someone good, strong and sane to someone useless or mad.

'If I was ill all weekend', she shouted at me, interrupting me, 'I didn't tell Janet I wanted to kill myself. I didn't want to worry her.' I spoke of her need for me to worry about her. 'You know why I was depressed over the weekend? It's embarrassing', she said turning away from me.

I said 'Yes, I know it's embarrassing for the grown-up Mary who has to tell me she felt like a little child and needs me and wants me to be with her all the time.' She nodded, looked at me and looked away. She picked up her handbag and threw it violently on the floor and said she didn't know why she liked it in the first place. I said the handbag represented what she felt about me. She liked me but liking me causes her pain when I am not with her. Then I turn bad like a rejecting neglectful mother who leaves her child instead of being there to attend to her needs all the time.

'It's all his fucking fault, if he hadn't fucked me, then I wouldn't be so fucked up now. I don't even like boys, not for long anyway. You know, I already had two showers today, I don't feel clean. Well, I am clean. I just don't feel it. I want to take the train today, buy some tablets, go and see him, tell him what he has done to me and take the tablets in front of him.' She looked around the room. 'I hate this room today. It's evil. I

81

don't like it.' Her voice had changed. She sounded lost in the grip of something frightening. I said she felt frightened. She didn't feel safe in my room. I had turned in her mind from someone good to someone frightening.

'Yes you have' she said slowly and very seriously and fear suddenly gripped me also. She looked at me, her face tense and frightened. She told me that she wanted to scream, throw things around. 'But I wouldn't touch you', she said reassuringly as if she picked up the fear that was gripping me. I said she wanted to keep me safe and divert her anger from me to the wall, so that something good would be saved. 'Don't make me think too much. I will have to leave soon, and if I let my thoughts come out I will get upset and then I will have to go outside in the street and people will look at me. They watch me, you know. My teacher keeps saying "Cheer up, Mary." Fucking cunt, why doesn't she leave me alone. I don't like people telling me to cheer up.' She looked out of the window, laughed hysterically and asked me to look at the clouds moving. It's the devil, he is watching me.' A funny smile played on her lips as she looked away.

I said she imagines the devil is watching her, telling her not to listen to me talking about goodness and not to think, because thinking would not make her feel better.

'Oh no, you are not going to make me think again and say that it's me and my feelings, not today ...'

'I know there is no devil only sometimes it feels that there is.' She looked away from me again and said that she really felt that she couldn't go on day after day being depressed. On Thursday she is going to come and see me, dressed like a tramp. Just because she is dressed nicely people think she is all right. Well she is not. At home she dresses like a tramp. She puts on her old dressing gown and worn out slippers. 'I want to go into hospital, no I don't. I want to kill myself but I want to come here too. That doesn't make sense. If I want to kill myself, I want to kill myself. I can't just not want to kill myself because I want to come here, but I do.'

I said she was struggling with herself. She felt desperate and hopeless towards the end of the session because she felt abandoned. But, at the same time, she believed there was hope and goodness and help from me and her therapy, a place for her to come and try to sort out her thoughts and feelings. She started to beg for half an hour more. She would pay me. She begged me to let her stay. I felt beaten, bruised, cruel and rejecting. When she left I became aware of my physical tiredness, as if a battle had taken place; her battle to fight off her devil and my battle to get her in touch with her good object and fight alongside her.

Beginning of Integration

My main task for some while was to contain her projections and avoid pushing them back at her, because she was still unable to deal with them herself. Persecutory anxieties continued up to the Christmas break. The negative transference came more and more to the fore, and though I was able to interpret it, I had to be very careful with her whenever I tried to bring the good and the bad together.

Mary began to bring her school work to the sessions to show me and though proud of the good grades she was getting, she was suspicious of the praise her teachers bestowed on her. She joined the dancing at school and, being a talented dancer, was asked to do solos and to sing in concerts. These activities had a constructive, defensive aspect; in dancing she could immerse herself in movement and be in a world of her own, and in singing she could express her pain through soul music. As the psychotic part of her personality was brought more into the therapy, she could function better outside.

She told me she was frightened of what was happening to her in therapy. 'It doesn't happen anywhere else, I don't know what happens. You make me think. This happens and then you tell me to go away.' Separation threw her back to primitive states of anxiety. She would struggle to maintain her ability to think in a more integrated way but when I disappeared, I became a very bad persecutory object. As the loved and hated objects were recognised to be one and the same she found this intolerable. She would shiver, hold herself tightly by stiffening her muscles then breathe deeply saying, 'There, it's gone away.'

'What has gone away?' I asked. She looked around the room then up at the ceiling and told me that she didn't like the room. A frightened anxious look came over her face. I said that the room and I had turned bad. She shouted that she hated me, that she was not leaving and begged to stay in the room underneath the bed. She began to laugh uncontrollably, asked me not to look at her, buried her face in her hands and said 'Oh God, I am crazy sometimes.' I said her laughter sounded like sobs, the sobs of a baby in despair. 'It feels just like that', she replied. 'There is something in this room.' I said she was suspicious of me now. She shook her head and said 'Go away, go away.' I said she was telling her bad and angry thoughts against me to go away because another part of her felt I was trying to help. 'You are a mind reader, I am not going today', and she curled herself up in a foetal position.

I suggested that she might think of lying on the couch. It might be easier for her. She looked at the couch suspiciously and shook her head. 'No, I don't like the colour of the cushions (deep pink and brown). They remind me of 'shit'. Involuntarily I added 'blood'. She shivered and said it reminded her of what it was like being in her mother's womb. 'I know you won't believe me but I do remember. I remember whizzing round

83

and round in there, being dizzy and then being born. It was all sticky, I was dirty, I needed a bath, needed to go home and have a bath. My mother was going to love me. She promised but she couldn't keep her promise.'

I said I was like a mother that promised to love her by being here sometimes but she felt that I didn't keep my promise because I was not there all the time. When she felt mad, it was like being inside a womb, a terrifying experience of her thoughts whizzing round and round, but when she left she felt just born, unprotected, dirty, like a baby left in its shit and neglected, left to clean itself up. 'I am leaving, I am just a baby.' She curled up in her chair. 'I want to stay a baby so you can't throw me out.' I replied firmly that part of her does feel like a baby but she is also a competent seventeen year old. She looked around and said 'They are here, they have followed me. I told them to stay in the room.' She listened, 'They are telling me to go to college.' She put on her jacket and said, 'I am not coming on Thursday,' then, 'I don't know why I say I am not coming. Of course I will.'

Mary also became preoccupied about what might happen to me. She felt I had been run over by a bus, or jumped in front of a train. 'It's awful, but nothing really happened' she concluded. The anxiety had shifted from fear of self-annihilation to loss of her good object. She began to talk less of suicide and became more thoughtful. She was more aware of what was happening, wanted to know why she had so many awful thoughts and how she could control them. 'It's awful what happens, because I feel good and it only lasts for a little while. I don't know why I prefer gloom to happiness.' She was aware that she was not swearing so much any more but also of the fragility of her good object which was constantly under threat. She complained to me that I was leaving her over Christmas to a drunkard of a mother and a family of drug addicts. There was nothing good there for her. She didn't want to go to them. My interpretations had to acknowledge the painful reality of this girl who did not have a good family. Before the end of the session she would withdraw from me and say 'I can't find my mother, I don't know where she is.' She knew where her real mother was but her internal mother was felt to go away and leave her feeling dead. She became identified with an object that was dying.

She came back from the Christmas break in an angry and morose state. She had dreamed of lying on someone's grave. She did not know whose grave it was and she had thorns all over her body. She showed me a poem which she had written for me, saying that she needed me to take the thorns and pain away. I interpreted to her that during the

Christmas separation she could not keep me alive and good in her mind and felt I had died, leaving her feeling very guilty and worthless.

During the break she had visited her foster parents. Her compulsion to go back to see them was too hard to resist. She felt that there must have been something wrong with her way of being, otherwise he wouldn't have done what he did. She was a bad little girl, a monster that I must not look at. She accused me of being uncaring, cruel. Sometimes I felt that nothing would satisfy her until she saw tears in my eyes or some visible proof that I was hurt too, that I cared.

The Effect of Sexual Abuse on the Development of Her Sexuality

Mary was now often in a more thoughtful mood, saying that she had been feeling well, not so angry with people. Instead she complained a lot about her pain inside and the sexual abuse. 'It's a scar that does not heal, a scar for life.' She also had a boyfriend with whom she had sex. I became very worried about a possible pregnancy.

She hated the idea of being pregnant. She said that she was going to have an abortion. She was not going to have some male doctor touch her. What she would do was to hit her tummy hard, or get someone to punch it so that the baby was killed. She didn't want a baby. If it was a boy she would throw it away, out of the window. She would get someone to put a needle through her tummy. Thinking of her brother, she expressed intense guilt and remorse for the damage she thought she had done to him when he was little. Her jealousy used to drive her to punch him very hard and jump up and down on his tummy. The fact that her brother had really been badly injured made all this unbearable for her. She would revert from blaming herself to blaming her foster parents. 'We were two healthy children before, now look at us, one mentally handicapped, the other one screwed up.'

When her period arrived she experienced it as a miscarriage. She imagined that she was damaged inside and would never have live babies. 'What do you expect when you have a great big dirty thing put inside you when you are little' she screamed at me. In her mind, men were always threatening the safety of women. She worried that she might be a lesbian and it took some time for her to admit that her feelings for me were passionate and eroticised because she thought I would be disgusted and would not want to see her again. In one session where she was describing her disgust with men and sexual intercourse, she said that it was not as easy to feel towards men as it is women. 'You can't cuddle them. If you cuddle them, they want sex.' I interpreted her wish to be

85

cuddled and comforted by me, and how abandoned she felt when she thought I chose to cuddle a man instead. She told me that over the weekend she would hold dialogues, telling herself that I was not coming back and that she would kill herself. She felt as though I left her in care while all she wanted was for me to take her home.

At this point, she began a relationship with a man twenty years her senior. She felt that he cared and understood her. Separation from her therapist became bearable and when I said to her that when she did not have Chriso to talk to, she had Jim, so never felt alone, she laughed and said with insight 'You think it's by chance I chose him, do you?' As it turned out, this man was good to her and encouraged her to go on with her studies and to develop her talent for singing, though he was also a very needy person who demanded a lot of affection and time from her. At times she felt suffocated by their shared neediness.

She began the session talking rapidly about what she had been doing with her boyfriend and other friends. Realising what she was doing, she turned, looked at me and said 'I talk and talk, don't I? That's because I don't want to tune into things. People laugh. It's not funny just because I talk differently. Do you think I am a cockney? Does it matter? You will have to help me tune in, you know.' I said 'By helping you tune in you want me to help you think, instead of talking and talking because you feel frightened. When that happens it is not funny, it is something that worries you.' I added that it was the first time she had asked me to help her think.

She smiled and asked 'When did we have our first breakthrough?' I asked what she thought. 'When I first came here, the first day' she said. I nodded and said that it was a breakthrough for her to allow herself to ask for help. 'Yes' she said, looking pleased with herself. She asked for a piece of paper. She was going to write a song, about therapy. She started to write, then scribbled it out, said that she shouldn't be writing poetry and started on another piece of paper. She showed me her drawing and asked me what I thought it was.

I said it looked like a mouth with a big teeth. 'Don't' she said shivering and putting her hands over her ears. I commented that it was unbearable for her to hear me say what she draws from deep inside the baby part of herself. She asked me to let her do something else. She took a piece of paper, folded it, then drew a vertical line, taking great care the line did not touch the edges. She asked me what I thought it was. I recalled from previous sessions the dead baby lying in a grave and her drawings of coffins with her name on them. 'I don't want to talk about it' she said sharply. I said it represented one of her deepest fears. 'You must know it does, but don't say it.'

She moved to the table at the side of the room and picked up a piece of plasticine. In a previous session she had drawn a heart and put a drawing pin in it to show how wounded she felt. She rolled the plasticine

86

into a penis shape and violently pushed the pin in one end. 'You know what it is', she said, screwing up her face as if in pain. 'It hurts a lot the first time, but it's not so bad the second time. It's a turnip, a carrot.' She took out the pin then pushed it back in violently. Then she rolled the plasticine into a ball and said that they were now trapped inside. They couldn't get out. This I understood as representing her most dreaded fantasy of a brutal sexual assault. She noticed the time and before I could say anything she told me that it was all right, that she was going. She placed the plasticine in the corner of the room and told me emphatically to be careful not to touch it. I said that the little girl part of her was very frightened to leave behind the bad carrot/penis with me in case I touched it and it harmed me. On the other hand she felt that if only she could leave those frightening thoughts with me then she could go outside and forget about it. 'Promise not to touch it', she said before she left.

Mary was haunted by this sadomasochistic phantasy. Very often she felt that she was the one whose baby had died because of being attacked by a bad penis. At other times she was identified with the baby inside mother being killed (Meltzer 1973). This phantasy deeply affected her sexual relationship with her boyfriend, and for weeks on end she would find it unbearable to have sex. She kept wishing that she could be with her boyfriend in a loving relationship without the horror of sex, which brought thoughts into her mind which she felt drove her mad. She often became angry with her sexual abuser and accused him of destroying her. She wanted revenge. It was not until she was eighteen that she was finally to talk about what she felt had happened to her. She said her foster father had fucked up her brains. She drew the face of a girl with a penis inside her head. The long frightening penis went from the girl's mind to the womb and killed the foetus inside it, thus illustrating her fear of never being able to have a healthy baby and her dread that every menstruation was a miscarriage.

Conclusion

On her eighteenth birthday, Mary expressed her amazement that she was still alive. 'I never thought I would still be alive. If I've survived up to now I'll see it through.' she told me. She brought me a present of a leaf and asked me to keep it safe for her. 'It's very fragile so be careful,' she told me. I understood it at the time as a symbol of something beautiful but delicate, in need of care and nurture. She told me also that even if the pain got too much she could not really kill herself now. Her boyfriend would be very upset. No, she couldn't do that to him, he loved her too much and her friends would be upset. She smiled and told me that she thought I would be upset too after all I had been through with her.

Mary's therapy lasted five years, after which, secure in the feeling that she could survive, she began to talk about ending the treatment. 'When I was 16, I thought I would never get to be 18, but look at me, I am 21. I am still here. I think I will stick with it although it still hurts.'

Acknowledgement

I would like to thank Hélène Dubinsky for her help in thinking about this case.

Discussion

Notes on the Impact of Sexual Abuse on the Inner World of Three Emotionally Deprived Girls

Alex and Hélène Dubinsky

The clinical material reported in the three preceding chapters shows clearly that the psychotic disturbances suffered by the three patients were linked to traumatic experiences to which they had been subjected. The three patients had either been sexually abused or had witnessed such abuse. In the present notes we will consider how sexual abuse was reflected in the patients' inner world and how it profoundly affected their mental functioning. We will see that these traumatic experiences led to the internalisation of extremely bad figures and to the domination of their mental world by sadomasochistic phantasies, and in particular by phantasies of intrusion. Their defences against mental pain had developed to an extreme degree, leading to psychotic states. A further pathogenic factor in these girls' development was that before the abuse they had received little emotional containment.

Extremely Dangerous Objects and Bad Objects

At the beginning of therapy, the protagonists in the phantasies of each of these three girls were plainly evil. Often their representations in conscious thought, or play, or drawings showed that these figures were not people but parts of the body (part-objects). Mary, for instance, an adolescent, was tormented by the thought of a baby-killing, mind-destroying penis. Jenny, who was four years old, drew a black phallic shape with small sharp points when her foster mother, in their first meeting with the therapist, talked of the child's difficult behaviour and of the possible abuse. This shape was a symbol formed by condensation

89

and combined the penis of the sexual abuse, the faecal penis of anal phantasies and the sharp small teeth of oral attacks. The corresponding extremely bad internal figures were formed by the internalisation of traumatic situations, but also of other early experiences. The latter included the apprehension by the child of her own sadism (the small teeth on the phallic shape for instance) projected into the external world. Mary drew a mouth baring its teeth when she became able to reveal her worst fears. Some of the figures internalised by the three girls corresponded indeed to the extremely dangerous objects described by Klein (1932, p. 6; Klein 1958, pp. 240-1).

The patients had also internalised a mother whom they reproached for failing to protect them. This figure corresponded both to the earlier external reality and to the mother who, in (sadomasochistic) phantasy, is thought to have allowed the bad penis to penetrate her and attack the babies inside. This reproach sustained Mary's feelings of hatred for the mother who had neglected her. Her idealisation of the therapist in the early stages of her treatment was motivated by the need to keep the therapist separate in her mind, not only from a terrifying male abuser but also from the hated neglectful mother.

As to Yvonne, her therapist described her as having internalised a mother whose goodness could never be trusted: the internalised object was 'suffused with confusion, incapable of differentiating erotisation from affection, and felt lethally treacherous'. This object could also appear as a narcissistic mother only interested in herself (Henry 1974). Jennifer's therapist also noted how, after the interruption of treatment for the holidays, the little patient would think that the adult was preoccupied with her own appearance and sexual pleasures, or with the babies she was supposed to carry in her womb. This would provoke paroxysms of envy in Jennifer, who then wanted to rip out the therapist's insides, or would masturbate and pretend she was a woman experiencing the greatest sexual delights.

The Sadomasochistic Phantasy and its Continual Recurrence

The patients' mental life had become dominated by a phantasy, which we will call the sadomasochistic phantasy, where babies are hurt, maimed or killed by a dangerous father or his penis.[1] The infantile part of the self identifies with either the aggressor or the victim (as in Richards' material in Klein 1945).

The sadomasochistic phantasy is part of humanity's common psychological baggage, since it expresses the inevitable conflicts between parents and children. Traumatic experience, however, gives it a central place in emotional life (Dubinsky 1986) as the experience is congruent with the phantasy in its essentials: a child is being hurt. The phantasy then becomes a schema for the interpretation of reality.[2] Thoughts, conscious or not, about the sexual abuse would indeed evoke the sado-masochistic phantasy. When, in the first interview, her foster mother talked of the abuse Jennifer had possibly suffered, the child gave symbolic form to her thoughts by drawing the phallic monster. She soon talked of it as 'cutting-up' children. Mary pushed a pin into a piece of plasticine rolled into a phallic shape when she spoke of the physical pain she had suffered when she had been abused ten years earlier. She then rolled the plasticine into a ball and talked of 'them' being trapped inside: it seemed she meant that a child was trapped with the dangerous penis inside the mother's belly.

The continual recurrence of the sadomasochistic phantasy in the three girls' mental life was also due to the fact that before the therapy they had little opportunity to internalise a capacity for thinking contain-ment commensurate with the traumatic experience. Emotional experience which could not be 'digested' remained as a concrete pres-ence in the mind (Bion 1962). One may wonder whether the internalisation of such bad objects, and the corresponding exacerbation of the phantasies where they figure, would have been avoided if these children had been able to talk of the traumatic experience soon after it had taken place with a sensitive and thoughtful adult. It has been noted that: 'When no adult intervenes to acknowledge the reality of the traumatic experience or to fix responsibility on the offending adult, there is a reinforcement of the tendency to deal with the trauma as an intrapsychic event, and to incorporate a monstrous apparition of guilt, self-blame, pain and rage' (Summit 1983).

The recurrence of the sadomasochistic phantasy was also in part due to the internalisation of an extremely dangerous paternal object. When this internal object was projected into the external world, people would be thought to present a heinous threat and the sadomasochistic phan-tasy would impress itself again.

The resulting anxiety often turned into terror. This would happen whenever this phantasy would be apprehended as being external reality itself. This confusion is characteristic of concrete thinking, which is further discussed on pp. 5-36. It meant that being in a room with the therapist was literally experienced as being trapped with a dangerous figure ready to attack. Concrete thinking was due to the intensity of the emotional experience and the lack of internalised containment.

Together with the extremely dangerous internal object, large fragments of the self, including destructive parts of the personality, could be projected out. Again, concrete thinking and terror would ensue, as when Mary was tormented by voices or when, in a temporary hallucination, she saw 'the Devil' watching her from a cloud.

Phantasies of Intrusion

The experience of sexual abuse was ever present in the patients' mind in the form of recurrent thoughts about a cruel intrusion. This cruel intrusion was a particular form of the sadomasochistic phantasy. For instance, many years after the abuse, whenever she had sexual intercourse, Mary, by now an adolescent, thought of a penis which penetrated a girl's head and which at the same time entered her mother's womb to kill the baby inside.

To give another example, in the first interview with her therapist, soon after Jennifer drew the black phallic shape, she moved the toy family to the roof of the dolls house and explained they were there because the monster was inside the house. After a moment she explained that she had a lot of monsters inside, and then pointed at the dolls house, saying: 'in there.' The dolls house now represented both her body and the place where her mind and sense of self resided.

The material quoted above shows that sexual intrusion was represented in the patients' thoughts as an invasion of portions of space other than those violated in the abuse. This corresponds to the fact that the child was identified with the mother, and that the mother's body is itself the object of phantasies of intrusion. Klein (1928), Meltzer (1967, 1992) and Rey (1979) have shown show that the inside of the mother (specifically the head, breast, genitals, womb and rectum – Meltzer 1967, 1992) and also the space thought to be occupied by the mind or the self, are of particular importance in this respect. As these authors indicated (see also Freud 1918) phantasies of intruding in the mother's body are common but they are pathogenic when they take over mental life. In the case of the three patients considered here, sexual abuse seemed to have much heightened the importance of these phantasies.

Phantasies of intruding in the mother's body lead to severe claustrophobic anxiety, since the infantile part of the self then fears to be trapped inside (Klein 1946). These anxieties were particularly unbearable for Yvonne. At such moments the patients would perceive the therapy room as a place of danger but also of erotic excitement. The breaching of boundaries protecting the self was often experienced and thought of as a breach through the skin. While Jennifer could not bear to be touched, when she identified with the aggressor she would scratch the therapist, or her own body, or the walls of the therapy room. The particular importance given to the skin indicated a return to a primitive level of functioning where the skin is both experienced and represented as an envelope offering the self protection and cohesion (Bick 1968, 1986). Thought and perception are not distinguished: mental phenomena are confused with bodily experience. The space occupied by the self is thought to be enclosed by the skin.

When persecutory anxiety is intense, this primal protection can be felt to have been lost. When Mary came to her first session, she slumped on a chair, shuddering like a small baby being undressed (Bick 1986). She had to be enveloped in a blanket before she could speak and tell the therapist of the sexual abuse she had suffered as a child. When Jennifer started therapy one of her phantasies seemed to be that her skin was full of holes through which anything could fall off or intrude. She literally feared that her insides would drop out in the toilet. Her doubting of the efficacy of sphincters, together with phantasies of intrusion into personal space, meant that she declared the therapy room to be safe only after locks had been placed on the window and the drawers, and after covers had been fitted over the electric sockets.

The Precariousness of Good Objects

Part of these patients' predicament was that they could not depend on a good internal object. Such an object provides 'a focal point in the ego. It counteracts the processes of splitting and dispersal, makes for cohesiveness and is instrumental in building up the ego' (Klein 1946). It provides the psychic envelope needed to hold the self together so that development can take place (Bick 1968, 1986). Instead of providing for the internalisation of a good object, grown-ups had neglected or ill-treated these children in their early years. They had abandoned them to abuse, or colluded with it, or perpetrated it.

The lack of a reliable good internal object left the patients in a most precarious state. Mary had managed to develop into adolescence by depending on good external figures but she had to idealise and control them. Jennifer's development was seriously delayed until she was adopted by a caring couple when she was two-and-a-half years old. Although she then grew into an intelligent girl, she was in fear of literally losing her insides when she started therapy a year and a half later. Internal containment barely existed for Yvonne when she was in

93

the therapy room. The ending of the therapy session or the interruption of treatment for the holidays were often very painful, and sometimes terrifying. Changes in care arrangements had a devastating impact on Yvonne and Mary. It is probably no coincidence that Mary was breaking down at the time of the referral for therapy as she had been moved from the children's home where she had stayed to a home for adolescents. The loss of internalised holding she frequently experienced and the resulting fear of falling were represented in a recurring daydream where she would sink lower and lower in a pool of water but would not drown since she would be woken up by 'an electric shock'.

Losing the protection of an external good object was often experienced as being abandoned to terrible persecutors. In a weekend daydream Mary had imagined that her therapist had left her, and she cried. Then, in her daydream, a man came and sexually abused her. After a holiday Jennifer jumped on the sofa and pretended that she was being attacked by crocodiles and sharks swimming in the therapy room.

The good objects that the patients had managed to internalise seemed to vanish when the bad objects took over mental life. When, in the first interview Jennifer put the toys on the roof of the dolls house, she explained this was 'because the monster was inside the house.' In her phantasy, good objects were driven away from the internal world by persecutory bad objects.

Defensive Processes Taken to the Extreme

In his paper on the 'Two Principles of Mental Functioning', Freud (1911) indicated that turning away from reality, as it is found to be 'unbearable – either the whole or parts of it', leads to mental illness. The patients we are considering here were turning away from the acute mental pain inflicted by the bad figures they had internalised and the terrifying fantasies which haunted them as a consequence of the abuse.

An important line of defence consisted in denying helplessness, a feature which Freud recognised as being central to the traumatic experience (1926). Identification with the aggressor provided a way of avoiding being cast in the role of the victim in the sadomasochistic phantasy. Manic excitement then gave the two younger children a sense of omnipotent invulnerability. Nevertheless, when concrete thinking would take over, the therapist would be perceived as the dreaded persecutor itself. In these moments, Jennifer and Yvonne could fend off the terror only by resorting to physical violence in what appeared to be a fight for sheer survival. At other times they would feel that something

94

Discussion

bad was literally pushed into them and in a correspondingly concrete manner they would try to push it back into the therapist. Often the excitement arising out of manic defence would lead to a state of mindlessness. Like many psychotic children, Yvonne and Jennifer would use this mindlessness to suppress mental experience, and in particular psychic pain and terror.

Splitting and disintegration, which are further discussed below, and projection were used massively. Yvonne in particular needed to project into the therapist her unbearable feelings and the part of herself which was experiencing them.

The defensive processes also played a role in terms of the organisation of the personality .A destructive part of the self often identified with the bad internal objects and the aggressor in the sadomasochistic phantasy, while more vulnerable parts of the self were projected into the attacked babies. Identification with the aggressor would lead to the temporary domination of the self by the destructive part.[3] Meltzer (1973, pp. 96-7) described how, when the destructive part of the self is not restrained by integration with the rest of the personality, this destructive part avoids 'becoming time-bound and subject to persecutory and depressive anxieties' by using methods which may lead to psychosis and, ultimately, to schizophrenia. In the cases we are considering here, the danger did not come from a particular virulence of the destructive part of the self, but from the despondency of the good parts. The abuse had shaken whatever trust in the internal good objects the children's difficult history had allowed to develop. In the absence of sufficient mental equipment to deal with psychic pain, there always was the temptation to turn to the illusory strength and protection promised by the destructive part of the self.

At other times, the good parts of the self seemed to have been in a relation of '*passivity* towards bad parts of the self, in a mood of *despair*': this is the type of narcissistic organisation, used as a defence against psychic pain, described by Meltzer (1973, p. 132) as 'addiction'. This addictive element can be recognised in Jennifer's and Yvonne's violence and sexual excitement, and in Mary's brief turning to marijuana and alcohol. When Jennifer masturbated in a session which followed an interruption for a holiday, she yelled: 'It's better than you'. The therapist asked her why. The girl replied: 'It feels good. I can touch it when I want. I have it all to myself.' Thus as Jennifer despaired of her therapist's love and attention she turned to a mode of gratification which she knew to be an attack against her object, as the rebellious tone indicated.

Defense mechanisms can be taken to the point where a radical impairment of the relation with reality, both external and psychic, ensues. In the case of the three patients considered here, such extremities in the deployment of the defences were resorted to because the mental pain was so great, but also because, as for many psychotic children, the capacity to tolerate pain was limited by a lack of internalised containment. This situation was self-perpetuating as the defences hindered the relation with good objects and their internalisation.

Disintegration and Fragmentation

When confronted with great psychic pain, defences such as fragmentation or even disintegration of the self were invoked. At times the states of disintegration were a passive response to the suffering. This was the passive falling to pieces referred to by Klein (1946) and the lack of a reliable good internal object which could hold the self together (Bick 1968) was a contributing factor. But active splitting (Klein 1946) was also well in evidence. The active splitting of the self into minute bits was a desperate attempt to avoid the pain through attacking the very functioning of the mind.

Passive disintegration was in operation when Mary came to her first individual session and slumped on a chair, shuddering and unable to speak. However, as she tried to talk, Mary attacked both the mental pain and her mind. She 'rapped on her forehead, shaking it as if she was shaking unbearable thoughts out of it.' She explained that 'she wanted to die, she couldn't stand the pain any longer ...' That night she pursued the attack on herself and attempted to commit suicide. When, a few weeks later, she showed her therapist photographs of herself and her brother when they were small, she said: 'I am a baby, I hate myself. I took something last night.' As Mary then tore up the photos, the therapist thought that she wanted to tear up her child self: Mary was attacking the part of herself which was exposed to the pain. The tearing up of the photographs, like the earlier rapping on the forehead, represented the active splitting of the ego used as a defence against persecutory anxiety (Klein 1946). When, after she had felt attacked, Mary would say that her brain was like 'spaghetti Bolognese', she was describing the minute splitting of the self. When, early in her therapy, she tried to describe her feelings about the abuse, she put it clearly: her mind 'felt as if it went to pieces.' At the beginning of treatment, besides states of disintegration, Mary also experienced depersonalisation (Rosenfeld 1947): she would say 'that part of her felt dead, everything was cracked inside. [She] would become listless, lifeless, [she would] begin to yawn and want to go to sleep.' As therapy continued, the disintegration was first replaced by the fragmentation of the self into larger pieces. The projection of these fragments resulted for a while in hallucinations as Mary heard voices, and saw the Devil.

Jennifer also went through states of disintegration when she started therapy. The first months in the treatment of this intelligent child 'were filled by chaotic stories, memories and fragments of phantasy.' In the first interview she showed how children were 'cut up' by the monster. For weeks on end she then went on cutting up toys 'into minute pieces that seemed like dust.' A destructive part of her personality was identifying with the aggressor. In her attack on her baby self and on small imaginary rivals, she was splitting them into minute bits. This phantasy probably contributed to her fear of losing her insides in the toilet: she may have feared that the tiny fragments would just seep out of her.

Facing Mental Pain

Mary, because she was older, had a deep sense of the emotional damage she had suffered through the abuse. The summary of part of a session conveys how she would mistake this depressive pain[4] for an experience of intense persecution and how her mental state would then deteriorate. Mary began by telling of her lonely aunt whom she had found eating on the kitchen floor. She was unconsciously expressing her feeling that she had been abandoned by her therapist during the weekend. As this grief became persecutory, Mary threw her bag on the floor, and exclaimed that she did not know why she had ever liked it. The bag was now representing a bad maternal object which had exposed her to pain. Mary then linked the suffering to the sexual abuse and talked of not feeling clean. The damage to herself was experienced as a persecution, not as something to grieve for. Again in the grip of the sadomasochistic phantasy, she thought of killing herself under the abuser's eyes. As the feelings of persecution escalated, the projections increased and she saw the Devil in a passing cloud. When the therapist managed to bring her back to thinking of her emotional experience, Mary described herself as a tramp. She now perceived herself as being damaged and talked of being in a state of constant depression. Mary seemed to be referring to depressive pain and to regard the depression itself as evidence of the damage she had suffered.

In the third year of treatment Jennifer started to show depressive concern. She became able to acknowledge the damage wrought by destructiveness in the outside world as she worried about the impact of war on babies. She also voiced her appreciation of the limits that her therapist had placed on her own destructiveness.

For a long time, the patients had to rely on external good objects to provide thinking containment. Only after the trust in such a relationship was established within the intimacy of the transference did the ability to tolerate mental pain start to develop. The patients had to learn from experience that while a good object would care for them, it could not protect them from all suffering. Instead of the distortion of external objects by the projection into them of exceedingly bad objects, or by processes of splitting and idealisation, or through the misapprehension of mental pain for the fantasised onslaughts of a cruel persecutor, the integration of diverse experiences of these objects began to take place. This integration was needed for the introjection of helpful and thinking parental figures to develop.

Conclusion

The impact of the sexual abuse on the development of their personality had exposed the three girls to extreme mental pain which led to psychotic states. The experience of abuse had exacerbated the malevolence of internal persecutors, and the importance of the sado masochistic phantasy and of phantasies of intrusion. The emotional deprivation suffered by these patients before the abuse had left them ill-equipped to bear the resulting persecutory anxieties. Defences against mental pain reached a level such that the apprehension of reality, external or internal, was disrupted to the point of psychotic disturbance.

Notes

[1] Meltzer (1978) explicates the sexual content of this phantasy and its links with Freud's understanding of sado-masochism (Freud 1918, 1919).

[2] In the case of Mary it became evident that the disability incurred by her brother, apparently through ill-treatment, played a role.

[3] This would constitute a narcissistic organisation of the personality as described by Rosenfeld (1964, 1971) and Meltzer (1967, pp. 28f., 1973).

[4] Depressive pain is the sorrow about damage which has been done to one's good objects and to oneself, and the grief at the loss, potential or actual, of the good objects (Klein 1935).

Part II
Psychosis and Developmental Delay

4

The Beginnings of Mind

Psychotherapy of a Six-Year-Old Girl

Ann Wells

It had become a glimmering girl (W.B. Yeats)

Helen was nearly six years old and 'severely mentally handicapped' when she was referred to the clinic with her older sister Clare. A diagnosis of chronic sexual abuse had been made nine months previously by the local hospital. When Helen was five, her intellectual level was about eighteen months. She had little language and was not toilet trained. Her violence to other children, extreme mood swings and sexualised behaviour alerted her special school, and an examination under local anaesthetic revealed 'recent and old' penetration of the anus, as well as other bruises consistent with physical abuse.

Helen's mother separated from her co-habitee, the alleged abuser, but the child's referral for therapy was a constant reminder of the abuse and was very painful for her. She could not accept help for herself, and proved unable to bring Helen three times weekly, both for emotional reasons and because of practical difficulties when she had another baby. However, thanks to an escort, we had fifteen months of reliable once-weekly work before the family suddenly moved away.

In spite of these disruptions, Helen managed to maintain contact with me and to benefit from treatment. My hypothesis is that at a very early infantile level, she was able to retain a wish for understanding and an innate preconception of a thinking object who could provide it.

Family Background

Helen was the second child of a working-class couple in a rural area. Her elder sister, Clare, is severely epileptic. The marriage was in

101

difficulties and Helen's father left soon after her birth. According to her mother, he was unable to accept the birth of a handicapped child. Mother then prevented him from remaining in touch with Clare.

After he left, Mother became pregnant by a casual relationship. She later met 'Eddie', the alleged abuser, who she said persuaded her to have the baby adopted. She agreed, feeling unable to cope both with a new baby and Helen's handicap. The birth of this sister has been kept a 'secret' from Helen and from Clare, who at the time was over four years old.

The family came to London with Eddie, who may have been violent towards Mother. Helen settled in at a school for children with learning difficulties, where she remained until the recent disappearance of the family. After initial doubts the staff were pleased with her progress in therapy, and very supportive of the work.

Since asking Eddie to leave, Mother has had a boy and a girl by another relationship, again possibly violent.

Personal History

Helen was a big baby. Mother was exhausted after a difficult two-day labour, and when Helen was finally delivered, the cord was tight around her neck, asphyxiating her. Mother said that she was blue and floppy, with no internal control of her body temperature and no sucking reflex. She was immediately admitted to a Special Care Unit, but Mother was unable to remember how long she had remained there or any other details.

Helen appeared to her mother as a 'good', quiet baby, but her maternal grandmother was alarmed by her lack of reaction when a saucepan lid was dropped near her. Investigations began, and the degree of Helen's retardation gradually became apparent, although tests at a teaching hospital, including a chromosome count and brain scans, revealed no organic abnormalities.

However, Helen suffered many severe early illnesses, including tuberculosis and whooping cough, which involved repeated hospital admissions. She did not learn to walk until the age of two. Her mother reported that she had an inoperable travelling squint and 'no depth of field' to her vision.

First Impressions: the baby doll

My first view of Helen, in the waiting room, was of a child, small for her age, dressed in a very short skirt. Her clothes were worn and slightly grubby and ill-fitting. Her long hair was tied back. Her face was sweet, heart-shaped, and almost pretty except for the vacancy and odd focus of her eyes. My feeling that she could not 'see' me got in the way of contact.

However, this preliminary impression of an alien, unknowable creature was contradicted by her purposeful behaviour. I quote from my notes:

In the room Helen immediately sat in the small armchair, away from her mother, and sat raising her head, reminding me of sniffing the wind as if to survey the room. Then she noticed the toys, and 'talking', went across to them and sat down next to them at the small table. She took a larger teddy with delight and as she took it across to the windowsill, Mother commented that Helen liked to have something in her hand. Mother distracted her, but Helen then returned with the teddy to the windowsill and moved him along it, saying loudly 'Walk.' She began to transfer animals one by one from the table to the windowsill and ended up with four or five animals on it. She then came close to me and held out the cow as if to give it to me. I reached out cupped hands. She then held it near to my face and said 'Moo.' Mother was talking now of Helen's birth and its difficulties. She told of her subsequent illnesses and the abuse. Towards the end of this Helen tried to open a locked drawer in the chest of drawers. Mother said 'No', and Helen immediately hit herself very hard until restrained by Mother. Mother commented that she often did this especially if arrangements or routines were changed.

Helen now spent a considerable time with the Daddy doll saying 'Lie Down!' She tried to post the baby doll down the slit along the top of the radiator grill and was stopped by her mother. She repeatedly walked the Daddy doll up the radiator grill saying 'Upstairs.'

Next she lay on the sofa by her mother, who was encouraging her to make the doll swim. Helen continued to say firmly 'Lie Down.' She protested about having to leave the room and again about leaving behind one of my small figures and refused to say good-bye to me as her mother insisted.

Helen's use of her mind was still very primitive. She sniffed to explore the room, as though body and mind were not clearly delineated. Words were experienced in bodily terms: she hit herself when Mother said 'No.' Feelings were difficult to pin-point. Helen's only hint of anxiety was in leaning heavily on her mother in order to climb the stairs. Her mother explained this in terms of a physical deficiency rather than emotional meaning, saying that Helen had no depth of field to her vision; but subsequently Helen was able to climb the stairs in an ordinary way. The second session illustrated her tremendous sense of confusion. Dress and undress, inside and outside, up and down were all mixed up and undifferentiated.

Helen habitually held a small toy, which fell absently from her hand once she arrived in the room. When leaving, she tried to take one of my toy figures, and screamed and fought when I stopped her. Since then, she has always preferred to 'travel' with a toy figure in her hand, now called 'baby'. Her word for herself at this time was 'baby'. I have wondered about this figure as being related to an 'autistic object' (Tustin, 1981), as used by encapsulated autistic children to give themselves a sense of existing by means of the sensations generated. (Winnicott, 1958 suggests that such an object represents the child having a sense of a 'bodily' – that is 'sensorially-represented' – separation from mother, before transitional activities of a more nearly symbolic nature had become established.) But most of all, this hand-holding-onto-a-figure serves (for me) as my image of Helen's capacity subsequently to use the therapy. For me now this figure represents an innate preconception in Helen, a 'form waiting for a content' (Money-Kyrle, 1968) which enabled her to use what was available to her. It was as if Helen were literally carrying a baby Helen about with her, ready for someone to attend to. This would be nearer to symbolic than to sensation-dominated functioning: in any case it evoked a caring response in me. I also have been interested to note the loyalty and affection this little girl aroused in the staff at her school and in her escort, both of whom would put themselves to quite a lot of trouble for her and respond to her hope for a containing object.

At the same time, the dolls were moved about, ordered around, dropped from her actions and thought in a terrifyingly casual and emotionless way. This handicapped child brought to mind the severely deprived children described by Hoxter et al. (1983), who treated their therapists in the way they felt they had themselves been treated.

Phases in Therapy

1. *Before Recognition: Mindlessness in the Patient and in the Countertransference*

During the first months Helen's attendance at therapy was extremely unreliable. Her play was exceedingly difficult to follow and to remember: she repeated actions over and over again with tiny variations. Small dolls were moved about, ordered around, treated casually. Their limbs were twisted; they were poked with pens, smelt, slapped and rubbed up and down the radiator. She would giggle hysterically, seeming quite mad as her hands twisted while her eyes looked blankly out of the window. I felt that she was communicating experiences of abuse, but in a partial chopped-up way that probably linked with her experience of the clinic, and of me, as fragmented, unpredictable and unreliable. I could only add brief comments and found it very hard to find words and phrases sufficiently short, quick and emotive to catch the rapid and fleeting moments of possible feeling.

Mothers by their words and actions provide a patterned context for their baby's sounds and movements. These patterns are sometimes active, sometimes soothing; out of them develops mutual communication and, eventually, language. The baby-in-bits in my room had to be shown that an object existed, in relationship and communication with her (Alvarez, 1992). My role with Helen in the first instance was to draw attention to the potential meaningfulness of her experiences and actions. Only after such attention and sorting have been integrated can the other more sophisticated aspects of interpretation, such as the location of a feeling or the reason for it, be approached.

During this time I never felt that she recognised me, but she came to recognise bits of 'me-ness'. I existed in the transference as a fragmented object – legs that walked to the room, hands that fetched or restrained her, a voice talking. Certainly she had no expectation that I would see her behaviour as meaningful. For instance, since Helen frequently requested the toilet though she was still in nappies, I asked how her mother usually responded. Her mother told me that Helen was incapable of sphincter control. 'Toilet' meant nothing: it was just a word she had learnt and sometimes repeated.

Helen's mother could probably not entertain the hope that her daughter was capable of meaningful speech or of becoming clean and dry. My experience, however, was that a communication was being stripped of meaning. In the sessions, too, I habitually felt thick-headed, stupid, unable to understand. This could be conceptualised in terms of attacks by Helen on our communication; but I think that she was conveying to me her experience and that of her internal objects.

Before long, she was able to begin the sessions by throwing the contents of her box across the floor and then excitedly throwing and scattering them some more. I think she was enacting her own fragmentation, but also exploring her potency. It was not she who was the recipient of scattered attention, casual cruelty: instead, she could chuck 'it', reject, hurl, abuse. Cruelty no longer occurred in the absence of affect: instead, she found pleasure in having the strength to throw.

105

My 'interpretations' were the simplest commentary: 'Throw it away', 'Don't want you', 'Get over there.' I relied as much on the tone, manner, rhythm of words as on the words themselves. I did not know who was being thrown, or where, or why, merely that things were being separated and that now Helen could be the cause of it.

During this first phase of treatment I felt overwhelmed, often helpless when confronted with the chaos she created, and also full of doubts as her behaviour spilled out from the room into the corridor and to school. I experienced feelings that would have been appropriate to her circumstances: that I was helpless in the face of a totally uncontrolled and violent maelstrom. I decided to set firm limits for her, establishing a clear difference between the session time, a clearing-up time, and out-of-the-room.

In her seventh session, for the first time, she commented on her actions in the way I usually did: she had internalised my function of attention.

'All out', 'Get out', I say. She sweeps (the toys) off the table like an excited whirlwind. 'Off '; 'Go there', 'Get down there'; I say. She picks up all the plasticine from among the debris and takes it to the desk, and sits on the desk with it in front of her. She pulls off pieces and says 'Off.'

It took me a while to realise what she was saying and that she was saying it.

2. Recognition is Established; A break has been helpful

Helen's ninth session followed a long and unexpected break. I quote from my notes:

I did not recognise her after the six week gap. She seems taller and has had her hair cut short which suits her. She looks elfin. She looked hard at me when I went to speak to her and then took my hand and said 'Room ...'

Quickly excited, Helen studies the marks she could make on (the plasticine) with her feet ... she twisted the man doll around and let him hang on the window bar for a long time. I wondered aloud about the long wait till she saw me today. She then lay and held the doll in her hand and was still, lying on the desk, quiet for a long time. I felt like I was watching a baby in her cot. This was interrupted by the doll in her hand slipping to the floor. She sat up and leant down looking after him. I felt expected to pick him up and rather automatically did so and then talked of it. She returned her attention to the window bar and now discovered that she

106

could wind the handle that opens the top window. She opened and shut it repeatedly with great delight, watching it.

She came down from the desk and placed the small doll on the edge of the small table in a very precarious position. She then leant over and hung her head upside down from the same small table for a long time ...

Helen collected the paper and the box lid and tore the paper into tiny strips carefully collecting them in the box. She put it onto the floor and hung again upside down with her head in this box of pieces.

It was time. She tried to take the small doll with her. She kicked and hit and punched at me when I said 'No.' I talked of her fury ... I was holding her to stop her hurting me. I said that the doll would stay in the box and be here when she came again. She flung a child-sized chair over and then placed the small doll very carefully and quietly in the box. I said that she was very angry with me, but that she knew the doll would be kept safely for her.

In these extracts it is clear how much Helen's language lagged behind the complexity of her expressed ideas. This may be linked to the way I found myself automatically behaving like a mother who does not expect her child to understand language. Thus, when she drops the doll and leans down to look for it, I feel impelled to pick it up and in fact, am doing so before I think and can only retrospectively talk of what has happened. Helen and I have enacted an assumption of 'no mind'. A mother would probably say 'Oh dear, you lost it? Where's it gone? Shall we look for it? Is it here? There? Oh look there it is, do you want it? Can you reach it? Shall I pick it up? What do you say?' While my automatic retrieving of the doll delighted Helen, who may have felt that she had an object, like the window, who would respond to what she did, I was perhaps at the same time colluding with a view of her as a handicapped person whom one would not expect to tolerate the delay of action that is involved in thought and speech.

3. *'Infant Observation' and Firm Limits*

As I mentioned in the above extract, I felt at this time that watching Helen was like watching a baby. Helen responded quickly to my attention and gradually I became an 'auxiliary ego' (Meltzer, 1975; Alvarez, 1992), a presence that commented on her actions and feelings. From this Helen began to make links and connections. She knew me. I knew her. Patterns emerged in her play. The sessions became sequential and possible to remember, instead of being a seemingly random jumble of fragments. At this time her school reported major developments in her capacities and her interest in the world.

107

4. The Continuity of Existence

After many months of uncertainty, Helen's therapy was finally established into a regular pattern as a result of the reliable work of a volunteer escort and the co-operation of her school.

Helen's play developed further. The plasticine, formerly scattered all over the room, was now kept in close piles of small pebbles. Then the lid of her box was introduced as their container. In this she explored their movement and motion as the box was itself wobbled. Helen, it seemed to me, had found a place for the bits of herself in the therapy-room, and in my attention.

Within the box lid, Helen made parcels of plasticine pieces wrapped in paper in combinations of numbers of pieces. 'Two' could stay together within a paper parcel; and paper and plasticine could come together. She tested out repeatedly whether the inside-thing still continued when out of sight.

Gathering the Bits

Helen's earliest drawings were ripped up quickly. She placed the pieces immediately in the bin. 'Bin', she announced firmly. Once therapy was more firmly established she would tear up the large sheets of paper and draw only on small pieces. These 'drawings' consisted of fragments – rubbings on furniture, experiments with colour in cramped and limited space. These were also firmly placed in the bin.

After one year, she drew huge circles and shapes on large whole sheets. These pictures were kept. The continued presence of the bin as a container for her fragments and adhesively collected bits of objects had permitted her to develop the notion of complete shapes and a more nearly intact self.

A Place for Mess

Concurrently, Helen differentiated clean from dirty, and learned to use the toilet. Her sorting was at first very concrete. The plasticine seemed to *be* 'pooh' rather than to symbolise it. She smeared it over the desk and windowsill, with graphic accompanying noises. Next she learned to clean it all away into a closed beaker, and she found that the clinic had sinks and toilets where she could be cleaned in reality. She began to play symbolically, disposing of pretend 'pooh' in the toy toilet and examining its origins, from the bottoms of the toy dolls.

4. The Beginnings of Mind

5. Perverse Confusions

Session 25 was a pivotal session in allowing her to use the lavatory. The very painful material may have been precipitated by my introduction of a doll's house and a large baby doll.

> Helen now explored the furniture. She found the toilet and said 'Toilet.' She said, 'Pooh.' She went and looked for and brought 'baby' to the desk and sat this large soft toy on the tiny toilet and made a peeing noise and said 'Toilet, wee wee.' She said, 'Baby, nappy.' I said she was now using toilets and her pooh and wee wee went into the toilet. Helen took the crib and said 'Baby' and placed a piece of plasticine in the crib and said 'Pooh' and 'Stink.' I said that the baby had a dirty nappy, 'Pooh in the nappy not the toilet.' (At this time Helen had a new baby sister at home.) Helen moved the baby from the toilet and then closed the lid and mimed flushing the handle with her finger and thumb in a delicate gesture.
>
> Then she picked up the toilet and licked it and stuck her tongue straight into the 'bowl.' She dropped globules of spit into the bowl and closed the lid and then opened it again and drank the contents. She repeated this. She sucked and licked and put this toilet right into her mouth. I said, 'The toilet – you are showing me you have a bad thing in your mouth. Exciting.'
>
> Helen spent a long time putting pieces of furniture in her mouth. She licked and sucked at the beds. I was feeling horrified and nauseous. The atmosphere was tense. She put an armchair right into her mouth so that I could not see it behind her lips. I kept wondering if she would be able to swallow it. I worried that it would go right down though it had seemed far too large. She threw pieces rather wildly around the desk area. She seemed very wild (crazed?) and things flew around. She slapped the table and banged the furniture and stuffed her mouth right up. I spoke of these things stuffed right into her mouth. 'Mouth full, like it? Hate it? Can Helen breathe? Frightened she might really swallow it?'
>
> Helen then said 'Bite', very loudly. I said 'You can bite the thing in your mouth.' She bit the toy table very hard. Helen slapped the table very hard. I said 'Take that, slap you, slap you hard' as she slapped it repeatedly. I said 'You really want to hurt it.' She continued and then slowed and patted it gently and said 'Hurt.' I said 'Oh, dear. Hurts. Poor table ... poor Helen.' At time, she ran out to wash her hands but unusually held them spread out in front of her, palms upwards as she ran. Today she washed my hands for me, and on the return to the escort, turned and said 'Good-bye' to me. These were all new actions today.

This terrible session marked a turning point. I felt a witness to tortures. I obviously thought of the possibility that she had suffered oral sexual abuse. I also felt that the new toys had brought up old fears that new

109

things, places, objects would overwhelm and suffocate her, as the cord had threatened to do when she was born. I thought of a baby-Helen who was full up with bad experiences, gagging and unable to breathe. Once I could feel the horror, and reflect my experience back to her, she was free to try another approach: instead of being the helpless one, she inflicted pain and enjoyed the power ('Bite'). Then a third possibility entered her mind: of being hurt or hurting – and even of making me better (washing my hands). I think that for Helen it became safe to explore the experience of her sexual abuse (and echoes of earlier infantile experiences) at this distance.

In the following session she allowed me to take her to the toilet for the first time, as if the split between clean and dirty was now established.

6. A Little Girl: Making the Face

After the first summer break Helen no longer seemed a 'little creature'. I felt for the first time that I was in the presence of a child, with many and varied states of mind. She remained profoundly handicapped with limited language, but I was aware now of finding a greater range of countertransference feelings and fantasies as well as the familiar thick-headedness or sheer emptiness that I had formerly experienced. For her part, she had retained her notion of me and of the clinic, and could now begin to explore this. Her curiosity and wonder were obvious:

> In the earliest sessions this term Helen looks around as we go to the room. She notices the lift (she comes up the stairs with the escort). She says 'What's that for?' She notices the window at the end of the corridor whose light floods in. Helen stops, looks, points and says 'Look, light.'

She stopped and stared at people passing. She named the doors, chairs, tables in the corridor. We studied the patterns on the lino. Reid (1990) has described how her patient Georgie revealed to her the beauty of the Tavistock Clinic staircase. Until this phase of Helen's therapy, I had never imagined that walking through the corridor could be so interesting.

With this comes a sense of her making links between her experiences. From our room she can see the front door of the clinic, and into the waiting room as well. She points both out to me. At the stairwell we look at the stairs she has recently ascended, then she is interested to see them continuing up and up. It seems to me at that moment that they ascend forever! Going down them is 'Home'. Helen knows our room,

110

her toys, and notices any changes. She searches for toys that she has in mind, expects them to be there, and asks and expects me to help her to find things.

Session 47: the face

Helen went back to the box saying something like 'elastic' which I then realised was 'plasticine'. She looked for it in the box. I said 'What does Helen want?' 'Helen knows what she wants, knows it is there.' She found it and poured it out and spread it out on the desk and said 'Look at that.'

I looked. She placed one piece on top of another and said 'On.' I caught this a few seconds late. I said 'On, together – like you and me here today.' She spread the plasticine around like a layer of stones. She said 'Look.' She looked then from my side, and then climbed onto the desk to look from behind.

Helen spent a long time moving the plasticine to various sites in the room, and arranging different patterns (lines, circles). We were both quite engaged in this exploration, me commenting and Helen making accompanying noises of hums and grunts. I then became aware that she was squashing a round shape onto the desk, and commenting, then I heard 'Eye.' She continued 'Mouth', 'Nose.' She had made a clear face. I was thrilled. Helen paused momentarily and then rolled them up again.

A face – an identity – had emerged, however momentarily.

Other People's Point of View

By now, Helen expected that I would think about her actions and comment. She would create a shape or situation with the toys, and then move across to look at it from my view point. I could expect the sessions to have a pattern and order that I could retain and write up. Helen was becoming interested in the qualities of her objects. She played symbolically, reproducing current events in her life.

I received reports of her improvements at school. She had been a very difficult child flying easily into a huge physically-expressed rage. She had wandered around in a solitary way, ordering small dolls around and attacking any child who got in the way. Now, when they explained a situation to her, Helen could listen, would reply 'All right, All right', but would negotiate the disagreement. She began for the first time to be interested in other children and share activities and play with them. She acquired new skills which she began to mention in therapy.

7. *The Pooh-Baby*

After the Christmas break, and against this background of greater strength, darker themes re-emerged in our relationship. I felt that Helen now was exploring my capacity as a thinking and feeling object to bear the horrors inside her. There were three strands to my countertransference: on the one hand, I felt a resurgence of the feeling that Helen was not quite human, that contact with her could harm me, as though I were identified with an object that hated and feared the baby. I often found myself 'waking up' belatedly to a new development. At other times, I felt real pleasure in something she achieved, or simply in being with her. Finally, I found myself not wanting to notice and process my experience of her. I found myself again living through periods of thick mindlessness, blankness, boredom. I think now that this was the turning away of the maternal object from knowing; – of opening her mind to the revelation of the mad and perverse world that Helen inhabited and the abuse-related material she presented. When I could feel and think it was particularly disturbing to notice the chronic and habitual nature of Helen's detachment of mind, as if she and I could easily witness awful actions with little affect (Bion, 1967). I carried a lot of worry about whether her actions were enacting present experiences of abuse or neglect.

From Session 44:

Helen fetched the large baby doll. She hit it, she said 'Sore' and pointed to its bottom. 'Sore', 'Wee', 'Pooh.' I said 'Oh dear, hurts.' Helen repeats this pointing at the bottom, and the leg. I said 'Hurts. Don't like it. Ohhhooo.' I was wondering what had gone on. Had Helen been hurt again? I had a real fear for her welfare.

Helen said 'Kicking' – 'Get there' – 'Shut up!' – 'Ohh God, Helen' – at different times. I said 'Someone hits. Someone hurts. Poor Helen hurts a lot.'

My (previous) mindlessness is gone. I feel convinced Helen is re-enacting recent experiences. She seems too concrete in her usual communications not to be telling me of recent concerns. I am alarmed.

Helen sat a doll on the toilet 'Toilet, wee.' She tried the doll on various seats. She looked hard at the woolly legs of the doll saying 'Jeans.'

Helen pointed again to the bottom and said 'Sore' and 'Wee' and 'Pooh.' I said 'Helen is sore when she does wee and pooh.' She clambered onto the desk. Her legs were wide apart and I had a view of her genital area. First I was surprised by her thin string of knickers, more like boys' boxer shorts, not girls' pants. Her genitals were on view and looked red.

I wondered if she was sore. I then wondered about my interest – concern? or abuse? ... Helen took one figure and tried it in various seats, and then on the roof. It slipped off. She tried to lay it on its front and again it slipped off. ... She placed a figure in her hand, again identifying to me the sore bottom and leg. I said 'Someone hurts a lot, there, oh there.' Helen held up her cupped hand and looked closely at the figure sitting in it. She said 'Shh'; I said 'Quiet now, sleeping'; and she held the little figure tenderly for a while. The session moved on to Helen drawing and 'cooking' with obvious enjoyment.

There is a time lag between her communication and my being able to 'see' the horrors it might contain. When I am able to, Helen can take care of the hurts, and she is freed to play more creatively.

Sessions such as this continued. I found it difficult to judge whether she was letting me know about real problems at home. 'Sickness' and 'Soreness' continued, and the violence of the relationships increased, focusing on Helen's explorations with a man doll. This doll was shut out of the house, pushed out screaming and kicking. Helen could become hugely excited and kick the walls of our room in a very wild way, screaming and often not calm until I intervened with the routine of leaving. The boundary between play and reality would easily blur, and it was important that I made the differentiation for her to allow her to know what was her doing and what was someone else's.

When I communicated my concerns to the social worker, it turned out that the home situation was deteriorating, with escalating violence and unreliable care of the children. Soon afterwards, the family disappeared.

Conclusions

Helen's handicap presents a complex problem of formulation. A traumatic birth was compounded by the emotional stress her mother was labouring under, which prevented her from noticing and remembering details of her daughter's earliest months. Helen's father was unable to tolerate the fact of his daughter's handicap, and it was undoubtedly a terrible blow for her mother as well. As Lussier (1960) describes, the mother of a damaged child seeks to protect herself from the loss of identity consequent on the narcissistic injury of producing a handicapped baby. The baby does not experience the sense of being valuable shining at him through his mother's eyes.

Anything that so profoundly affects the mother must profoundly affect her capacity to perform for her baby what Bion (1967) called alpha function. By this function, the overwhelming impact of the baby's early experiences is tolerated, and the feelings are identified and made meaningful. Psychoanalysts and child development researchers agree that it is the social attentiveness of caregiving adults that is paramount: 'The characteristic that determines whether or not a particular adult will become the object of the baby's separation anxiety is the social atten-tiveness of the adult to the baby, not physical care' (Bower 1977). In the normal situation, cognitive achievements develop within emotional relationships: Bower (1977) describes how new-born infants when spoken to 'move their bodies in precise rhythms that are perfectly co-ordinated with the basic units of adult speech.'

Therapy provided Helen with careful attention, coupled with the assumption that her behaviour had meaning. I have documented the steps in her development, leading to a realisation of her own identity, the capacity to be interested in another point of view, and concomitant improvements in her social relationships and ability to learn. As Bion (1967) puts it, an infant denied the chance of exploring 'his feelings in a personality powerful enough to contain them' is faced with the destruction of the earliest feeling link between infant and mother, which leads 'consequently to a severe disorder of the impulse to be curious on which all learning depends.'

Fragmentation of experience and of the self can come about through splitting (Klein, 1946; Rosenfeld, 1987; Bion, 1967); through uninte-gration as a consequence of defective holding (Bick, 1967 and 1986); or through the dismantling processes described by Meltzer (1975). Despite suffering a primary deprivation of containment as well as sexual abuse, Helen was able to achieve substantial improvement with very limited help. I have suggested that she had been able to retain an innate expectation of a thinking person, and that this expectation was not attacked. Even so, work could proceed only by means of the 'million tiny integrations' of which Alvarez (1992) writes.

5

Symbolisation and the Sense of Identity

Daphne Briggs

This paper is based on the psychotherapy of an adolescent boy whom I shall call Alexis, which began once a week when he was thirteen, was intensive for three years in his middle teens, and continued thereafter on a reduced basis into his early twenties. In it I want to explore the part that his use of symbols has played both in his psychotic functioning and in his recovery. By symbols I mean something – whether a pattern, a thing, or a concept – which is employed to hold emotionally charged meaning that does not intrinsically belong to it. At the simplest level in this sense a symbol simply stands for something else, as Klein typically used it in talking to children (e.g. Klein 1961, p. 24).

Alexis

Alexis was born prematurely, weighing only 3½ lbs, and before his mother had actually seen him, was taken as an emergency to an intensive care unit in a big city far from his place of birth, where he spent the next six weeks. Because of the distance and his mother's condition, his parents were only able to visit him once.

Alexis's mother had had two miscarriages before he was conceived, and had become desperate to bring a baby to full term. She was devastated by Alexis's premature birth and never recovered from her guilt and disappointment. While he was in hospital she was convinced Alexis was either dead or horribly deformed, and that people were lying to her about his progress. She remained locked in this state of mind right through his childhood, insisting upon his utter 'uselessness', and saying despairingly that he would need institutional care for the rest of his life against all the evidence for his steady progress towards independence. 'I can't see it', she would say, and to some extent she was justified, since Alexis would crumple emotionally and withdraw into himself when

115

faced each weekend with the seemingly impossible task of inspiring and sustaining hope in his mother.

When Alexis first came home, small but healthy, his mother seems to have been rather frightened of handling her baby.[2] She remained frightened of him into his teens, projecting a considerable measure of her own unacknowledged hostility into him. Her fear communicated a greatly exaggerated sense of his own dangerousness to Alexis himself, something that inhibited intimate relationships of every sort. In a session a couple of months into treatment, when he first began to explore the room with a sponge ball, Alexis threw it rather forcefully at my locked cupboard, glancing at me, and I commented that he might be wondering what would happen if he felt like throwing it at me. He replied, with a look of utter tenderness, by touching my arm gently with the ball, and saying, 'I wouldn't hurt you; you are nice.' Much later, he dramatised another aspect of his feeling that even his affectionate advances could be dangerous when, in the midst of a struggle to distinguish intrusive curiosity from legitimate interest, he played at being a lion roaring for a mate, grinning at me and telling me that the lion was going to eat his mate, he loved her so much; and then crawling across the table at me with laughter in his eyes to pretend to bite me, then sitting back to say with amused delight, 'You don't understand the danger!', and we could talk about it.

Alexis is said to have been a sleepy baby, but otherwise affectionate and sociable, and was beginning to talk early in his second year, a reassurance to his parents. Then, at fifteen months he lost his mother again as she was rushed to hospital with another late miscarriage, and was kept in for three weeks. Again Alexis did not see her, and during her absence is said to have stopped speaking and relating to people. He refused contact with his mother when she returned, and his parents trace his later difficulties to that period. His depressed withdrawal was to deepen during the course of his childhood. A brother was born when he was three – at last a healthy, full-term baby – but Alexis is said not to have taken much notice of his arrival apart from asking the next day when he was going away again. Although seldom actually rough, his jealousy of Stavros became more open in later years, as the younger boy began to overtake him in the ordinary achievements of childhood. Alexis would sometimes talk guiltily about a time when he pushed Stavros down stairs and hurt him, and a time when Stavros cut his hand, and he laughed.

According to neighbours' reports, Alexis was left alone for hours on end as a young child, often in the garden, where there was little to play with, and would occupy himself by scratching patterns in the soil with sticks or fingering the contours of parked cars in the drive.[3]

While it is possible that he suffered some degree of brain damage around the time of his birth (Alexis himself certainly thinks so), no organic damage or disorder has ever been identified. Physically he developed well, reaching puberty at twelve. But he had difficulty learning, needing special education, and his condition worsened as time went on. By eleven the only thing he seemed to take much interest in was front-loading washing machines, and when asked by the school psychologist to draw his family, did a splendid row of washing machines in a kitchen. When asked about the people, he became highly anxious and added a few sketchy pin figures.

By thirteen Alexis's education had come to a virtual standstill. He was incapable of social interaction, could do very little for himself, almost never spoke, and seemed to live in a world of his own, accompanied by open masturbation and many bizarre stereotyped gestures with his hands and head. He was obsessed with big machines, particularly on construction sites, but had little recognisable interest in anything else. He baffled the people involved with him. Educational tests repeatedly produced incongruous, unclassifiable results, suggesting that he was performing at a dismally low level, but probably well below his potential. Despite his social isolation and oddities, adults liked him and felt drawn to help him, responding perhaps to a wordless appeal for help. For Alexis could communicate powerfully in an inarticulate, atmospheric way, and for a long time this most primitive of all modes of communication (Bion, 1967, pp. 91, 102 ff.) dominated his work with me.

Alexis was brought up as mentally handicapped, but his history and development raise questions about the nature of his difficulties. The degree of any absolute mental impairment he might have had is almost impossible to assess because it was so massively overlaid with the secondary handicap that resulted from identification with the handicapped child that others, above all his parents, saw in him (Sinason, 1986). Throughout his childhood he was nakedly sensitive to the light in which others saw him, for good or ill. He would respond vigorously, sometimes openly with joy, to the experience of being treated as worthwhile and with a future, and this attitude, wherever it was found, seemed to promote personality growth in him (cf. Alvarez, 1991; Reid, 1990). By contrast, being treated as 'useless' or criticised, would provoke personality collapse.

Alexis made successful use of the psychotherapy he was offered, and

117

his progress was strikingly steady, resuming the development that had come to a halt in his infancy. From the beginning of my contact with him I was struck by his tenacious grasp of a sense of reality even at times of extreme disturbance. He would, for instance, spontaneously interrupt a wild outburst of confusion to check the time or make some down-to-earth comment. Despite a number of very stressful events during the years of treatment, he never suffered a serious setback, and indeed sometimes complained half-seriously that he wished he *could* 'go backwards', because it would be easier to be handicapped and looked after than to cope with the shame and realistic difficulty of being a disadvantaged young man in such a competitive world. Like his parents, Alexis is not fundamentally a thinker, but more practical in his approach to the world, and has never had grandiose ambitions. All along, he has wanted to lead an ordinary life, have a place of his own, get married, and raise a family. In his twenties, though still under-confident and subject to occasional very depressed moods, he is well on his way to independence.

It is striking how Alexis's physical appearance, and especially his face, have changed as his identifications have altered. In the composed states of mind that increasingly held sway, he grew into a tall, attractive young man, with a balanced, open expression and smiling eyes. In the withdrawn, psychotic states that beset his childhood he was collapsed and shrunken, conspicuously 'different', with a grotesque, lopsided face that appeared visibly crazed. It was, however, difficult for Alexis to shake off his entrenched identification with the handicapped child his parents and many others had seen in him over the years, partly because it was the only identity he had ever known, partly because of its secondary benefits to himself (little was expected of him, and he could do more or less as he liked), but also because of a chronic entanglement with his mother's disturbance.

Attachment to a Depressed Mother

Alexis was well aware that his mother needed him and could not let him go, despite her continual complaints about him. 'She won't let me go; she wants me to be a baby', he said simply and acceptingly after one discussion about his future. Leaving home was an unresolved issue for many years. Alexis was devoted to his mother, desperately anxious not to hurt her further than he believed he already had. He would describe, near to tears, how he would try at weekends to comfort Mama when she cried, or make her a cup of tea, but she would ignore him, or call for his father. It was apparent from independent observation that she was completely unaware that she was hurting his feelings.

Against this background, it is understandable that Alexis should have built into the core of his personality a model of anxious, eroticised, clinging dependency upon a depressed and needy mother from whom he could not part without irreparable damage to one of them. Much later, as he was in fact finally discovering a new, independent, sense of his identity, he represented the sheer impossibility of separating the two parts of this depressed and depressing dyad by drawing the outline of part of one half of a male figure: the side of a head, one eye, part of an arm and a torso – then, communicating bleak anxiety, asking, 'Is this like me?' He also represented this state of fusion in terms of pairs of semi-detached houses. 'His' house was never fully drawn in; 'mine' was generally given much detail and lovingly coloured in. Part of the point of drawing semi-detached houses is that they are, by definition, permanently attached and cannot be separated. Alexis once represented in action how this state of fusion was related to the threat of object loss. I had had to cancel a session at short notice because I was ill. In his next session, visibly upset, he went up to the tall cupboard where he knew I kept my own things, gave it a big hug and kiss, tugged in vain at its door, and then flung himself violently face down onto the couch, grinding himself frantically into its surface as though seeking to disappear into it, and conveying an illusion of being merged with it.

Alexis felt his very life still depended upon a huge and powerful 'Mama' who was continually 'telling him off ', as he would say, tenderly cuddling the pillow that represented her. He also represented this in numerous drawings in which he, portrayed as an empty, rather penis-shaped blob, was being embraced by a large, colourful, angry little girl-woman in a tee-shirt. In his favourite of these pictures, which infallibly aroused him sexually, the woman's fat arm had the head of a penis for a hand and a nipple for an elbow: a pure culture of sexually desirable qualities, so far as Alexis was concerned.[4]

This situation was not a promising context within which to negotiate Oedipal development,[5] and his earliest fully triangular Oedipal representations in psychotherapy were replete with the non-human objects he had substituted for people in his infantile despair. He came back from one holiday, for instance, to tell me with glee that he was writing a film script; it was called the Frilly Pink Thing, and was set on a construction site. In the plot there is a shoot-out between a baddie and a goodie for possession of a massive concrete mixer which stands by

119

rather helplessly, getting battered, and needs repairs afterwards. The goodie wins.

It seemed that Alexis and his mother were locked into an interminable repetition of the traumatic events and unworked-through grief that beset his early years, when their relationship broke down in reality. These traumatic 'unthought knowns' (Bollas, 1987) were active agents in Alexis's personality, structuring and distorting what he made of life around him. It is relevant here that it was only when focus on these aspects of his early infantile transference in psychotherapy had enabled him to begin to rebuild his internal world on a more realistic footing that he at last became able to respond appropriately to – and accept constructive criticism from – the many other people who had all along sensed the best in him but had been continually frustrated in their efforts to help him realise it. Detaching himself from his core phantasy of fusion with an ambiguous maternal object was a painful and depressing pro-cess, though was finally accomplished with an enormous sense of relief. 'I'm building a house of my own, a bungalow, a detached house.'

Mental Handicap and Psychotic Functioning

By the time he was thirteen, Alexis was seriously handicapped by psychotic functioning. In his second session he represented his predicament very expressively in a drawing of his family approaching a fairground, and himself, far behind, running to catch up, but weighed down by the enormous tape recorder he was lugging around under his arm. At that time, this machine had quasi-animate properties, embodying aspects both of self and his maternal object, inextricably confused. His drawing was an apt representation of a non-psychotic but undeveloped personality bogged down by psychosis, and Alexis had a striking capacity for self-observation. He had thoughts which he could represent very clearly, but no apparatus with which to think them (Bion 1962, pp. 83 f.; 1963, pp. 35 f.; 1967, pp. 117, etc.). It was, I found, useful in working with him to think of Alexis in terms of psychotic and non-psychotic parts of his personality and their relationship (Bion 1967, pp. 43-64). Alexis was well aware of their coexistence, and of his difficulty in maintaining identification with the sane part of his personality. Later in treatment, during particularly wild sessions he would spontaneously say things like, 'I must control my madness', or, 'I want to stay better, I don't want to be like this any more.'

Early in his first session, Alexis told me he was handicapped, wasn't he,

120

but could he catch up with the others, especially Stavros? He said he wasn't a baby any more, was he – could big boys still play on the bouncy castle? He scratched the stubble on his cheek audibly, and when I said that he was showing me that his body was no longer a little boy's, but that he still felt inside him like a little baby who needed Mama's bouncy lap, he said, 'I sound different now, don't I?', then gave me a sweet, mad look with a twist of his head, and let his body sag from the waist exactly as though he were a baby a few months old who could not yet support either his head or his back.

Alexis's psychotic functioning protected him from awareness of unbearable feelings of loneliness, worthlessness, and loss, but at the cost of almost complete withdrawal from ordinary relationships. It presented some autistic features, but was mainly characterised by such comprehensive projection of aspects of his own personality and feelings into things, primarily machines, and of even his entire self, when perceived as potentially healthy and alive, into any individual or group with which he was in contact, that he could lose touch almost completely with himself as a separate being (cf. Klein, 1955, pp. 141 ff.).

At the end of his first session, Alexis asked me if I could help him with his worries. 'Catching up' in psychotherapy involved working through the aftermath of specific infantile traumas as well as exploring and reconstructing his inner world more generally. As time went on, memories-in-feeling were identified and worked upon, gradually evolving into a sort of infancy narrative that helped him to make sense of his ongoing feelings and reactions. This area of experience was vividly communicated in non-verbal, atmospheric ways (see note 19): blinding lights, physical pain, an aching head, the crushing onset of gravity, difficulty in breathing, overwhelming helplessness and loneliness. This form of communication could be distressing to receive. On one occasion in the midst of such material, in a moment of silence I momentarily felt, with an actual shock, that he had died, and was relieved to see that he was in fact breathing.[6]

Alexis also communicated an equally strong sense of his keen appreciation of the beauty of the world he had entered, represented even at the beginning of treatment as fairground lights in a night sky, the glint of sun on shiny objects, or an open sunlit sky, as well as by his vivid use of colour and actual outbursts of joyous excitement or delight. He desperately needed shelter from all the extremes of emotional experience – rage, ecstasy, or despair – in order to begin to sort them out and find meaning in them instead of swiftly evacuating or hiding from them as too much to cope with.[7] He certainly elicited a filtering function from me. In the first few months of treatment I was spontaneously very still and unobtrusive with him, and spoke very softly. Later he took over something like this function himself by pulling the curtains and turning off the lights during sessions when he said the light hurt his eyes.

Problems with Communication

I think responding to Alexis's need for shelter in such a concrete way within the context of an intensely dependent early infantile transference was important in providing an interpersonal situation which he could recognise in his own time as adapted to his needs, as a prelude to gaining confidence in his ability to communicate, and internalising thinking functions for himself.[8] I will illustrate what I mean from the first months of his psychotherapy.

Although he was already a tall young man, being with Alexis at the beginning was more like being with a timid and terrified child, even at times a small frightened animal. This atmosphere was all-pervasive. He himself spoke so hesitantly and softly that I often missed what he said, and if I asked him to repeat he would react as though I had attacked him physically. Years later, he told me that in those days whenever he tried to talk, he felt there was a man standing over him with a gun, holding him down and forbidding him to move or to say anything.[9] He experienced communication with other people as actually putting some sensitive but invisible part of himself into them that might get cut or mangled by their reaction. In truth, this was quite an apt image of the most primitive kind of emotional transaction, in which 'feelings' reach out to and affect other people.

Countertransference is an essential instrument in psychotherapy with psychotic children. The predominance in them of non-verbal modes of communication also helps to account for why it is so very difficult to convey adequately what their psychotherapy is actually like. Session notes, and narratives such as this one, can look deceptively coherent and intelligible, selecting as they generally do the more describable elements of what was done and said, whereas what is overwhelmingly predominant is often the non-verbal atmosphere, attention to which is an absolute precondition for any progress at more evolved levels of the personality.

Alexis anticipated pain in encounters with other people, identified in his mind with his father's occasional angry outbursts, and he was terrified of being criticised in any way.[10] For at least two years he felt even the slightest faltering in my understanding (and such lapses were frequent) as a painful stab or hit that would provoke frantic flapping, or thumping the back of his head with a clenched fist, or a burst of seeking reassurance, sometimes accompanied by physical symptoms like a headache, breathlessness, or a racing heart. Being 'told off ' was worse still, like being electrocuted, shot, or cut to pieces. For a long time, Alexis very rarely initiated conversation, though he seemed to appreciate my talking to him, and certainly listened carefully, mainly responding to me in the three or more drawings he made most times, from which I could judge what he was making of his session. This already-developed use of his capacity to symbolise performed an important secondary function of screening him from direct emotional contact with me, one that could on occasion be abused. It was to be several years before Alexis could endure much direct, unmediated discussion of his feelings.

Confusion Between Mind and Body

One of the first objects of emotional significance to which Alexis introduced me, early in his first session, was an electric table-saw. This was soon to become familiar, with its large toothed circular blade mounted in a workbench, and various different controls and accoutrements according to the state of his mind. I will say more about his psychotic objects below, but this one was used at the beginning to represent aspects of an undifferentiated maternal body-mind that was irresistibly attractive to him but very dangerous. Alexis readily assimilated impressions of me and my functions into these drawings, for instance colouring the bench to match my clothes. It was apparent from early on that he could slip into a state of complete identification with these bizarre animated objects, as though they were people.

As he drew, he said that what he especially liked about table-saws was the way they cut wood into squares that he could nail together and make boxes with, and he commented on how sharp the blade was. He seemed contented, drawing all the details of the machine with its safety guard, switches, tool rack, and a pile of wood ready for sawing. He began to make a continuous buzzing sound. I eventually said that perhaps he felt he was being the saw as he drew. This put him in a panic, and he flapped his hands frantically. I said I thought he was frightened. He said that if he was frightened he would 'scream, and that would make monsters go away.' I said he felt I had become a monster just then, and he calmed down, continuing to draw. A few moments later, taking the material from the other perspective, I said that perhaps he felt I was the saw and that my words or thoughts were sharp and could cut his feelings. He nodded,

123

added the platform that the saw stood on, and told me that he was under age so would be in trouble for using a saw and would be told off – he said he only 'practised' on the saw at school, he didn't really use it.

While I think he *was* identified then with the saw and its functions, it was to be a long time before Alexis could accept 'patient-centred' observations such as the one I made without flinching (cf. Steiner 1992). However, a connection with me had been made, and material in the session moved on to anxiety about his continual masturbation, and Oedipal aspects of his transference: fantasies of being in a man's place at the bench, feeding wood into a maternal saw, which he readily agreed was coloured like my sweater, and could cut the man if he wasn't careful.

> I took up the need he had for a mind to sort things out into useful bits he could make things from (noting inwardly that it was containers he wanted to make), and his perception of my mind as a saw he could use, but that was sharp and could hurt him. He relaxed, and pointed out for himself that he had given the man clothes like his own. He drew a table coloured like the one we were sitting at, and when I said his drawings were connected with this meeting, he nodded. He added a window to the workshop in his picture, glancing up at the one in the room, and told me I would recognise the floor as he drew it.

Basic Emotional Containment

Continual movement between nameless anxiety states, psychotic confusion acted out or represented in drawings, and straightforward perceptions of everyday realities, external and emotional, was characteristic of Alexis's sessions for a very long time, sometimes alternating with bewildering speed. A lot of my work with him consisted in trying to keep up with these shifts and help him to tell states of mind apart and ultimately bring them under his own control. Most important of all, looking back on it, was making sense of previously nameless, unknowable anxieties, communicated non-verbally in terms of sometimes barely tolerable atmospheres.[11] Alexis, very aptly, represented these states by sawdust, introduced later on in the first session.

> I fell silent for a couple of minutes, thinking, and in the silence Alexis's anxiety began to mount. I explained that I would sometimes be silent to think, but that my silence seemed to worry him. He replied by drawing a pile of sawdust, rather large and tending to increase as he coloured it yellow. I said I thought the sawdust represented the feeling that had filled

124

the silence just then, and I wondered if he had been afraid that I had gone away from him in my mind and left him, or was criticising him. He did not reply, but his anxiety abated, and he said he was making a box (I mentally noted that this was another container), and he started a new picture.

After the first holiday, which had gone well, externally speaking, it became clearer that sawdust represented states of unbearable depression that Alexis had suffered from helplessly all his life.

> First, he depicted his loneliness during the holiday by means of clouds in a huge empty sky – an eloquent metaphor in anybody's language – and, in his private idiom, a table-saw working on its own outside in a field, unconnected to any obvious power supply, expressively drawn so as to appear very isolated and far away. Its blade was edge-on so that it looked 'thin' and almost invisible. There was a mounting pile of sawdust next to it, and as he drew and described this, I began to feel very sad. I took this as a mute communication, and asked him what he felt would happen to the sawdust. 'Nothing', he said, 'No-one clears it up. Maybe the rain will wash it away.' I spoke to him about the feelings that pile up inside him that he feels nobody clears away when he is left alone, unless maybe tears wash them away if he cries. In response he drew a roof on four supports and said it had struts to keep the roof on; then he drew a saw seen more fully from the side. I linked this with a sense of having found me again, and he drew 'clips to hold it together – you and I are together now, aren't we?'; then began asking over and over, conveying absolute panic, whether he would come back to see me again, and I could take up his despair about separations, since as a baby he had felt, and still did, that Mama-me might be gone and never come back again, even if he cried.

A session shortly after this, building on the same themes, marked a turning-point for Alexis both in his transference to me and, as I soon learned, in his life outside, where his bizarre behaviour and open masturbation suddenly stopped, never in fact to return except transiently, under exceptional stress.

I have been asked at various times what makes me think that psychotherapy rather than just life and getting older makes any difference to children like Alexis, or, if it does help, what makes me think anything psychoanalytic rather than just being nice makes the difference. What follows – and there were several other sessions like it over different developmental issues in the course of Alexis's psychotherapy – is a partial answer to these questions, while also exploring Alexis's use of symbols in the process of internalising a sense of basic emotional containment.[12]

125

For the first time, Alexis came to a session very obviously depressed, muttering to himself. He drew a broken tape cassette with a bit hanging out; a saw was cutting something up, but he didn't know what; a radio was already full up with an 'ordinary tape'. He was grim and withdrawn, and I interpreted in various ways during the long, difficult silences: feeling that Mama was full up with her ordinary baby and could not cope with a broken little boy (he glanced up at the mention of 'broken'), feeling that in my absence he had turned to his own body for comfort and damaged himself like a broken cassette (by now a familiar concern of his); he smiled fleetingly when I spoke of the baby teeth he felt did such damage when he was angry, and so on. For half an hour or so the atmosphere was leaden, yet despite his despair, he retained a thread of contact with me. It was characteristic of Alexis never, even at his most negative or chaotic moments, to sever all his links with sanity.

Gradually his drawing became bolder. He drew a more solid table-saw with controls that made it work, and said that he would make it work. I took up his determination to make his mark on me, and make me work in the way he needed. He drew a tree, so far always a representative of growth and hope, but after starting to colour it let the pencil slip from his fingers, and showed me the unfinished drawing with a look of utter despair. For the first time with Alexis I actually felt a direct emotional appeal, an important departure. Since he could say almost nothing that day, I said to him, 'Maybe you would like to say to me 'Why do you make me hope when I am hopeless?' He gave me a radiant look for a moment, rising slightly, then crumpled again. I talked to him awhile about the pain of growing up, and how it takes time. He finished colouring in the tree, adding branches and twigs.

I think the most crucial work of the session had now been done, though Alexis took it further still in his own unconscious idiom. He fished the pencil sharpener out of his box and began to sharpen a pencil absent-mindedly onto the floor between the two of us. Without thinking, I fetched the waste-bin and placed it under the trickle of shavings, and then wondered inwardly why I had done that. I thought of the sawdust that just piles up. I now think I was reacting automatically and unconsciously to an equally unconscious appeal from him for help with emotional overspill, represented in very concrete terms. Sometimes primitive, non-verbal communication can only be picked up and made sense of by observing the way one has in fact reacted to it. Alexis went on sharpening slowly for a while without taking any obvious notice of the arrival of the bin he was now sharpening into, and eventually said he was sharpening 'the teeth', and said pencils were like saw blades that get blunt. He was still rather listless.

Suddenly the sharpener slipped from his fingers and landed with a clang in the bottom of the bin. Alexis suddenly came alive. He laughed, saying 'That's better!', looked me full in the face (I smiled), took two pencils and began to tap a rhythm on the rim of the bin. I said he had found a drum to play on. He said it would be a bass drum if he played on

126

the other end (he liked puns, and was already developing a marked enjoyment in using words). 'But' he said 'What will happen if the shavings fall out?', giving me an enquiring look. I said he wondered if I would mind if they fell on the floor. He accepted the implicit permission, upended the bucket, and began banging its sides and base in various rhythms, like a baby exploring a container. I commented that he seemed to have found a good drum, and found in me a container with sides and a bottom that can hold in mess and unhappy feelings. He said he was happy now; 'The sun came out', and that he liked to be happy.

I said something else, he frowned, and I said the clouds had come over. He said 'Yes', brightening, and added, 'The sun can come out again, can't it?', and I said today was a day with clouds and sunshine (metaphorical discourse). There followed a disappointing period in which I could not follow his material, and he crumpled, but when I interpreted his disappointment he recovered, and, for the first time speaking in a strong voice that also elicited the first ordinary speaking tones from me, he asked me whether I would be glad when he was finished with this work – he was glad he was coming – how long would it be – as long as he needed? I said I hoped so, and he added that he would come again next week, 'all being well'. He could bear realistic uncertainty in this state of mind, and I could take up with him his great fear of having to leave me too soon, as he had had to leave his mother's body before he was 'finished' as a baby.

It was now ten minutes before the end of the session. Alexis put away his pencils, dropped the sharpener in his box with a decisive plop, and began to play with the sponge ball for the first time, tossing it carefully in the air between his hands, and touching it very gently to his face. He lay down gingerly on the couch, also for the first time, and seeing that I was not going to stop him, began to bounce on his back, holding the ball above him. I said he was showing me a little-baby feeling of being held by Mama and holding her breast in his hands. He nodded, and then said 'Watch'.

Alexis finished the session by exploring the room, something else that was new, and reminiscing about the first time he had met me, with his family. He bounced the ball again, with open delight, and said he liked this, that he 'should have done it in the first place.'

From this session onwards for the next year or so an important part of most sessions centred upon the ball and later a pillow, on the couch. At the same time, there was a marked step forward in the maturity of his relationships outside. Next holiday he thought the pillow would absorb his tears if he cried. Most of the time during this next period in his psychotherapy he was mute, and I myself was in effect conducting an infant observation, making comments describing what I was watching, or could sense in the countertransference: sometimes an unborn baby, sometimes a baby behind glass in an incubator, sometimes a feeding baby in Mama's lap, or one who feels lonely in Mama's presence. He threw himself enthusiastically into this area of transference relationship. The ball seemed to represent a means of connecting with me as a separate object, a theme he explored in a variety of ways over the next few months, sometimes using it vigorously to explore the room with. He also elaborated on the theme of containment and making sense of himself, for instance making paper covers for his wad of drawings, tying it all together untidily with string and labelling it 'My Book'.

From then on the issues of connectedness and how to cope with separation became very prominent themes, and were important in forging a new identity for himself, in the process of which his capacity to use symbols – graphic, dramatic, verbal, and musical – was fully employed, developments that lie outside the scope of this paper.

Symbol Formation in Psychosis

The last theme I want to explore in this paper is the light which work with Alexis sheds upon the process of symbol formation in states of mind where there is no underlying sense of mental containment. Alexis's psychotic functioning was probably in origin self-protective, and the methods he used were primitive. Finding insufficient shelter from the forces of his own emotional states, his overriding priority was to achieve some sense of equilibrium, a tolerable minimum of discomfort, and if possible, a kind of manic 'happiness' which he could pump up artificially for hours, exhausting himself in the process. Emotional and bodily comfort (or discomfort) were as confused with one another as they probably were in his earliest infancy.

In this situation, Alexis sorted and organised his experience and perceptions according to purely tactile and sensory impressions which gave either pleasure or pain. The most important such distinction, that prevailed early in treatment, was between a sharp, cutting, painful reception by his object (the saw of his first session), and a soft, bouncy, delightful one (the bouncy castle for children to play on of the second session). The use of such primitive, sensation-based distinctions as a basis for organising experience promoted the zonal confusions that abounded in Alexis, as in all psychotic children. The specific functions and properties of different bodily parts were much less important, if they were even discriminated between at all, than the sorts of sensations associated with them at a given moment.

For most of the first three years of his psychotherapy there was constant work upon identifying the sets of distinctions that Alexis employed to organise his universe, and helping him to make further or different distinctions that were more useful for development. His primitive objects, both paternal and maternal, were ambiguous in quality, both attractive and dangerous, and the only form of idealisation he seemed to use was based upon trying in imagination to divest these objects of nasty sensory qualities and focus upon a pure culture of the remaining pleasant ones, a procedure achieved and accompanied by physical activity such as masturbation, rocking, or bouncing on the couch while making stereotyped hand gestures. He used the latter to rid himself, and protect himself against the return, of the nasty elements of which the idealised sensations had been stripped.[16] For a long time he equated being happy with being in a state of masturbatory bliss. It was to be a year before Alexis could make a new and developmentally more satisfactory split either in his primal objects or in himself between bad and good aspects – complex, intangible qualities not available to sensory perception, which only take on meaning within realistic human relationships.

He seems also to have used bodily sensations, including genital masturbation, stereotyped gestures, and inarticulate noises, to create an imaginary barricade (or 'guard rail', as he called it) around himself, beyond which unbearable feelings could in phantasy be ejected.[17] In this omnipotent state of mind, which could generate a sense of oblivion, Alexis was relatively impervious to anything coming back to him from outside, accounting for some of his learning difficulties. This procedure left him feeling empty (cf. Klein, 1946, pp. 8ff), but at least he was not in a state of unbearable distress. Its developmental drawback was that it precluded owning and working through feelings; and for this to begin to happen his feelings had to be received and understood by another person, and returned to him in tolerable form.[18] When undigested feelings returned to Alexis from behind his makeshift barrier, they were no more use to him than they had been when ejected. When I first knew him, he was fascinated by echoes, usually imagined as reverberating around large empty buildings, perhaps unconsciously drawing upon life in an incubator. Sometimes in lonely moments he would make the sound of his voice bounce off the corner of the consulting room as he lay on the couch, feeling its reverberation as much as listening to it. At one point he complained, 'Why does everything come back at me? If I am nice to people, they are nice, if I am horrible they are horrible', referring to something like an emotional echo. One of the earliest expressions of real curiosity on his part was asking me how I knew that he was making echoes, as awareness dawned of empathic mental contact between two separate people.

In states in which Alexis felt alone and preoccupied with his own survival, he used his capacity to imagine and symbolize to manipulate, control, or alleviate mental states, and avoid the human relationships that confused him. This process compromised his contact with reality. He made extensive defensive use of projective identification,[19] evacuating feeling states beyond his makeshift barricade and attributing them to things or people outside himself, so that whatever was employed in this way lost its own identity and became identified with the meaning projected into it. This gave rise to a world of symbolic equations (Segal, 1981, pp. 49-65), bizarre objects with animate properties (Bion, 1962, p. 25; 1967 chapters 5, 6.). Alexis and many others like him employed their capacity to symbolize to evolve an alternative, psychotic universe to live in, one that was under their own control, being unable to make sense of human relationships.[20]

When Alexis gazed at an everyday scene in a psychotic state of mind, he saw electricity pylons standing proudly erect, confidently carrying power supplies to other machines, and warning off interfering little boys for their own protection, like someone's father at work. Lorry-mounted concrete mixers churned away contentedly, exuding an irresistibly attractive cuddly charm like someone's mother at work in the kitchen. Many other machines were imbued with similar qualities, and watching them made Alexis feel that he, too, had their properties – huge, strong, constructive, and dangerous if misused. I have employed metaphorical language to describe all this; Alexis himself was not using metaphors, nor the sort of childish as-if that animates Thomas the Tank Engine. Alexis's machines *did* have personalities, intentions, and feelings that he could understand and cope with. Real people simply terrified him, and he sheltered himself from them.

Using objects in this way, however, had serious developmental drawbacks. Bizarre objects substituting for people cannot process or modulate the emotional states they are imbued with, so that any feedback from them is illusory, like muddled echoes. An inevitable confusion reigns between the rules of emotional life and the laws of physics; no such difference can in fact be conceived of. When I first knew him, Alexis equated himself physically and emotionally with his stereo tape recorder, whose self-object significance has already been outlined. This made him abjectly dependent upon the actual condition of the machine. If a tape was damaged, or, worse still, the machine itself got broken, Alexis himself entered a state of helpless personality collapse.

Symbols used in this way do not function satisfactorily as vehicles of communication with other people, who are apt to get bored, puzzled, or dismayed by psychotic children's obsessive 'interests', and the difficulty in achieving any sort of meaningful dialogue with them.[21] What Alexis and I meant by a tape recorder or table-saw were categorically different entities. A lot of my work with him involved trying to recognise, and relate to, whatever emotional state was being contained within these bizarre objects, in order gradually to arouse an awareness in Alexis himself that it could be made sense of and worked upon. Symbolic equations seem to hold or bind emotionality that is deliberately divorced and kept apart from its appropriate context,[22] a sort of obsessionality motivated in Alexis not only by catastrophic or persecutory anxiety, but by the desire to spare himself and me (or any other person he was involved with) the impact of his extreme emotional states, which he experienced as omnipotently powerful.

One of the most difficult tasks of psychotherapy with psychotic children is helping them to relinquish these omnipotent illusions and put feelings back into people, where they belong. Alexis took an important step forward in his later teens when he began to realise that while machines might mean something to him, they had no feelings or intentions of their own. He could only do this after he had begun to gain confidence from experience of real human relationships, renegotiation of which at depth was initiated in his transference relationship with me.

Finally, these defensive uses of projective identification interfere with the perception of self. For most of his life, Alexis had projected healthy aspects of his own personality into others, giving rise to a feeling that all the life and happiness that he longed for resided outside himself and was unattainable except by fusing with a lively object, represented in his many drawings of the large vividly drawn Mama/wife hugging himself in the form of an empty blob. In this state of mind, Alexis could feel he was actually taking part in a situation when he was in fact standing silently on its margins, gazing. He would represent this state of affairs in drawings in which a lively and well observed scene – for instance the school playground – was being watched by himself in the foreground, portrayed as an empty shadow.

It was difficult for many reasons to emerge from these habitual defences against anxiety. They were well entrenched aspects of his personality by the time he was thirteen, and it was acutely embarrassing

131

for him to glimpse himself as he then really was. He could see nothing about himself that he liked. He felt unbearably clumsy and ugly. What is more, his psychotic states were seductive; masturbation was fun; he could do as he liked and be what he liked; and they sheltered him, as he later told me, from the noise of family rows. He portrayed his predicament in an especially poignant series of drawings just after his first summer holiday from treatment, which seemed among other things to have reawakened anxiety connected with his mother's absence when he was fifteen months old, and guilt about his reaction to it.

The first drawing showed a black bridge over a river. This bridge had first appeared in his sessions just before the summer break, and had then represented an important sense of connectedness with me. Now he drew it so that one end of the bridge was next to me on the paper. He said it was wobbly. It had two 'staples' at either end joining it tenuously with the banks, reminding me of the way that he never quite lost his thread of attention, even in his most withdrawn states. I related the drawing so far to the holiday gap he had had to cross. The bridge, he said, was held up by 'strings or ropes or chains', and he drew the shadow of the bridge on the river, and then himself standing on it. He said the bridge wobbles when there is a fight: he is fighting 'someone' on it, but does not know who or why. I spoke of a fight inside himself, perhaps with a Papa who took me away over the summer, or perhaps a fight between nice and nasty feelings, the man standing for his rage. He drew, on the far side from me, his 'wife', whom he later also called 'Mama' in full colour, sitting knitting him a jersey to keep him warm. 'She never gets cold; she loves me.'

Then he drew another version with himself, still in black, listening to his own music on his Walkman on the black bridge. He said the bridge could break if people fought on it or bounced on it too hard (which I took to refer to his masturbation). His wife, again in full colour, was on the shore at a table making him a meal with sauce and drinks. She was calling him, he said, but he would not come. He said he was angry and did not know why, and himself reminded me of a picture he had drawn after another holiday of being driven in the rain in a car by Mama who was furious with him, and looked like thunder. I spoke to him about his anger with Mama/me after the holiday absence, leaving him as Mama had left him when he was a little boy; and about his conflict over wanting to be by himself, needing what Mama had to offer, and being very frightened of how dangerous his anger was, so that he did not want to come. He then said he was coming, but slowly, and his wife was telling him to hurry up. I asked if he felt he was coming in his own time. He said 'Yes, but it's too slow; she loves me and wants to feed me.'

I was able to relate this to his own actual history, but also to his feelings now, in his transference to me, and the next few weeks saw the scene

132

in the drawings acted out in sessions, as he retreated into silence behind a dense screen of masturbatory activity, bouncing on the couch, hugging the pillow, plugging his mouth with his tongue behind his teeth, and holding his breath for long periods. Yet he was not altogether out of contact; he seemed to listen as I talked to him about the way he was using body sensations to screen out unwanted feelings and amuse himself, listening to his own music, and depriving himself of the real human contact that could feed his mind. This inaugurated a long but ultimately successful struggle with the idiosyncratic activities that played such an important part in perpetuating his disturbance. From then on Alexis's psychotic functioning became increasingly less of a protection – widespread improvement in his life was rendering it unnecessary and in his rapidly growing self-awareness he realised it was not 'normal' – and instead it became more blatantly omnipotent. Its last bastion was in his sexuality. It was tempting to go on masturbating excitedly to pornographic drawings of his favourite erotically charged psychotic symbols or to pictures torn out of magazines instead of trying to relate to real women and girls, but it was typical of Alexis that, confronted very starkly with these alternatives in the course of treatment, he should have given up his masturbatory retreat, and been grateful for having done so.

Conclusion

Human beings seem to have an inbuilt urge to use symbols, but whether they are used creatively, in the service of personality development and expanding relationships, making tolerable contact with realities outside the self, or defensively, leading away from objective realities into a developmental cul-de-sac, depends upon many things, including the quality of emotional attunement of an infant's earliest caretakers.[23] If all goes well, symbols will be used as metaphors, in which the symbol retains its own separate identity while containing and communicating the meaning attributed to it. This enables new meanings to be evolved. Use of symbols as metaphors presupposes a background of accurately attuned, realistic human relationship, and fosters the development of mind and personality.

There is a delicately poised, grey area between productive and unproductive use of symbols. At its best, the capacity to symbolize spares everyone involved in an interaction from uncontained extremes of feeling, while allowing emotionally charged communication to take place. Well on his way to recovery, and having recently been told that

133

in a year's time I would be reducing the number of his sessions each week, Alexis became very preoccupied with conserving supplies of all sorts. He brought to one session a chart he had been given to fill out as part of a fund-raising exercise for a day-centre he attended that was facing closure (!). The idea was to stick objects onto it against each letter of the alphabet. The chart was almost complete; 'A' was still missing. Alexis said Apple would do, but he didn't really want to spoil an apple for it – he would have had to cut a piece off. Then it occurred to him spontaneously that he could draw an apple. His face lit up: he could represent the apple without damaging it in any way. It strikes me that this is one of the most important elementary functions of symbolism, which can also be used to spare other people's feelings, something richly illustrated in Alexis's material.

By extension, symbolic representations can equally be used to mask or distract from emotionally charged situations, and there are times when the effort to spare self and object in this way may block progress in personality development. Towards the end of his intensive psychotherapy, Alexis was beginning to face up to awareness of feelings of disappointment and rage towards me and other people that he could never previously have acknowledged as his own. It was very necessary for him to discover that such feelings were truly not omnipotently destructive, and that, however painful, they could be communicated appropriately to the person concerned without wrecking the relationship, as he felt they had done with his mother.

Once I had to cancel a session at short notice because I was ill, but he was brought by mistake and turned away. Naturally, this upset him deeply. During the session that followed (the session of the semi-detached houses), he represented his feelings in every way he knew, short of direct confrontation. Finally, he made a drawing of a house. You could see right through from the front window to the other side, and it had a dismal brown interior, but a flower on the back windowsill. This picture had been the focus, with other material in the session, of interpretation on my part of his present and past agonies at times of separation. When I took up how he feels the inside of himself and Mama/me is dark and miserable and that he is only attached on the outside, so that separation means being literally torn apart, he came over to stand very close to me, forehead brushing mine, looking at me, and holding my attention with his gaze, but pointing to the picture on the table, saying 'Look at this.' I said he was afraid to ask me to look at him, so asked me to look at his picture instead, as though it were more real than him. This, I think, deprived his picture of its function of protecting him and me from an upsurge of emotion – for he immediately flung himself onto the couch, grabbed the pillow, and began pounding and smashing it against the wall and radiator, shouting 'Slag!' and saying he was the burglar, he had 'Smashed Caroline's house up' (Caroline was by now the standard representative of his bad maternal object, and bad me in the transference), 'Gone in and smashed her up' – all accompanied by a stream of dizzy non-verbal projection. He calmed as I talked to him about what I thought lay behind his feelings, and at the end he sat up saying, 'This is why I come here, isn't it.'

It will not be possible here to explore more fully Alexis's healthy use of symbols in the process of recovery. Suffice it to say that he did employ his capacity to symbolize to very good effect. Well into the second year of work, shortly before the session described above, he succeeded for the first time in his life in making a useful split in his primal object of attachment, so that there was a whole good Mama/me to love and a bad slag Caroline to hate, and a good whole loving self to identify with as well as an angry Jaws-self who could in play be put out of the door for peace of mind during his sessions. 'I like people!' he would exclaim, 'I want to help them!' From then on he worked steadily towards acceptance of the realistically mixed qualities of himself and other people, asking sorrowfully after one painful confrontation with me, 'Can you have an argument with somebody and still love them?'

Notes

[1] I am particularly grateful to Frances Tustin for her help when I was first working with Alexis. She always thought he would recover, and taught me to recognise and foster signs of healthy growth in him amidst the tumult of his psychotic functioning.

[2] Alexis confronted her, among other things, with an unbearable irrational sense of failure (Druon, 1988).

[3] I wonder whether this was a precursor of his considerable ability to express himself by drawing.

[4] During his long weeks in intensive care, Alexis may have been keenly aware of people's arms and hands reaching into his incubator to attend to him. In his longing to be held and cuddled, something that remains deeply unsatisfied in him, he may have invested women's arms with meaning more usually attributed to the breast or face.

[5] See Ogden, 1989, pp. 146 ff.

[6] This was, I think, an example of primitive communication by projective identification of the fear that he was dying, appropriate containment of which may avert deterioration into nameless dread (cf. Bion, 1963, p. 27 etc.).

[7] Cf. Bion, 1962 chapter 3, 1967 chapter 9; Tustin, 1986, pp. 147f; Meltzer/Williams, 1988, pp. 15 ff.

[8] I find Bion's concept of pre-conception (1963, p. 23) useful in this kind of work. If pre-conceptions of basic relatedness – such as the need for realistic emotional containment and understanding – do not meet with adequate realisation in infancy, permitting the gradual evolution of more mature forms of relationship, they seem often to be carried over intact into later life, going on seeking realisation at the primitive level. This can have unfortunate social consequences, since other people generally resent the 'manipulative' pressure that this crude unconscious appeal inevitably puts them under.

[9] I think this is a manifestation of the extremely primitive savage super-ego that attacks non-verbal communication, described by Bion (1967, pp. 91-2).

[10] Here he seemed to project a more evolved primitive super-ego into other people, cf. Klein, 1955b, p. 133; 1958, p. 241.

[11] Bion's beta elements, fit only for evacuation (1962, pp. 6 f., 13; 1967, p. 27. etc.).

[12] I take the essence of *psychoanalytic* psychotherapy to be selective attention to transference phenomena, including the most primitive forms of relatedness, and helping the patient to recognise and make sense of these for themselves. Without the sort of conceptual apparatus described in this paper I do not think I could have made any useful progress with Alexis.

[13] This is not intended to idealise countertransference acting-out and other technical mistakes, although sometimes mistakes can be picked up very profitably. I have found the literature on psychotherapy with borderline states very helpful in this connection (e.g. Joseph, 1975, Alvarez, 1985, Steiner, 1979, 1992).

[14] The importance of rhythm in establishing a fundamental sense of safety is relevant here, (Tustin, 1986 chapter 15).

[15] Alexis was never breast-fed, but the preconception of finding a feeding breast remained, (Klein, 1952, p. 117).

[16] These manoeuvres seem to be derived from the sensation shapes described by Mrs Tustin in autistic children (1990, pp. 38 ff.). Close observation of what Alexis was actually doing with his hands revealed that each gesture was composed of a sequence of movements that held specific meaning – getting together, reaching for his object, warding off monsters, shaking off nasty bits, holding on for dear life with his mouth, and so on. Attention to these details enabled even his stereotypes to lead into meaningful communication about infantile states of mind.

[17] Cf. also Mrs Bick's second skin (Bick, 1968), and Bion's beta-screen (Bion, 1962, pp. 23-4).

[18] Bion's alpha function: (Bion, 1963, p. 27; 1967, chapter 9).

[19] Bion was the first to describe how projective identification is employed in two different kinds of unconscious mental activity, but satisfactory terms to differentiate them have not yet been generally agreed upon (for one suggestion see Meltzer, 1986, p. 69). One use of projective identification is to achieve the most primitive known form of emotional link and non-verbal communication (Bion, 1967, pp. 91-2), employed by many animals who have no articulate

136

language at all, and by human beings alongside and underpinning language. It is the only mode of communication available to very young babies, and seems to work by mobilising congruent feelings in any available recipient of the communication. Attention to difficulties in this area of absolutely essential communication is one of the most important tasks of psychotherapy with children like Alexis. The second sort of projective identification is the omnipotent phantasy that Klein first described in 1946, in which parts or even the whole of a person's inner world is extruded into objects or people outside the self. This is not so much a single procedure as a cluster of related imaginative activities, which have in common that they defend the personality in illusory ways against awareness of realities that it cannot for the moment cope with. Such activity is overwhelmingly predominant in psychotic states, where it has become a developmental dead-end. Each sort of projective identification has its own particular clinical implications, some of which I hope to illustrate here. So as not to introduce clumsy neologisms, while maintaining a conceptual distinction, I shall distinguish the two sorts of projective identification here by referring to the first by such expressions as non-verbal or atmospheric communication, and the second as the defensive use of projective identification.

[20] Freud 1911, pp. 69 ff. (Schreber's psychosis as a form of self-made recovery from internal disaster), or Bion, 1967, pp. 91-2 (another view of the underlying primitive catastrophe).

[21] Cf. Bion, 1967, p. 119: 'an important function of communication is to achieve correlation.' Psychotic children are primarily seeking to control emotional states; achieving correlation remains an unfulfilled pre-conception.

[22] Fetishistic and pornographic objects would come into this category. Alexis had several such sexually charged objects that were infallible turn-ons: the sexual desire projected into them appeared to be seducing *him*. For a short while, little boys were objects of such narcissistic erotic significance – human bizarre objects – perhaps shedding light on one of the components of paedophilia.

[23] The sort of playful interaction between mother and young baby in which the mother shows attunement to the baby's emotional states with a range of different but congruent sounds and gestures (Stern, 1985, 138 ff.) strikes me as being an important prototype of more evolved uses of symbolisation, including language.

6

'Here I Am!'

Self and Object in a Developmentally Delayed Boy with Autistic Features

Sara Rance

Introduction

Anthony began intensive psychotherapy at the age of three. Concerns both of his parents and professionals centred on his marked language delay, which, combined with poor social interaction, had given rise to worries about autism. This account of his therapy focuses on the emergence of language and on what this reveals about his growing sense of self and his capacity for object relatedness.[1]

History

Anthony is the first child of Mr and Mrs M, a professional couple both actively involved in the care of their children. Anthony's birth was normal, but his mother suffered from severe post-natal depression, and she felt it had been virtually impossible for her to bond with him. Her attempts to breastfeed proved unsuccessful and she became racked by despair, readily blaming herself for Anthony's difficulties, and feeling immensely isolated despite her husband's actual presence. It was six months before she received medical help in the form of medication for her depression, which lifted during her second pregnancy, but returned after the birth of Anthony's brother when Anthony was sixteen months old.

It was a time of great emotional upheaval for the family; the stresses of a first baby's arrival characteristically reactivating internal conflicts for each of the parents, as well as exacerbating tensions in their relationship. Contact with both sets of grandparents was regular, but they tended to experience it as critical and intrusive rather than suppor-

138

tive. Despite the problems with breastfeeding, Anthony took to the bottle and was weaned onto solid food, which he initially took to with enthusiasm. By fourteen months he had started to walk and spoke a few words. However, during the months surrounding his brother's birth areas of his development ground to a halt or even regressed. His language failed to progress beyond the use of two or three single words, and he began to refuse most solid foods, accepting only milky foods such as yoghurt or cereals. He showed no readiness for toilet training. His parents saw his lack of speech as a refusal which they felt had become a 'rule of life' for Anthony.

Anthony was referred to a speech therapist and was subsequently enrolled in a professionally-staffed play group. At first he was unsettled and unable to play. He wandered aimlessly, or paced back and forth in an agitated way, sometimes walking on tip-toe when entering the room, arching his body and averting his eyes when approached. He was either rigidly focused or easily distractible, and seemed to enjoy the sensations of wading through piles of toys or mouthing objects. Initially unresponsive to verbal requests, he appeared to be unaware of, or to avoid contact with other children and adults, but he did gradually begin to make eye contact and occasionally showed some interest in interacting with others, particularly those at a distance.

By now concerns had been expressed about autism. A referral was made to Child Guidance when Anthony was two and a half, and the whole family was seen for a number of months by a social worker before an assessment for psychotherapy was requested. Anthony's mother was finding it increasingly difficult to respond to him and appeared fearful of making real contact, as if paralysed by her despair. Her own suffering was powerfully conveyed as she sat, at first largely silent, her eyes downcast. In time she became able to describe her feelings of inadequacy as a mother and her fear of being blamed for Anthony's difficulties. However, beginning to express her anxieties seemed to enable Mrs M. to respond more readily to Anthony, and to recover some hope of being helped.

Anthony's father seemed worn down by the combination of his wife's depression and the children's needs. At the clinic he could appear reproachful towards his wife, not easily empathising with her anxieties about Anthony, and suggesting that language would develop in time. He was open to further professional help, though seemingly sceptical of its value at this stage.

Both parents conveyed the impression that their own internal objects were inadequate to contain and support them through their difficulties.

139

Expectations of abandonment, condemnation and failure permeated their relationships with professionals. Yet they were seeking help for Anthony. Over the three years of Anthony's therapy their social worker provided ongoing support in which his parents were able to explore their concerns about Anthony, and their affectionate responsiveness towards him grew to meet his own growing relationship to them.

Anthony's individual assessment was beset by problems in separating him from his parents. However there were hopeful signs. He did not display flamboyant autistic features, but appeared to have withdrawn defensively, and his parents, encouraged that he used more language immediately after the assessment sessions, accepted the offer of three-times-weekly psychotherapy for him. He was also offered part-time childcare by a project for children with special needs.

In gathering together Anthony's early history it is possible to understand how constitutional and environmental factors intertwine. A child's sensitive temperament can interact with its mother's depression in such a way that exposure to each other's distress overwhelms their fragile relationship. Anthony's extreme sensitivity made him excessively permeable to his mother's emotional state, like those children described by Meltzer as being 'naked to the wind' (Meltzer et al., 1975, p. 9). Mr M felt helpless to alleviate the downward spiral, and professional help was not prompt enough to limit early damage. If unbearable mental pain is what is mainly shared between mother and infant, a recoiling from contact into mindlessness is an understandable response. Murray and Trevarthen (1985) found that two-month-old babies showed signs of distress, including avoidance of eye contact, when their mothers adopted a still face. Primitive fears of persecution and of damage to the object inhibit reaching out into the world. The process of differentiating self from other may go into reverse, and in this more fused state symbolisation and language development are impaired.

Klein linked inhibitions in symbolisation to the excessive and premature strength of a child's defence against sadism and an incapacity to tolerate anxiety (Klein, 1930). The relationship between internal and external objects is crucial to the possibility of modifying such inhibitions. If a child's mother is depressed, sadistic phantasies towards internal objects would appear to be confirmed by reality, thereby increasing anxieties about sadism, whereas a child with more resilient external objects will discover that his destructive phantasies do no real damage, and is thus helped to differentiate phantasy from reality.

140

6. 'Here I Am!'

The Beginning of Therapy

When I first met Anthony in a family meeting he was peripheral to the group, flitting round the edges of the room. He lacked a central focus, a sense of self or of place within the family. He largely ignored me, although twice he approached and peered at me, craning his head forward, and squinting through outspread fingers. Conflict was apparent between his healthy curiosity, and his defensive need to break up the impact of new experience.

At the outset of therapy Anthony's speech was still limited to a small vocabulary of single words, mostly names of familiar things and people. He lacked a firm sense of what Meltzer calls 'a suitable audience for speech', that is 'an object in the outside world which has sufficient psychic reality and adequate differentiation from the self to require vocalisation of inner processes in order for communication to take place' (Meltzer 1975, p. 193). But he did seem to be searching for such a presence. His father said that Anthony would sometimes wake in the night, refusing to settle until a word had been repeated back to him. It was like echolalia in reverse, a verbal equivalent of the need for a gaze to be met and held, and an expression of a primitive anxiety that his communications would drain away into nowhere and nothingness. In the countertransference Anthony's unresponsiveness evoked similar anxieties in me – 'has he heard me?' 'Can he see me properly?'

Anthony was immediately interested in the therapy room and its contents, though he would not involve me directly in his play to begin with, and sat with his back to me. I often felt that he was impervious to my presence, and at such times found my own attention wandering, yet I discovered that he was acutely sensitive and would suddenly look up at me if my mind drifted from him.

A fascination with water was Anthony's major avenue for autistic withdrawal in his therapy. He would turn on the tap and leave it running endlessly, put his hand and face into the stream of water as if to dissolve into it, or fill his mouth and then open it, passively allowing the water to flow out of him, mingled with his own saliva. He poured water back and forth from the toy tea pot to a cup, creating the illusion of it never running out.

At these times Anthony was at his most silent and inaccessible: his fused, sensation-dominated state allowed no distance between self and object within which thought, let alone language could evolve (Segal 1957). Although apparently mindless, his activity with water aptly conveyed the formless, fluid quality of his more autistic states. It was

141

congruent with his repetitive play; his regression to milky liquid foods; as well as the constant leaking of saliva and mucous from his nose and mouth; his incontinence and the prolonged open-mouthed vowel sounds which would accompany his pacing up and down the room. They all manifested what I called his 'on-and-on-water-world'. Under the sway of this amorphous state sphincters would not close, the articulation of consonants would not occur, nor the biting of solid food or the formation of discrete thoughts which could be transformed into inner speech. All these depend essentially on processes of separation and differentiation: of inside and outside; body and mind; self and other – the necessary preconditions for symbolisation and language development to occur (Meltzer, 1975). With his on-and-on activities he protected himself from knowing about absence, the experience of space opening up within him, or a gap to be bridged. It became apparent, for instance, that his pacing would occur mostly when the end of a session was looming. It became necessary to limit such activities in order to draw him back into contact. Initially he would respond with panic when I did so but in time angry protest took its place, a sign of greater resilience in his internal world.

Anthony was particularly interested in the 'car wash' and played repeatedly at making one in the garage of the dolls' house. Being in a car wash would of course perfectly fulfil his wish to be encircled in a never-ending flow, its slushing pulsating sounds recapturing the sounds of intra-uterine life, and a delusion of watery fusion with his object. Although the beginnings of pretend play were evident in this car wash game, the play was repetitive and more concrete than symbolic in quality, aiming to replicate exactly the actual place he knew. Having 'set the scene' he was unable to elaborate on it in phantasy, but recreated it over and over again, like an assistant stage manager who brings on the set and props but cannot take part in the human drama.

Anthony could tolerate only a world which was utterly predictable. This is characteristic of a state of adhesive identification (Bick, 1968). In this two-dimensional state he lacked 'an internal space within the mind in which phantasy as trial action, and therefore experimental thought, could take place' (Meltzer, 1975, p. 225). The concept of internal space in the object is also missing, and consequently surface properties of the object are desperately clung on to and mental functions cannot be introjected. Anthony was anxious if furniture in the room was at all 'out of place': if I moved a chair so that he could reach the sink more easily, he squealed. He was unable to adapt, and equally unable to respond to an object that might adapt to meet his needs. This fear of change would inevitably have a profound impact on his intellectual development, inhibiting curiosity and imaginative conjecture. He had a good recall for names of things and people, but could not retain information about how things worked or fitted together – how to turn the tap on, or open the catch on the doll's house. He would frantically try to wrench this apart, as if convinced that his object was inaccessible to him.

Anthony used various mechanisms to diffuse threatening experience. He would hold bits of plastic fence or his outspread fingers close up to his face as if to distort his focus. Donna Williams (1992, p. 3) describes how she learned as an autistic child to 'lose herself ' in patterns of spots in the air, or patterns of sound, which allowed her to 'ignore the gabble' and soothe herself. Anthony also used rapid clapping, as if to disperse intrusive thought or sound. He came to depend far less on such devices, except at times of stress. (For instance much later, when talking about the ending of his therapy he began blinking repeatedly and rapidly). I knew it was crucial to retain my own focus, carrying the ego functions that were weak or lacking in Anthony, in the hope that he would become able to introject a thinking object. Yet his anaesthetising actions meant that it took great effort to remain alert.

Beginning to Reach Out

Five weeks after therapy began Anthony was trying out the chairs in the room. This later developed into an interest in the Goldilocks story, to which he frequently returned. He sat in 'my' chair leaning his head back and then to the side, fully exploring the feel of it. He then looked at me from across the room saying 'no good, it's no good.' He was beginning to tell me about his own 'no good' feelings, but also, said from the perspective of a mother's chair, I think this described Anthony's anxieties both about his maternal object and the mother-child relationship. It was not a comfortable fit. This moment evoked deep sadness, but it also contained hope. Anthony was endeavouring to reach out and to verbalise his experience of loss and despair, rather than denying it through compulsive dependence on the comfort of bodily sensations. Here he made contact with me across the length of the room and communicated his sadness through his gaze and with words, for the first time using language descriptively. He had also begun to call me by name.

Notes on another early session illustrate Anthony's growing responsiveness to my efforts to understand, and the primitive infantile quality to his communications.

143

He got up on a wide shelf under the sink, on which a large tipper truck and the doll's house were placed. He looked at the eyes painted on the front of the truck, and turned away, squinting, as if frightened by a vacant staring quality in them. He began to play with the door of the garage, moving it up and down. Then he looked up at the pipes over his head and I began to talk to him about what he could see, about his interest in the water and where it goes. He lay on his back and began to make happy gurgling sounds, followed by babbling. He was smiling like a contented baby. He was somewhat hidden behind the dolls house and I peered at him through the open garage door – he was able to look into it from the door at the back. I said 'hello Anthony', wondering at first if he would be frightened, as he was of the eyes on the truck, but he laughed. This developed into a peekaboo game in which he would move out of sight, but peer again at me through the door when I asked 'where's Anthony gone?' He then reached round the outside of the doll's house and put his finger to my mouth, as a baby at the breast might do. After this he reached again and took my finger, holding on to it for a few minutes.

There was a compelling intimacy to the relationship which was disconcerting at times, but which seems to have been an essential key to Anthony's emotional development in therapy. Meltzer describes how the intensity of the breast-relationship can wither, when depression or other disturbance in the mother 'dries up her attentiveness, warmth, chatter and sensuality towards the baby', and how 'the dismantled self will float away for longer and longer periods of mindless activity' (1975, p. 16).

In a fluctuating manic-depressive illness, a mother's need to engender liveliness in her infant, and her frantic efforts to recover lost contact might be experienced as bewildering bombardment by the baby. The peekaboo game allows the infant to take control of the to-and-fro of contact, working through not only the experience of separation, but also the challenges of reunion. When Anthony and I played this game he would always be the one to hide his face and have me come and find him, conveying his wish to be retrieved from his mental hiding place (Alvarez 1992, re more active technique).

Struggles with Separation and the Drawing Forth of Language

Following the first break in therapy Anthony returned excited but very uncontained. Contact was fleeting and sparse and he kept his back to me. His dribbling had returned, and his nose ran, as if nothing could be held in. There was a recurrent theme of falling, and he spent time scattering things aimlessly and wading through the mess, evoking in me feelings of chaos and hopelessness. Before a later break the theme of falling returned and he spoke of 'poor Humpty', pitifully expressing his fear of falling into a state of disintegration from which he would never recover.

As Anthony's tendency to dissolve into autistic withdrawal became less pronounced, he found new ways to manage the difficulty of separation. With a growing capacity to consciously face separation, communication with an object who was other, rather than merged with the self, became necessary, and Anthony drew increasingly on gesture and verbal language. He began to anticipate the endings of sessions, and would look at the clock, then put his hand against the door, saying 'Not yet.' Later he would step into my shoes, pre-empting my control of the ending by announcing 'Nearly time', 'Five more minutes' or 'Finished now.' Thus his experience of abandonment was projected into me, and I was to be the little one left behind as he busily organised his departure, turning the light off as we left the room. Evidence was increasing of a capacity for projective identification, in which the mental functions (as opposed to the surface bodily qualities) of his object were perceived and entered into in phantasy. Here projective identification was used communicatively and it represented an important step towards the capacity for introjection.

By this time Anthony was saying 'goodbye' when leaving his family in the waiting room. There was now a sense of their 'going on being' in Anthony's mind when he was not actually in their company. The crucial link between a capacity to experience loss and the development of symbol formation and therefore language is emphasised by Segal (1957), and also explored by O'Shaughnessy in *The Absent Object*: 'before you can 'think about' you must develop the prior capacity to 'think of '. This latter is essentially linked to things absent; developmentally speaking, to the absent breast.' (1964, p. 34). Indeed it was his growing capacity to contemplate and tolerate parting and absence that provided the context in which Anthony spoke his first full sentence to me.

Hearing noises outside he stopped what he was doing and listened attentively, then looked out of the window. This day his father had, unusually, left the clinic after dropping Anthony off for his session, and I suggested that Anthony was looking for him. He then said to me 'Daddy's gone to work.' He was beginning to understand that 'gone' meant 'somewhere else'. The knowledge of his father's continued existence meant that Anthony could both construct in his mind a place where his father might be, and find the words to tell me about it. Also striking on this occasion was the precision in his language and the unusually crisp articulation, compared to many of his garbled mutterings.

The direct relationship between Anthony's conscious acknowledgement of loss and separation at any one moment, and his clarity of thought, verbal expression and articulation at that moment became increasingly apparent, and was highlighted in the months leading up to the termination of his therapy. Within a broad trend of developmental progress, his capacity to use language continued to fluctuate according to oscillations between more autistic or object-related states.

This can be seen in material following Anthony's return after the first summer break. His mother told me that he had asked for me and became angry and distressed if they passed the clinic while I was away. He was able to convey to me powerfully, though without words, how hard the separation had been.

> He lay down on his front, head away from me, looking rather collapsed, with one leg dangling over the edge of the bed, which he swung listlessly. I watched from the other side of the room, saying that it had been a very long time for him to wait and now he was not sure if he was ready to look at me yet. Then I went over to the bed and sat on it a little distance away from him. He peeked up and then resumed his position with his head facing away from me. He was breathing heavily and slowly, conveying a mixture of relief and sadness. His turning away did not feel particularly hostile or cut off. I talked about how very tired he was from all that waiting; perhaps he thought I'd never come back. As I talked he remained still and with his eyes wide open, his hand held near his face ... He sighed a few times and then I had the impression he was falling asleep. He remained quiet for some time. When I looked again his eyes were open. I talked about his relief to be back but also his sad feelings that I had been away all this time. He had not spoken at all during this time, but then, as I talked, he was looking at his hand, and curled and uncurled his fingers one by one, muttering quietly to himself, counting them, one to five, as he unfurled them. I said that he was counting, like he did over the five weeks I was away, when mummy and daddy reminded him when I'd be back, but it was so hard for him to believe it.

Kanner described how 'the personal metaphors of the autistic children can convey 'sense' only through acquaintance with the singular, unduplicated meaning which they have to the children themselves' (1973, p. 47). This applied to the uncurling and counting of Anthony's fingers. It is also true of many gestures and idiosyncratic sounds made by infants who are just beginning to speak. Typically only their parents can understand their meaning. In *Symbol Formation* Werner and Kaplan describe how in normal development language gradually becomes 'the medium par excellence for the communication of precise, objective reference, and inner experiences tend to be embodied in internal feelings and strivings, imaginal forms etc' (1984, p. 260) whereas in pathological states distinctions in the functions of different media of expression such as language, gesture, imagery, dissolve. In autistic regression 'the sharp distinction between an autonomous, interpersonal medium of language, necessary for communication to others, and personal idiosyncratic media of imagery and gesture used in communicating to one's self ' breaks down. Anthony had survived my absence without returning to autistic withdrawal, but the strain of prolonged separation was unmistakable. Here he was occupying a borderland in which expressive gesture had more of the quality of inner speech, though it held a unique shared meaning in the therapeutic relationship. The counting and unfurling of his fingers had something of the quality of transitional phenomena, and Anthony's state, which appeared to be in-between sleeping and waking, was also suggestive of this borderland, from which he needed gentle encouragement to emerge. In order to draw him further into interpersonal contact, Anthony would need to be persuaded of the attractive potential of language to establish the psychic experience of being with a differentiated other.

Anthony's growing sense of self and of relationship were vividly conveyed on the day he arrived at the clinic and exclaimed to the receptionist 'come to see Sara!' Knowing about my separateness would also increase his awareness of others in my life. Towards the second year of therapy Oedipal conflicts and sibling rivalry emerged increasingly in the transference and in his external relationships. His parents reported that he was taking more notice of his brother, and I witnessed growing curiosity and jealousy towards other children in the clinic.

Anthony found it difficult to negotiate the transition back into therapy after a break, struggling to find the right distance between us. Increased vulnerability in his more separate state led him at first to burrow into me or into narrow spaces in the room in an attempt to get inside his object. This then led to claustrophobic panic, followed by shrugging off and getting up too high, adopting an omnipotent position on top of the lockers, from which he would then cry piteously 'help! I stuck.' He was expressing greater ambivalence towards me with more passionate seductiveness and rage.

Ordinary mischievousness was also appearing, and Anthony would describe things he was doing as 'naughty'. He began to defy me and to enjoy a playful pantomime exchange of 'Yes!' 'No!' 'Yes! 'No!' It had its serious edge, but like the peekaboo game was a manageable way of establishing our differences, and discovering the resilience of self and object in the face of disagreement. New phrases which popped up in his play, such as 'Don't worry', revealed the presence of a containing internal figure helping Anthony to hold himself together and to manage anxiety and frustration.

'Here I Am!'

It was during the second year of Anthony's therapy that tentative beginnings gave way to a surge of progress. He was spending far less time in the continuous loop of timelessness and mindlessness which had characterised his more autistic states. There was some progress in toilet training and tantrums and no-saying increased, which his parents recognised as important developmental steps. Freedom of thought and symbolic expression were still relatively inhibited and as this inhibition lessened, the use of obsessional mechanisms to protect himself from feelings of uncertainty and helplessness became more pronounced. Obsessional features emerged in his language development: his unusual familiarity with product brand names, advertisements, and names of TV programmes, for example, like an armoury of lists with which to bolster his fragile ego.

The important contribution to his development of greater tolerance of aggression became more evident. (If the start of therapy is thought of as a form of psychological re-birth, the second year of therapy may hold developmental features typical of the second year of life). When Anthony came into therapy he lacked potency or 'bite', and although frantic and stubborn at times, he was not prone to aggressive outbursts. The dynamic internal process of differentiation was now resumed and he was facing the frustration of separation. His mother's greater resilience and the experience of containment in therapy was linked with increased tolerance and expression of aggression, and this in turn allowed a more confident, adventurous and curious frame of mind to develop.

For some time Anthony had been proudly using his full name, but had continued to refer to himself in the third person. He now began to use 'I' and 'me'. One day he ran to the waiting room at the end of the session, calling out to his father 'Here I am!' In his joyful anticipation of welcome the inviting internal object (Alvarez 1992) is revealed: Anthony unmistakably held in mind a father with an Anthony in mind, a father awaiting him and looking forward to his return. The importance that he could now assume in his family's life was a major breakthrough, and they, in turn, were able to greet his progress with delight.

Anthony's subsequent use of the possessive pronoun 'my' coincided with a more expansive use of the therapy room, and greater possessiveness towards me. Fuller exploration of Oedipal conflicts was possible. He was using imaginative play to explore problems such as going to sleep, and to re-enact and work through troubling experiences. By the end of the second year he could tell me 'I pretend to sleep', and further evidence of his conceptualisation of mental processes were to follow: 'I know', 'I think', and in the third year of therapy 'I remember.'

Anthony's wish to claim me to himself led to attacks on parental figures and sibling rivals in his play. Anal and urethral sadism came more to the fore with spitting (more active than his earlier passive dribbling), and play about 'weeing.' He painted his first face, 'a lady', to which he gave a name like mine. There was as yet no outline, merely eyes, nose, mouth and hair. (The features in his later pictures were enclosed in round faces, suggesting the movement from permeable to more containing internal objects). Anthony subsequently took the miniature father doll and stuck its head into the black paint, then filled the hollow base of the doll with water, saying 'oh no' as he did so. Both the defiance of the rivalrous little boy and the protest of the parental figure under attack were expressed in this sequence, revealing the emergence of divergent points of view and of conflict between internal figures. At the end of this session when I was clearing up, he said 'poor daddy.'

He was now expressing much greater extremes of emotion, frightening and surprising himself with the extent of his passionate rages. On one occasion he hit me with his fist, afterwards expressing sorrow and anxiety about what he'd done, but also working through his rage and reparation in a playful re-enactment of the event. He returned again to the Goldilocks story, through which he continued to explore his identity and to search for his own position in the family. One day he got under the loose covers of the bed, pronouncing it 'soft and comfortable', then afraid that his intrusion would bring reprisal, he called for my help in smoothing back the covers.

His Oedipal preoccupations and curiosity about the parental couple were ever-present in the transference. After a Bank Holiday he asked indignantly 'Sara Rance where *were* you? where have you been!'. Later still, as the ending of therapy approached, he protested fiercely about my departure, telling me 'You're not going anywhere, you're staying right here!' He would place the mother and father dolls together end to

149

end, face to face; often he would say they were 'fighting.' His violent perception of intercourse could be seen as a projection of his own aggressive phantasies towards the parental couple. He tried again to unite the two of us, giving me his surname (telling me my name was too short) or adding my surname to his.

But he was worried about the repercussions of taking a father's place. He talked about a Daddy being hurt and needing the doctor, as well as letting me know how extraordinarily afraid he was of retaliation or even total annihilation. He told me a story: 'once upon a time there was a little boy called Anthony, and he lived with his mummy, his little mummy, then ... crash! crack! and that was the end of Anthony.' The way in which Anthony's internal and external objects interrelated was again significant, as Anthony's father did appear precarious and under considerable strain around this time, magnifying the depressive concern which came to Anthony rather too readily.

Once when playing rather messily with water, Anthony asked anxiously 'Are you all right Sara?'. He continued noisily, telling me 'Anthony naughty. Anthony cross. Poor Sara ... Jesus Christ, what a mess!'. He was outraged when I stopped him squirting water from the tap, yelling 'I want more' ... then 'I shout!', utterly astonished at himself. As his inner strength increased he was to declare 'I am king' and referred to me as 'my little lady.' But the need to relinquish this omnipotence was dawning on him, and one day he arranged the doll's house figures around the table with all the adult partners paired next to each other, saying 'shall we sit together?', and placing the Anthony doll firmly with a group of children, where they all had 'a nice cup of tea.'

Characteristically Anthony's more autistic states returned at times of separation and heightened anxiety. Before the second long summer break he became the TV-news reporter and weatherman, pouring out a monotonous litany of weatherspeak. Whilst the subject matter inherently lent itself to metaphorical expressions of fluctuating mood and impending dangers of separation, the deadening on-and-on-ness of Anthony's delivery served to keep meaning at bay, stultifying my thinking capacities, and placing what felt like a screen between us. However, hidden in his news broadcast was a reference to 'five weeks' – the length of time I was to be away. The unpleasant reality was surfacing at an unconscious level.

Anthony became better able to manage changes which formerly would have overwhelmed him. At five he started nursery school and had to leave his child-minder (protracted delays in the statementing-process meant that no specialist educational provision was available to him for

150

another six months). His openness to new experiences was accompanied by an on going need to reclaim the baby position he had left in his new identity as a bigger 'going to school' boy. The to and fro between these baby/big boy positions was like a typical two-years-old's forays into independence. Sometimes he would drink alternately from a cup in one hand, and a bottle in the other, portraying the conflicts over weaning, and his yearning for this process to be reversible.

On one occasion after his fifth birthday Anthony drank, like a baby, from the bottle, then told me nostalgically 'it tastes ... five years ago.' This evocative phrase is typical of idiosyncrasies in his speech and a capacity to get to the heart of the matter with poetic vividness. His early speech resembled a kind of short-hand in which bridging words and phrases are absent. It provides a window on his primitive states and the intense quality of emotional experience which is not mediated by conscious thought. As in 'primary process': the world of dreams and the unconscious, the dimensions of time and space are condensed, and transitional functions such as memory and anticipation are lacking.

How Do You Spell Lost?

When the stresses of actual separation were too great, Anthony regressed to a confusion of self and object. This resulted in an impaired capacity for symbolisation and a return to concrete thinking. For example, when for the first time his mother went away for a few days without the children, Anthony took the mother figure from the doll's house and put it in his mouth, saying 'I eat her!' In this phantasy of incorporation the distance between object and symbol had broken down and the doll was equated with his lost mother. It was also during her absence that I noticed the occasional reappearance in his speech of the reversal of personal pronouns 'I' and 'you'.

It was through Anthony's particular use of language that the persistence of concrete thinking was most evident. Words and letters were related to concretely rather than symbolically, and Anthony became obsessed with spelling: dismantling and storing the contents of any new term. Abstract qualities such as colour, relative size or position were constantly objectified, or even personified. Instead of saying 'Where's the blue one?', Anthony would say 'Where's Blue?', 'Where's Middle?', or 'Where's Little?' etc. This persisted until towards the end of his fifth year, despite otherwise growing sophistication in his use of language, making elusive qualities seem tangible and secure. It also revealed his failure to perceive relativity and his resistance to being one of many.

151

And as in his verbal 'shorthand', the collapsing of distance between self and object meant that context was taken for granted.

One day Anthony asked me yet again about a red spoon from the tea-set which had been lost some time before. Naturally it had troubled him when it first disappeared, and perhaps in its absence had come to represent the nipple, lost so early for Anthony because of his feeding difficulties. When I reminded him that it was lost he asked me 'how do you spell lost?' He seemed to believe that herein lay the answer to the problem; that if only he knew how to spell 'lost' or 'spoon' he could recover the lost object and secure it in his mind in a process of reification. This was not a relinquishing of the lost object but an attempt to magically restore it, and it continued to impede Anthony's creative expression in language and play. His capacity to symbolise was still rudimentary and precarious: I think the red spoon had been used symbolically at times, but he returned to concrete levels of functioning when his capacity to bear loss was overwhelmed.

When he was five and a half Anthony finally started in the reception and assessment unit of a special school, where he was amongst the brightest in his class. Predictably his development after starting school was mixed. His language flourished and he appeared happy, interacting more readily with his peers, and popular with the staff. But I was to witness a further increase in obsessionality, for which early school work could provide a fertile breeding ground (Hoxter in Meltzer, 1975). He was far less prone to retreat into states of autistic withdrawal, though I found he continued, in the face of anxiety, to resort to a sensuous writhing of his face and body against smooth firm surfaces. For a while he became very manic, denying his littleness and dependence in pseudo-adult stances, but then would very touchingly recover his delight in infantile games such as peekaboo, which held an enduring significance in his therapy.

Conclusions

The difficulties which Anthony presented when he came into therapy have been explored in relation to the combined forces of his predisposition and early deficits in containment. He lacked a sense of self and an inner space in which phantasy could develop. Psyche and soma were insufficiently differentiated, and the lack of a psychic skin was expressed somatically, in symptoms of incontinence. His inability to bear loss and to differentiate self and other impeded the development of symbolisation and language. In response to uncontainable anxiety he seems to have fallen readily into states of autistic withdrawal which could be recognised in therapy in his repetitive tendencies, his sensation-dominated play with water, insistence on sameness and his stunted language development and symbolic play.

Anthony's relative inaccessibility in his more merged states required in his therapy an active technique of coming to find him and drawing him into contact, which helped to elicit both a stronger sense of self and the development of an inviting object. Over time his capacity to acknowledge separation and loss increased, leading to the growth of an inner world in which symbolic thought and language could develop, though his symbolic functioning remained immature. Greater discrimination between phantasy and reality allowed Oedipal conflicts to come more to the fore and to be explored in his therapy.

Although chronologically speaking he was delayed in relation to many developmental mile-stones, areas of 'immaturity' were usually congruous with his level of emotional development, and with the very early infantile relationship in therapy. For instance babbling and playing with sounds increased alongside more sophisticated language development. Anthony seemed in therapy to be 'making up for lost time', and addressing gaps in primitive emotional experience as a necessary prelude to broader cognitive development. Meltzer writes of the 'loss of maturational mental lifetime', and suggests that 'the degree of arrest in the development might well have a near arithmetic relation to the waking, and perhaps the sleeping, life-time spent in the state of autism proper.' (1975, p. 16).

The more vulnerable exposure to anxiety that accompanied his emergence from states of autistic undifferentiation led Anthony to resort to obsessional defence mechanisms. With the realisation that his objects were separate, these obsessional mechanisms were used in an attempt to ward off levels of mental pain that he could not tolerate, and to bring his objects under his control. His family and his educational environment must play a crucial role in managing his complex and uneven development, for there is a risk that in the fostering of narrow areas of precocious intellectual development, his emotional deficits and the impairment of creativity will be obscured. If this is not to happen, he will continue to need considerable help beyond the therapeutic setting in discovering what Meltzer calls 'the "why" and not merely the "how" of things' (1975, p. 222).

153

Note

1 There are many whose personal and professional support helped me in this work. I am especially grateful to Peter Bradbury, Beta Copley and Margaret Rustin, and to Anthony's parents for their dedication to the therapeutic process.

7

A Little Boy Who Did Not Want to Learn Anything

Alex Dubinsky

Introduction

This chapter is concerned with an attempt at understanding the psychological component in a child's severe developmental delay. I first saw this boy, whom I will call Paul, when he was three years old. It seemed clear that he was capable of symbolisation and his obstinate fascination with gaining access to enclosed space suggested that the representations of his phantasy life contributed to his lack of cognitive and emotional development. I thought that one should attempt psychotherapy, and not abandon Paul to a future of very severe retardation. After some months when he was seen together with his mother as they refused to separate, he started twice-a-week individual psychotherapy.

During the first years of his long treatment, which has now lasted for eight years, progress was very limited. There was no known medical cause for Paul's developmental delay, but there remained the possibility that his restricted mental life reflected some great poverty in his cerebral endowment and that he would not develop significantly. Very slowly, however, Paul internalised the emotional containment provided by the therapy. As treatment continued, small changes could be observed. Little by little he became more able to tolerate anxiety. He eventually started to put his words into simple sentences. Gradually, his tiny vocabulary began to expand and indicated a widening of his interests. However slowly, he was responding to the psychotherapy, but I was left with feelings of despondency which reflected some of the helplessness which is at the very root of Paul's emotional difficulties. Indeed, since he was little, and for a long time, because of this very helplessness, he had taken refuge in phantasies of omnipotence which affected his contact with emotional and external reality to the point of psychosis.

More recently, and in particular in the last fifteen months, Paul, who

155

is now eleven, has made very considerable progress, both in his emotional and cognitive development. He is, however, still quite limited in his intellectual abilities. Only continued work might eventually indicate how far he can develop, but I have no doubt that the earlier psychotic turning away from reality has seriously contributed to his cognitive delay. The progress he has made has depended on his newly acquired capacity to internalise a good father.

It will be suggested below that, while Paul had not yet developed the psychological equipment needed to tolerate mental pain, early experiences of profound helplessness had fostered feelings of rivalry with figures representing his father and siblings. The internalised parental couple became split into a persecutory father and a permissive idealised mother. This led Paul to turn to an impoverished phantasy world of perpetual conflict, reflected in mindless repetitive play, at the expense of emotional and cognitive development.

The Beginning of Treatment

Paul lives with his parents and two older brothers. The middle brother is four years older than Paul. The parent's difficulty in providing Paul with intellectual stimulation, even now that he is making progress, suggests that they continue to both suffer from some form of depression. For as long as I have known him Paul has had severe eczema.

He was referred to me when he was three years old by a colleague who was seeing his mother professionally. This colleague had become worried about Paul's passivity as he was kept in his push-chair during the interviews. The referrer also told me that Paul was crying a lot and that he had started to knock his head against the furniture. In the second assessment interview I had with both Paul and his mother, he deliberately hit his head against the seat of a chair. Although he was very upset, his mother did not seem to believe that she could help him until I talked to both of them of how much Paul wanted to be reassured. It seems that these few words had a considerable impact since, very rapidly, his mother came to represent comfort for him. However, as we will see, little of this comfort was internalised until recently.

When she first came to consult me, Paul's mother said that he had been an easy baby. At first, however, he had refused to take the breast until the nurses showed her how to feed him. Later he refused to take the bottle. It took him a long time to learn how to use a spoon: his mother said he did not allow her to teach him how to use it. According to her, during the early months, Paul showed no interest in the people around him and he did not smile before he was three months old. She described Paul as clumsy and thought he had a vocabulary of only twenty words. I was also told that his play consisted solely in lining up cars. When he was taken out of the house, he would often cry when brought to an enclosed space.

The extreme poverty of Paul's language play made me worry greatly about his intellectual abilities. However, I became convinced that, at least in part, he was held back in his development by his inability to deal with anxiety. My own impression when he started therapy was that he was not using more than ten words. His pronunciation was also very poor as he has the greatest difficulties in forming the sounds. His use of language during the first years of treatment fluctuated considerably: there were periods when Paul would barely speak in his sessions with me as he seemed discouraged by his relative incapacity to express himself. More recently, his vocabulary has expanded considerably and he can speak more clearly. During his early years the provision of speech therapy for Paul was interrupted over long periods of time but he has now received speech therapy on a regular basis for more than two years. After attending from the age of five a special unit for children with language difficulties, Paul has been attending, since he is eight years old, a school for children with moderate learning difficulties. He is learning to read and write and both teacher and speech therapist are pleased with his progress.

Intrusiveness, Fears, Terrors and Phantasies of Omnipotence

For many years Paul's therapy was dominated by the perpetual repetition of certain closely related themes. Already in the first sessions, Paul was interested in spaces with clearly defined boundaries and in the means of access to them, and he would represent symbolically his coming into the room by pushing a ball into a cup. The doors of the room, the doors of a Wendy house which was then in the room, and the doors of the patients' individual toy lockers would arouse his interest or anger. I also noticed that he wanted to get under his mother's chair. The space under the tables or in a little cupboard under the sink kept their attraction through the years. Often he would seek refuge there. When he felt very anxious he would fall asleep under his coat, but sometimes he would be even more persecuted when he would re-emerge. He found much comfort on top of a white cupboard and, appeased, would also fall asleep there. This space on top of the cupboard seemed to represent the maternal breast, or rather its inside. If

157

only because of the different emotional meaning attached to various corners, the whole room seemed indeed to represent the inside of the mother's body.

I think that his mother's depression, and maybe also the depression in his father, left Paul with the experience of a parent who cannot make space in his or her own mind for the child's painful emotions. He developed instead a fascination for the intrusion into physical space. Meltzer (1982) has contrasted the mental 'container' of emotion, derived from the parental ability to receive the child's projections (Bion 1962) with the claustrum, the mother's internal bodily space into which the child may intrude in phantasy. In the child's phantasy access to the claustrum is disputed by its imagined residents, other babies or Daddy's penis, as these become terrifying rivals enraged at the intrusion. The phantasy of intrusion thus exposes the patient to feeling pursued by a proliferation of persecutors instead of providing him with the experience of having his emotions modified by a receptive mind. It does not provide him with the possibility of internalising a protective thinking parent who alleviates the feelings of persecution.

Paul's feelings of rivalry, which, for a long time, corresponded in phantasy to a struggle with the legitimate inhabitants of Mother's body, have been quite obvious. When he started therapy with me at the age of three, he would climb on the table and, in his omnipotent elation, announce he was as high as the ceiling, as high as the sky. Later, and over a period of time, he attacked savagely some cuddly toys. Still now, on occasion, he violently kicks the chairs in the room. These are symbolic attacks on me and my children when we are thought to be his rivals. The competitions he used to imitate from television programmes were again symbolic fights. They aimed at asserting his position of mastery in the room and his superiority over any rival. They started as soon as he went through the door. For a long while he mimed the wrestling bouts he had seen on television. On the other hand, if he hit me or some toys with too much violence, he would fear retaliation and run out of the room.

Through the years I also learnt to recognise that often, after he had been briefly asserting himself in some way, he would scratch himself, sometimes until he bled. The intense itching was the somatic representation of attacks from envious persecutors The scratching of his skin represented Paul's own attacks on these persecutors. He would also cause his eczema to itch by tickling his skin with a hair or by rubbing chalk into its cracks. When I would question him, he would agree that in this way he was setting up a fight with the innumerable children he

158

has been attributing to me. He kept hoping that he would triumph over them once and for all.

Persecutory anxiety led Paul to resort to either manic or obsessional defence mechanisms based on a delusion of omnipotence. Early in the treatment, he spent months jumping from chair to chair shouting 'the apparatus, the apparatus' (this turned out to be the equipment for gymnastics that the janitor would set up every week at the nursery school). Through the years he has often spent the best part of his session in frenetic football games, sometimes driving himself to utter exhaustion. There was a manic quality to his aspiration to be the master of the room, as when on one occasion he gave a thorough beating to a large plastic bus which on that day he called the 'giant' (Daddy's penis inside Mummy). As to the obsessional defence, it could be recognised in the long periods of time he spent controlling the movements of the toy cars, lorries and buses that he would align on the table and which were supposed to be on their way to school. Fear of his rivals' envy made him put at the end of the queue the little truck which was supposed to be driven by his mother and which carried two little dolls representing him and his friend.

The delusion that he himself was omnipotent led Paul to attribute (by projection) an immense power to his persecutors. For instance, he believed for years that there were wolves hidden behind my windows or inside my cupboards. The pleasure and relief that his defence mechanisms gave him were thus ephemeral since he had to repeat without respite the manic or obsessional behaviour in order to fend off the terrifying revenge of the rivals over whom he was triumphing or exercising his control. The ceaseless recourse to these defence mechanisms constituted a psychotic state.

The always repeated manic or obsessional behaviour left him also little time to learn. Moreover the intense feelings of persecution did arrest the flow of his thoughts. For years indeed, on the rare occasions when he would allow his play to somewhat develop and represent his thinking, it would be suddenly interrupted as his imaginary persecutors would again threaten him.

Also, when, through the delusion of omnipotence, Paul believed that immediate mastery had been given to him, he would not take the time required for the task at hand. Still now, the wish to communicate instantaneously sometimes reduces his sentences to inarticulate grunts.

The Beginning of the Healing of the Split in
the Internalised Parental Couple

When Paul was ten, his mother expressed the wish to stop his treatment. This resulted in an interruption of two and a half months in the therapy because the meeting with both parents where we were to discuss this issue had to be postponed twice, first because I had fallen ill, and then because Paul had to spend three weeks in hospital as his eczema had got much worse. We reached a compromise: Paul would only attend once a week.

The four sessions which immediately followed this forced interruption indicated considerable development in Paul's capacity for sustained thinking. The anxiety lest he might lose his therapy had moved him to use his mind and represent this crisis symbolically, through play, for the entire duration of some of these sessions. Thinking, instead of action, was offering an alternative method for mastering the perceived threat (Freud, 1911). This was now possible for Paul since, little by little, he had through the months and years of therapy begun to internalise a capacity for containment which was demonstrated by a greater tolerance of anxiety. Now, at last, there was a balance between the anxiety which makes the child resort to new symbols and the required capacity to tolerate this anxiety (Klein, 1930). The developing containment enabled Paul to tolerate the oscillation between the feelings of persecution and the moments of integration (the oscillation PS < = > D in Bion, 1963) which accompanies the emergence of new thought.

These sessions, which are discussed below in more detail, threw some light on Paul's phantasies. The splitting apart of the internal parents had exacerbated his fear of his displaced rivals' possible revenge. This had led him to an exaggerated recourse to phantasies of omnipotence. On the other hand there were now clear indications that a good paternal figure was making its appearance in Paul's internal world.

On the day he restarted therapy, it was clear that he liked very much the nice room I now use. The clinic had moved to a different location during his absence and Paul asked me whether the toys of the waiting room had been left in the other building. Soon, however, he seemed to be getting in a manic state and I noticed that he had considerable difficulty breathing. He built a tower with the small chairs, which are made of red or yellow plastic, and put the waste paper bin on top of it. He threw the ball in it and announced that he was a champion.

He then pulled a small table in a corner. I asked him whether he knew that from now on I would see him once a week instead of twice a week.

'No.' I explained this had been decided when I had met his parents the previous week. He piled on it the contents of his locker, including a whole lot of crumpled paper. He kicked the yellow chairs. The red chairs stood for his allies. He threw the yellow chairs and the crumpled paper in another corner but he kept his toys on the little table. He hid the red chairs under a big table and said they were 'saved.' Soon he used his cup to fill the waste paper basket with water.

At the beginning of this session, Paul was obviously pleased to find himself in a new therapy room, spacious and freshly decorated, but he was also in touch with the experience of losing the familiarity of the old clinic. He might also have been thinking of all the sessions we had missed during the long interruption in the treatment. For a moment, however, the sense of loss was replaced by feelings of persecution against which Paul defended himself by asserting that he was a champion. I think that he was conceiving of this loss as an attack by robbing persecutors and wanted to assert his superiority over them. What happened next was that he wanted to stake a claim for what was his. The announcement that I would see him now once instead of twice a week seemed only to confirm him in his plan, after he had a brief symbolic fight against his persecutors (represented by the yellow chairs). He wanted to keep and save what he felt was precious. He was now fully aware that there was a loss but that his therapy had been preserved. Paul seemed to transform this passive experience into an active splitting whereby he kept what was good and got rid of his persecutors. This was achieved by splitting the internal mother (represented by the therapy room) into a good compartment where he and I, as a good object, were allowed to remain, while the persecutors were relegated to another compartment. The crumpled papers he was getting rid of probably represented ineffectual aspects of himself, but also, I think, the difficult experiences of the recent months when therapy had stopped and he had gone to hospital. On the other hand, with the filling up of the bucket with a cup, Paul was demonstrating, I believe, how much he wanted a good experience, but also how he felt it was difficult to obtain it.

Paul was unable to attend the following week but the material developed when he came two weeks later.

The beginning of the session was not promising: the first thirty-five minutes were taken up by his playing football. He started with calm and efficiency but soon he was troubled by flatulence. He was now breathing with some difficulty and his play deteriorated. When I interpreted that he was feeling the need to fight his enemies, the splitting reappeared as he again threw the yellow chairs into a distant corner. He sat at the little

161

table in another corner with some paper and a pencil, some adhesive tape and a ruler which he used to draw horizontal lines over a sheet of paper. He filled his cup with water, put it carefully to his mouth and drank with concentration. But he did not manage to cut the adhesive tape which crumpled into a ball. I pointed out that he didn't think I could help him. He asked me to cut the adhesive tape, which I did. With my help (I had to spell most of the words) he wrote that he would soon go on a school trip with some boys in his class. At the end of this session he showed proudly to his mother what he had written and suggested that he would also show it at school.

Paul had started this session by asserting again his omnipotent control over the room, but soon he felt threatened by his persecutors (his rivals for the possession of the room and of the inside of the maternal object). The splitting reappeared when I pointed out to him his preoccupation with his persecutors: again he relegated them to a distant corner while he became a competent child receiving instruction, nourishment and practical help from the adult. I was thus allowed to see a sober and competent part of his personality of which I had only caught a glimpse before, as most of the time it was also split off (this division of the personality in distinct parts is a splitting of the self, as described by Klein 1946). Moreover, his sitting down to write, his drinking of water and his asking me to help him with spelling suggest that, for a moment, Paul had a clear sense that I would protect his achievements, and that I would allow him to internalise the capacities he needed to acquire.

The next session was characterised by Paul's wish for omnipotence and by feelings of persecution which turned into claustrophobia. He was upset by the approaching interruption of the therapy for the holidays and he left the room on all fours.

This takes us to the fifth week since he had restarted treatment.

This was his last session before the holidays and at first he did not want to come into the building. He then went up the stairs backwards and stopped to smile at me. His wish to assert that he was in control of the situation made him then run in the direction opposite to that of the room. When we eventually came in, he pushed the chairs away and once more he started to play football. When I suggested that it was a fight against other children who would take his place in the room, he wanted to throw some heavy toys against the window. However, perhaps for the first time, he did not have to be stopped physically. He paid attention to my telling him not to throw these toys against the window and threw them instead against the patients' lockers. He then stuck balls of adhesive tape on the lockers and punched them with small, repeated jabs: the balls of adhesive tape represented the rivals who wanted to take his place.

7. A Little Boy Who Did Not Want to Learn Anything

He stuck adhesive tape across door of a cupboard and looked at me with a satisfied smile. He then threw chairs next to those he had already thrown in the middle of the room. I came to realise that these chairs were forming a barrier between him and me. At first he used his cup to fill the overflow in the sink. He then used wet paper towels to clean the blackboard and the window. I established that I was not supposed to go over the barrier. I interpreted that Paul thought he had taken Daddy's place and was cleaning Mummy's inside. As he sighed I suggested this was a big task for a little boy (Williams 1990). He took a good look at me but went on with his cleaning. Suddenly he looked at me furtively over his shoulder.

While, with some trepidation, Paul had taken over the place of the good, cleaning, reparative father inside the mother, I now represented in the transference the bad father relegated to a distant, segregated part of the mother. The splitting of the mother, which was reflected in the division in two of the room, was manifest during these weeks. It gave a structure to his phantasies which can also be regarded as an attempt on his part to set limits. It is clear that at the beginning of this session he was finding it very difficult to accept the boundaries imposed by the pattern of the sessions and holidays. He agreed however to my putting a stop to his throwing of toys at the window. He then stopped the bad father, projected into me, from having access, first to the cupboard, then to the part of the room where he stood: while emulating a good father, Paul was setting limits to one of his internal persecutors.

This splitting of the internal father into a bad persecutor and a helpful adult, like the splitting of the internal mother represented by the room, was benign. It allowed Paul to explore the reunion of a good internal parental couple (although, as we see in this last session, this was done at times by usurping the good father's place inside a good part of the mother). It allowed Paul to take a first step in healing the pathogenic split of the internal parental couple into an idealised permissive mother and a persecutory father. This pathogenic split had been demonstrated on the countless occasions when feelings of persecution would escalate and Paul would run away from me and go to his mother in the waiting room. The splitting of the internalised parental couple would in turn encourage a splitting of Paul's self as the little champion in him needed his sense of omnipotence in order to face the persecutory father, while the ineffectual child could call for Mummy's protection and also would often seduce her into this role through his vulnerability.

The pathogenic splitting apart of the internal parents reflected an actual split in the family, whereby the father was kept at some distance

163

by the mother and the children. (In Paul's phantasies, siblings can be rivals or allies.) Persecutory feelings were exacerbated since a split in the family where the child allies himself to the mother induces a fear of the father who, in the child's mind, might feel supplanted. Furthermore, the split does not allow the two parents to modify this particular anxiety. The phantasy of usurpation of the father's place inside the mother can then raise this persecutory anxiety to a psychotic level.

The restoration of a good internal couple is also essential to the establishment of the limit setting necessary to mental functioning. The mother's mind can be perceived to provide thinking containment for the child's emotional experience only if it is sufficiently protected from intrusion by jealous persecutors and if, in phantasy, the mother's body is sufficiently protected from the child's intrusion. A crucial role for the internal father is to preserve boundaries and thus protect the thinking containment provided by the mother. In the transference this was represented by the preserving of the therapy agreed at the recent meeting between his parents and myself.

The Next Year of Treatment

When Paul came back after the Easter holidays, he returned to playing football during our sessions. After repeated interpretations of his anxieties (he would readily agree that he thought my children would break into the room), after repeated explanations that this repetitive activity did not help him in his development and prevented him from using his sessions, and after repeated occasions when I told him to put a stop to the football playing, Paul finally responded to firmness when, in the autumn term, I asked him to go to the desk and use the toys.

By then I had observed a change in his mother. She had recently been promoted at work and now dressed in a more adult fashion, instead of wearing her eternal track suit. She had approached the school and expressed her deep anxiety as to Paul's future. She now kept setting simple tasks for him: reading the signs at the clinic, saying good bye. She was now much firmer in handling him, for instance when he would wish to stay in the waiting room.

There was a clear sense that Paul's play in the therapy room now had a 'form'. This corresponded to the development of his capacity for sustained thinking which could now manifest itself as prolonged symbolic play. As Paul's movements slowed down, I became more aware of his clumsiness and of how uncertain he felt even in planning simple actions. In fact, despite his phantasies of omnipotence, Paul seems to

164

have always known that he is quite small and clumsy. In part, this seems to have been projected into him through his mother's view of him as an ineffectual baby. However, as we saw above, recently, she had been consistently trying to encourage him to develop.

A meeting with his parents indicated that Paul was now making good progress and that he was determined to assert that he could acquire a new competence as he was obtaining badges for achievement at school for cooking a meal for his parents and for joining various new activities. His parents said he was asking endless questions. His constant worrying as to what would happen if his parents and his brothers were not there to take care of him confirmed that there was a significant decrease in his belief in his omnipotence. In this meeting, his mother, for the first time, was able to rejoice in his progress. After a while, however, his father looked crushed as he came to reflect on the uncertainty of Paul's prospects in life.

At school, both his teacher and the speech therapist were pleased with Paul's development in the last year. When he had joined her class, the teacher had found that she had to be quite firm and stop him flailing about the class. Both the teacher and the speech therapist are obviously fond of him and work on helping him to assert himself in the group. They are pleased with the new clarity of his speech. His grammar, however, remains very limited and incorrect. The articulation of phrases into sentences is still at an elementary stage. His teacher also told me that Paul knows his numbers well but has great difficulty in learning arithmetic. He does well in the science class. He is well accepted at Cubs, and at a club where he plays football with younger children. He has been able to go camping with the school as he has now learnt to rub his body with the cream against his eczema. Both parents are now co-operating with the school.

The Sense of Helplessness and the Relationship with the Internal Father

The session reported below took place just before Easter, a year after the sessions which were discussed above. In the previous week, Paul, who was now eleven, had been very pleased with my offer to give him for the following session a new roll of adhesive tape. He had then asked me to wrap some toys in towel paper and to give them to him as 'presents'. (During the previous months he had on occasion carefully left toys wrapped in towel paper in the dolls house.)

165

When, at the entrance door, I told him to be careful, as the floor had been washed and was slippery, Paul stepped in very, very cautiously. His mother told him to go and do the code (on the lock on the first floor), maybe to accelerate his climbing of the stairs. At the second attempt, he managed, for the first time ever, to open the door. He read, as he now does every week, the 'fire exit' message on the next door: it seems that competence is all the time on his mind. At the therapy's room door he got out of his jacket and handed it to his mother.

Once in the room, like the week before, he told me to wrap him five presents, and after pulling two soft chairs together, he lay on them face down. I was to put the presents next to him without any noise. I suggested that, like the previous week, I was to be Father Christmas. He was quite interested in the elephant I had wrapped up, and in particular in its tusks (Paul allowed to have a penis) and he was delighted when I wrapped the adhesive tape, which I had promised. When he asked for more 'presents', I told him that now he should make believe, so that I could watch him and think of what it meant. His play changed and soon he went behind a cupboard. At the back of this cupboard he drew with white chalk a circular shape which he then shaded. I interpreted that he wanted to be in charge of Mother's breast. At the end of the session, he wrapped himself in adhesive tape and he agreed when I said he wanted to be a Power Ranger (Power Rangers are the heroes in children's programme on television and are dressed in a futuristic garb).

What seems to have been important to Paul was not only the contents of the parcels, but the way they were delivered. However gently I had tried to do this, my refusal to continue with the wrapping and giving to him these parcels was felt by him to be a humiliation, which he attempted to overcome by turning to a phantasy of omnipotence and trying to become a Power Ranger. As we will now see, the material further developed the following week, which immediately preceded the Easter holidays.

Paul said his name on the entry phone and opened the coded lock on the first floor door. When he came into the therapy room, he pulled together two soft chairs face to face, thus making a pretend bed on which he laid face down. As he had done the previous two weeks, he asked me to give him 'presents', that is, to wrap some toys in towel paper and to place them next to him without making any noise. As I did this, I interpreted that Paul wanted to establish that I was a good Daddy and that he wanted me to be like a sort of Father Christmas, who would want him to have good things, for instance the mother's milk, and not a bad Daddy stopping him … I had first wrapped the toy elephant, but he said 'not that' and got me to wrap for him the felt eraser used for the blackboard and some sticks of chalk, then I wrapped some toys from his

166

locker: a car, then a cup together with some felt dolls, scissors and a pencil sharpener.

Paul then got up, arranged some plastic chairs by the sink. He announced he would make some school dinner and asked me what I wanted. I told him I wanted steak and chips. He flattened a piece of paper in the sink and, apparently, drew on it in brown pencil (later I did not see any trace of it). He then put little bits of green towel paper on this sheet of paper: these were the chips. I became aware that one moment he was talking of feeding me, the other of my feeding him. He asked me to prepare some food for him. I drew on another piece of paper a plate with some food on it and gave it to him.

He put it aside and staged a football match on my desk: the players were cars pushing the pencil sharpener. I tried to get him to respond to my comments. He agreed to my suggestion that he had thought my drawing of the plate and the food was better than his. I interpreted that he had found it painful to see me as the big Daddy and himself as the little child (and, I could have added, a little child feeling incompetent) and I suggested that he had staged the football game because at football he felt competent. After this interpretation the protagonists in the game started fighting, and I pointed out that he was quite angry.

He eventually went to lie again on the two soft chairs pulled together and he organised a football match between the pencils. He then went to look through the window at the building site, where there is a huge crane. (Work there had ceased an hour before the time of his session.) When I told him it was time to go, he first refused, saying that he wanted to sleep in the room, but then agreed to return to the waiting room. His mother told me that he had wanted to come and see me with his parents on the next day. (During the session I had reminded him of the appointment his parents had with me on the following day, and I had also reminded him this was our last session before the Easter holidays.)

This material demonstrated that despite Paul's progress, his phantasy life still takes place at times inside the mother's body. Indeed the chairs pulled together, on which he lay down to wait for his presents, represented not only his bed where he was waiting for Father Christmas, but also a place inside the mother's breast where his infantile appetites could be gratified. Again, when he returned to these chairs to organise his football match, he was staging the Oedipal conflict inside the maternal object, in the way described by Klein (1945). The possessiveness he felt for the inside of this object was indicated at the end of the session by his refusal to leave the room. On the other hand his readiness to involve me and talk with me, even at these moments of the session (except when he arranged the football match) suggest that, by now, even when he intrudes into his (internal) object in this manner, he is

167

able to maintain a relationship with his internal and external objects. In other words, although his phantasies are still often staged inside the maternal object, already for some years now, he does not 'live' inside this object.

At the start of this last session I represented for Paul a generous father who dispensed bounty: the maternal milk, but also the virile competence represented by the felt eraser. This was also the competence he was aspiring to when he opened the coded lock. The material was confirming the emergence of a good internal father which we had witnessed a year earlier, and the importance of this figure for the evolution of the process of internalisation. However, probably in order to avoid remaining the dependent child, Paul then decided to cook the food. He was emulating the good father who, in his phantasy, had contributed to the making of the maternal milk. And when later in this session, Paul wanted again to be fed by me, he found that he could no longer tolerate it. His sense of his own developing competence was challenged, he felt angry and humiliated and he moved back to his chosen field of achievement: his repetitive game of football.

He had become again a baby who felt belittled and humiliated by a nipple which seemed to flaunt its capability. Envious rivalry had turned him against the nipple in what seemed to be a re-enactment of the earliest form of the Oedipal conflict, where the protagonists are the breast, the nipple and the child.

It is interesting to note in this context that the emergence out of a psychotic or borderline psychotic condition of two young adolescents I have seen for psychotherapy for some years has also been marked by the appearance of a good paternal figure in an internal world which, until then, had been dominated by persecution. Like Paul, they had found themselves confronted, as children, with experiences of a profound helplessness which they could not contain.

The therapy was showing that the figure of an internalised protective father, with whom Paul was identifying, was continuing to develop. The following session took place three and a half months later.

Paul insisted to take into the therapy room two plastic toys he had found in the waiting room, although his mother tried to discourage him, telling him these were 'baby toys'. He chuckled as he brought them in. There was a telephone with a rattle in the receiver, some squeaky push buttons and a button which made a picture of a bear pop out. The other toy had three levers which dropped one of three plastic bears respectively into a cubicle, a straight slide and a curved slide. Paul explored the workings of the toys and showed the delight of a one year old. As I had already done when he had entered the room, I acknowledged his enjoyment of these baby toys.

Paul said the doll's house would be for the bears to use, and put the telephone in it. For the second time, he tried to make the bell ring. He then turned to the bears, and worried that one of them was missing. He told me, in an authoritarian tone, to look for it – thus showing his worry that I would not be a good parent. I commented on the authoritarian tone, but later, I looked for the missing toy bear: indeed, through the whole session I felt the urge to act as a protective parent. The two little bears went inside the doll's house and talked to each other. I asked Paul whether these were a mother and a father but he told me these were children. One of the two bear dolls talked on the telephone to the bear on the picture which popped out. At first Paul did not know what they were saying to each other Then he told me that this bear was telling the other one to rescue the missing one (which, by now, Paul had found in the toy's cubicle). In my interpretation I linked this to Paul's sense that I was a good father looking after him.

Paul played with the three bears, getting them down the slides. He then told me they would go to the swimming pool. He stopped at this and asked me whether the three bears could go in to the water. I paused to think and said 'Yes'. 'But they are babies!' protested Paul. He soon told me that one of the bears was the teacher and that the two others were children he was taking in the swimming pool. I repeated the previous interpretation.

Paul prepared some paper towels (which he later used to dry the toys) and took the bears to the sink which he had filled with water. The teacher and the children were clearly differentiated. The first child hesitated before he jumped into the water, the second one hesitated also but then swam competently. I suggested that he had learnt to swim, and I linked this to how Paul had indicated before the session that he wanted to learn the new code on the door. At one moment the playing in the water became animated and Paul explained that 'they' (the children) were splashing water. The playing remained delightfully good-natured and relaxed. In fact this was the first time ever that I had seen Paul relaxed.

Paul's view of the external world is reflecting the change in his inner world: from a place exclusively dominated by power and persecution, it is becoming a place where children can develop under adult supervision. When his vulnerability needs to be recognised, adults can protect the baby in him. I think that the maturation indicated by this last session corresponds to introjective identification and that the little bear on the telephone represents Paul listening to what his good object has to tell him.

Conclusion

I think that, as in the case of many borderline or psychotic children and adolescents, a profound sense of helplessness lies at the centre of Paul's difficulties. I would link it to his experience as a new-born, when he seemed at first to have been incapable of managing the mother's nipple. But first and foremost, I would link this sense of impotence to an early experience of not being able to evoke an appropriate response from a mother who is emotionally distressed. I think these early experiences were represented in the baby's phantasy as his being kept out of and away from the mother by a hostile paternal figure, hence the premature onset of the Oedipal conflict, the envious rivalry with the father and the splitting apart of the internal parental couple. Phantasies of omnipotence, and in particular the phantasy of intruding inside the mother, were the means used by the infant to avoid the experience of helplessness.

The price paid for this evasion has been high. Phantasies of omnipotence and of intrusion inside the maternal object severely limit the child's relation with reality and thus prevent learning from experience. Emotional and cognitive development, and the development of physical skills are delayed. Furthermore, the phantasies of omnipotence and intrusion expose the child to the revenge of displaced rivals, in whom envy and omnipotence have been projected. This leads to a vicious circle as the child feels even more helpless and thus feels ever more the need for omnipotence. Also, when at last he succeeds in emerging out of these phantasies, the child has become genuinely helpless since he has not developed. The temptation to return to these phantasies is thus great, and this explains why progress is so slow until the introjection of sufficiently good objects capable of protecting the child has been achieved.

The material discussed suggests indeed that the internalisation of a good paternal object has been essential to Paul's progress. For a long time achievement was understood in phantasy as triumph over dangerous rivals, the internal father and siblings, thus again exposing the child to their revenge and thus to more persecutory anxiety. In contrast, achievement can now proceed from introjective identification with a helpful, competent, reparative internal father protective of his children, and from the emulation of this figure. Quite significantly, thinking containment by the mother is made possible by this emerging internal father as he sets limits both to the little boy and to his internal persecutors. The change in this patient's internal world has enabled the development of a new capacity for sustained thinking.

7. A Little Boy Who Did Not Want to Learn Anything

Acknowledgement

I wish to thank my colleague, Margaret Goldwyn, who made this work possible by her constant support and who helped me to think about this case through many discussions. Both she and my wife, Hélène Dubinsky, pointed out the importance of splitting mechanisms in this case.

Note: this is a much expanded version of a paper given in April 1994 in Larmor Plage, France, at a conference organised by the AEDPEA, which has now become the Centre d' Etudes Martha Harris.

Discussion

Maria Rhode

Theoretical Background

Historically, emotional disorders have been sharply distinguished from cognitive impairment. As Spensley has pointed out, this division follows the tradition of classifying psychological faculties as cognitive, conative or affective. 'In this way, mental disorder has been deeply split into two diagnostic categories seen to have very different aetiologies and prognoses' (Spensley, 1995 p. 90).

In 1931, in her paper 'A Theory of Intellectual Inhibition', Melanie Klein suggested that the capacity to explore the outside world and to take in knowledge depended fundamentally on the child's confidence about what he expected to be revealed by an exploration of the inside of his mother's body and of his own. She traced a patient's specific scholastic difficulties to paranoid fears concerning the inside of his mother's body, and put forward the idea that many children's intellectual inhibitions were based on psychotic anxieties leading to a break with external reality to a greater or lesser degree.

Since then, Winnicott (1948, 1949) has written about the part played by psychosis in cases of apparent 'stupidity'. Although in general the assumption that a certain minimum intellectual capacity was necessary in an analytic patient has been tenaciously maintained, therapeutic work with intellectually impaired patients has been undertaken by workers with a number of different perspectives (Alvarez, 1992; Balbernie, 1985; Sinason, 1992; Symington, 1981; Spensley, 1985). Castets et al., in 1962, went so far as to suggest: 'It does not seem inconceivable that idiocy, imbecility and feeblemindedness are in many cases merely a form of autism ... are, in short, merely psychotic forms, and should be treated as such.' Maud Mannoni, who cites this opinion, gives examples of many cases in which an intellectually impaired child became capable of dramatically different use of his capacities following psychotherapy,

172

without any change in measurable IQ (Mannoni, 1973). She stresses the importance of the use made of the IQ rather than of the IQ itself. Her work illustrates the interplay of organic and psychological factors in children with severe mental impairment. She describes the way in which the child's deviation from the norm and the consequent intervention of professionals as well as of parents makes it impossible for him to experience himself as a (Lacanian) Subject, or autonomous agent. Striking improvements were seen when psychotherapy allowed the child to achieve the status of Subject. Similarly, Negri (1994) has stressed that the degree of neurological impairment in premature babies is a poor predictor of the development of cerebral palsy: emotional factors play a vital part. Psychotic and autistic anxieties are increasingly reported in children and adults with various forms of cognitive impairment. For instance, Kilchenstein and Schuerholz (1995) have recently discussed the importance of autistic coping devices in adults being treated for Attention Deficit Disorder.

The work of Bion has made it possible to overcome the split between affect and cognition, and to understand the bearing of emotional factors on the development of the capacity for thought. In his theoretical framework, the K-link (knowledge) is one of three (along with Love and Hate) that define the relationship each person has with the world. The capacity for verbal thought depends on the transformation of beta elements, fit only for evacuation, into alpha elements, which are the building blocks of dreams and thought. Without the capacity to dream, as Bion's patient demonstrated (Bion, 1955), it is impossible to think. The transformation of beta elements into alpha elements depends on alpha function (Bion, 1962). Developmentally this function is provided for the baby by the mother's capacity for reverie, in which she is open to the baby's communication of powerful primitive feelings. These are modified by their sojourn in the mother's psyche: she experiences their impact, prototypically the impact of the fear that the baby is dying, but is able to retain or regain a balanced state of mind. Because of this modification, the baby comes to experience his feelings as being encompassable, possible to think about and to name. When a baby who is seeking such help has experienced enough of it, the baby's internal mother can provide him with this capacity for alpha function even when his actual mother is externally absent. This developmental process can be interfered with if the mother is insufficiently open to the baby's communications (a 'brick wall' mother), or if she is overwhelmed by them and unable to regain a sense of perspective. Equally, if the baby is unable to tolerate his need of the mother as a separate person, and of

173

her capacity to bear what he cannot yet bear, he may attack the containment she provides for him. Bion (1959) has described adult schizophrenic patients who attack their capacity for verbal thought because any link is reminiscent of the link between the parents and therefore cannot be endured. He has shown how the most economical way of obliterating an external reality that is felt to be unbearable is for the patient to attack his perceptual apparatus, which is the link with this external reality. His schizophrenic patients attacked their own mental equipment, including their capacity for thought, in the same ways that Melanie Klein described in the case of infants attacking their mother's bodies (Bion, 1957).[1]

Such a model does not exclude the importance of organic factors in relation to mental impairment (or indeed in relation to other forms of mental illness). What it does do is to show how organic and emotional factors can interact. A body of work is growing which emphasises the plasticity of the nervous system and strongly suggests that the strength of neural connections, which depends on the degree of use of a given pathway, is open to modification when habitual emotional responses change (Grigsby and Schneiders, 1991; Fox, Calkins and Bell, 1994; Perry et al., 1995). Even in a situation in which there is no detectable organic impairment, thinking may be grossly disturbed for emotional reasons. Conversely, the condition of a baby with an organic problem may be secondarily aggravated by the impact of the baby's condition on the mother's capacity for reverie. This factor was of great importance in the cases of Helen and Alexis.[2]

The capacity to learn implies the capacity for creative interchange with the external environment. Meltzer (1975) has suggested that the degree of development, intellectual as well as emotional, that is possible in children emerging from a profound autistic state may depend on the amount of time they have spent in this state; that is, on the quantity of life experiences they have missed and learning opportunities they have lost. Alvarez (1992) has shown how an impairment that may look like a purely cognitive deficit, implying what she calls a one-person psychology, may in fact be the consequence of an emotional deficit within the infant-mother relationship and thus imply a two-person psychology. For example, a child whose internal mother does not see him as capable of curiosity or of meaningful interchange may well approach the world without curiosity. She links this with developmental research of the kind reported by Trevarthen, who has documented the pre-linguistic foundations of language development proper (Trevarthen, 1977; Trevarthen and Marwick, 1986). Emotional reciprocity between

174

mother and baby, expressed over a long stage of their relationship before the baby develops speech, is essential for the emergence of such a seemingly purely cognitive achievement, and the precursors of verbal interaction can be precisely traced in developing patterns of play (See also Stern, 1985, and Brazelton et al., 1974.)

Alvarez gives examples of the way in which a child may adapt to the view of him that his parents or therapist appear to have. This allows a sense of identity, but one which may be severely limited, and the therapist must be careful not to collude. In the words of Maud Mannoni, 'The trap into which the analyst falls is that, despite himself, he has built up an idea of what constitutes feeblemindedness, and accepts as true coin what is merely a type of relationship between mother and child.'

Sinason (1986) has made related points in her treatment of secondary handicap, which derives from the emotional consequences of the primary impairment. In addition, she has documented how the capacity for intellectual functioning can be shattered by the invasive trauma of sexual abuse (Sinason, 1992). These intellectual capacities can often be restored when patients are able to work over their experience with a therapist who believes that they are telling the truth. This links with Balint's argument that a major part of the traumatising effect of abuse stems from the undermining of a child's belief in the proper ordering of the world when adults in a position of trust do not behave in a trustworthy way (Balint, 1969). This is compounded when the child cannot find an adult, usually the mother, who will believe his version of events.

Sinason (1990) has reported a case in which a child's apparent 'stupidity' turned out to embody his allegiance to a distorted view of the world. This child had the misfortune of having parents who colluded with his own destructive tendencies. During the therapy, he stopped speaking in his 'stupid' voice, and made marked intellectual progress. However, when progress meant abandoning his parents' world view, with the implicit danger of losing those he loved and depended on, he chose instead to abandon the therapy and reverted in the last session to speaking in his 'stupid' voice.

This case illustrates the interplay between external figures and the child's inner world, and shows how 'stupidity' can sometimes be a denial of the truth. (Steiner, 1993, has made a related point in his treatment of perversions as being primarily a perversion of the truth).[3] Similarly, Cecchi (1990) has reported the case of a normal two-and-a-half-year-old girl who reacted with complete autistic withdrawal to the trauma of seeing her parents carried off by secret police in the middle of the night during her mother's pregnancy. Cecchi suggests that the external world had come to embody the worst features of the child's aggressive impulses, and that she reacted to this by breaking with reality. This formulation is in accord with Melanie Klein's view of her autistic patient, Dick. She saw his failure to produce symbols and to approach the world with interest as evidence of his excessive fear of his own aggression. When his aggressive impulses were described and contained in the therapy, symbolic play and speech increased dramatically (Klein 1930).

Clinical experiences of this nature make it understandable that a therapeutic containment of the child's emotional experience, carried out as truthfully as possible, should help to establish or to re-establish those truthful links with the world that are indispensable if learning is to take place. It has long been known that the intellectual capacities of neurotic children improve as a consequence of treatment, and much has been written on this from the 1920s onwards (Klein 1923). Work with psychotic children illustrates the extension of these previous insights to more extreme cases.

Bodily and Emotional Integration

Intellectual impairment is not the only characteristic of developmental delay. Physical milestones are often achieved later than the average, and even when they have been achieved, there may remain failures in bodily integration including general physical clumsiness and impairment of fine motor skills. Recent psychoanalytic work makes it possible to consider these physical difficulties under the same theoretical framework as emotional ones.

Whereas Klein (1961) wrote of hypochondriasis and psychosomatic illness as an expression of the patient's relationship to damaged internal objects (see also Rosenfeld, 1964), later work has shown the connections between physical symptoms and the inadequate containment of emotional experience (Bick, 1968; S. Klein, 1965; McDougall, 1989; Taylor, 1987). In Tustin's work with autistic children, the importance of the body becomes central: she describes how trauma is experienced physically by children who typically feel broken rather than hurt, and how they take refuge in a world of self-generated sensation which reassures them of their continued existence. She attributes this aberrant way of life in large part to a failure between mother and baby to process and metabolise what has been experienced as a traumatic separation in which they were wrenched apart from each other (Tustin, 1980). In *Autistic States*, she gives a detailed process recording of a session, including her own countertransference experience, which illustrates the means by which a child caught up in sensation becomes able to have thoughts as a consequence of the therapist's capacity for reverie (Tustin, 1981, Chapter 17).

More recently, Geneviève Haag (1991) has applied the work of French psychoanalysts on the coming together of vision and touch in the mother-baby relationship to developmental sequences of bodily integration. Her thesis, supported by material from clinical sessions and infant observation, is that the mother-baby link comprises the physical interpenetration of nipple and mouth together with emotional 'interpenetration' mediated by the eyes. When all goes well, the interaction of these two means of contact leads to a situation of proper 'embodiment', in which the individual feels in harmony with his body. Haag suggests that the dual link between mother and baby is 'incarnated' in the major joints ('articulations') of the body, in a developmental sequence beginning with the experience of the head being properly joined onto the shoulders. When this is achieved, the baby is able to support his head, typically at about three months of age. At about five months, the baby is able to sit unsupported; finally, at some point between ten and fifteen months, the legs and feet have been emotionally linked to the rest of the body, and the child is able to walk. This proposal ties in with Bion's distinction (e.g. Bion 1991) between internal and external sources of strength (the endoskeleton and exoskeleton), which in turn is related to Alvarez's delineation of 'becoming vertebrate' as an important step in children emerging from autism (Alvarez 1980). The link is also clear with descriptions of children who experience states of catastrophic physical unintegration which have not been healed by the mother's reverie (Bick 1968, 1986; Tustin 1980; Winnicott 1988). The relevance to the physical impairments encountered in developmental delay is obvious. Besides, many children who are not developmentally delayed but who retain symptoms of physical lack of integration and clumsiness can be helped by psychotherapeutic approaches to primitive anxieties, just as children and adults with learning difficulties of various kinds, including short attention span, can now be helped in this way.[4]

Environmental Factors

All four of the children presented here suffered from an interference with their mothers' capacity for reverie. This can come about in different ways, and no doubt the four children's circumstances were not identical in this respect or in any other. As various authors have pointed out, with differing emphasis in each case, disturbances may occur because of difficulties in the parents' marriage, because the mother is depressed, because she feels cut off from her own external and internal sources of support, because she does not feel that her internal parents allow her to have a healthy child, because she feels alone in a foreign country, because she has suffered a bereavement, and so on (Tustin 1980, 1994; Meltzer 1975; Alvarez 1992; Tischler 1979; Lewis and Page, 1978; Klauber 1997). Often, these difficulties are temporary, and the effects are easily reversed when circumstances change (Robertson 1965); sometimes the effects are longer lasting (Murray 1992). Equally, most children of depressed mothers do not go on to show developmental delay, so that factors in the child must be operative. Findings such as those by Sinason and Cecchi illustrate this; no doubt children also vary in their sensitivity to their mothers' state of mind.

Williams (1992, 1995, 1997) and Briggs (1995) have discussed varieties of failed containment. Instead of receiving the baby's communications, the mother may present a 'brick wall'. In more extreme cases, the mother is unable to contain her own emotions, and these are thrust into the baby.[5] This need not imply any malign motive; it can occur particularly easily if the baby's parents find it difficult to see him as himself. Instead he may represent a figure from their own past lives (Fraiberg et al. 1975), or indeed a problematic aspect of their own personality.[6]

All four of the children presented here were born to parents who had suffered some of the dislocations mentioned above. In addition, Helen and Alexis both had physically difficult births and suffered some degree of damage. Instead of the more than average degree of attunement that they would have needed, their mothers were able to offer them less, partly because of the trauma of having produced a damaged child.[7] Helen was then exposed to the extreme form of reversed containment that is sexual abuse: since sexual and other forms of physical abuse take place in a context of bodily violation, it is understandable that they can sometimes have an even more shattering effect on the processes that keep mind and body in balance than does the kind of reversed containment that constitutes emotional abuse.

We can only speculate about many aspects of the inner worlds of these children's parents. It is clear, however, that neither Alexis's mother nor Helen's was able to believe that her child was capable of growth.[8] It is important to keep such facts in mind so that the child can come to recognise clearly how his parents might need to see him. He can then begin to be freed from this projection, and to take responsibility for factors within himself that are holding him back. Alexis's unrancorous statement about his mother, 'She wants me to be a baby', was the outcome of much carefully balanced work, in which he needed to discover that his therapist was unlike his mother in many crucial ways if he was to be able to acknowledge and modify the negative part of his own personality.[9]

The whole issue of parental contribution to children's difficulties is a very delicate one, and will be returned to in the concluding chapter. It cannot be emphasised enough that blame and guilt are unhelpful categories in thinking about these important issues. There can be no question of saying that a parent has 'caused' his or her child's difficulties. The majority of parents, certainly including those described in this section, make the utmost efforts to do the best for their children. Otherwise they would not be able to seek therapy for their child or to support it, a difficult task requiring much persistence and devotion. It is more helpful to think of an interaction between difficulties in the child and the parents that has led to a vicious circle of discouragement and 'stuckness'. Intervention from an outside source may then be necessary. In some cases, as with Helen and Alexis, treatment can raise issues that parents find too painful, or they may feel too hopeless about being able to have a healthy child to be able to notice improvements. Often, however, as with Anthony and Paul, improvement in the child gives the parents new hope and enables them to make positive changes of their own.

Internal Factors

Paul's therapist emphasises the importance of his overwhelming experience of helplessness. This, according to Tustin (1981), is also the central factor in children who protect themselves by means of autistic devices. Other factors will be relevant to therapeutic outcome and length of treatment – more particularly the defensive mode that the child has adopted, and the degree to which he has been able to retain a preconception of helpful figures in the external world.

Helen and Alexis both showed clearly that they had been able to do this. Both of them inspired in the adults involved with them strong feelings of love and a desire to help them. This should not be understood in the context of sentimentality, seduction or collusion; it is a general observation (Boston and Szur, 1983) that those children who have undergone much deprivation and trauma and who do end up in

179

therapy are usually those who inspire adults with such feelings. This is indeed necessary if the therapist is to be able to endure the despair (and often the violence) that is part of such children's therapy: it is a good prognostic indication, suggesting that the life-seeking aspect of the child's personality remains strong. Helen and Alexis both took to therapy as though they had an instinctive idea of what it was for. As Helen's therapist writes, it was as though she had been able to maintain an idea of a thinking, helpful external person in spite of all the trauma she had gone through and all the disruptions to the therapy. Indeed, she came back from interruptions having grown emotionally and with a more firmly established sense of self.

Although Helen's therapy was so fragmented, distinct phases may be discerned. In the first, characterised by Helen's failure to recognise her therapist as a separate person, mindlessness was the striking feature both of the patient and of the countertransference. Then, following an interruption in the work, recognition of the therapist as a separate person was established. (A similarly helpful break was a turning point in Paul's therapy, though probably not for the same reasons.) In Helen's case, we can sense her pleasure and relief at discovering that her therapist was still there in spite of the break. She had clearly been able to retain some of the experience of therapy; finding again after an absence someone who remembered her made it possible for her to risk being dependent on someone else. In the next phase, she brought to treatment aspects of her infantile self that could now be integrated by means of an activity on the therapist's part that was like infant observation. Such a phase occurred in Alexis's treatment too. In view of the deprivation of early maternal attention that these children had suffered, it is possible that this does not represent a regression. Instead, the children may have been taking advantage of an opportunity to integrate aspects of their personality, functioning at very early levels, that had not previously been brought within the realm of object relationships. The infant observation phase of these therapies mostly concerned bodily activity that had not been linked with feelings: the therapists' task was then to put appropriate words to these bodily enactments.

Helen's dependence on her therapist's capacity to do this went together with the establishment of firm limits to the setting. The location of the work then moved to the doll's house. Again, this is frequently observed in the treatment of children who for one reason or another cannot yet trust the therapist to act as a safe container for their feelings. The doll's house can be a safe area in which things are enacted 'out there', where they will not threaten to overwhelm the child as they might do if they were experienced directly in the transference, in terms of 'you-and-me' rather than of 'they'. The child can show his experience of things that happen to him: he may not feel that they happen for any meaningful reason (Alvarez 1992). Another way of thinking about this would be to say that traumatised children face the difficult task of sorting out what is their own contribution to their predicament and what is someone else's. This cannot be addressed until they feel safe enough within the therapy. Alvarez has argued this persuasively in respect of autistic, traumatised and borderline children, who may feel hopelessly undermined by a premature emphasis on their destructiveness (Alvarez, 1992, p. 117). This is not a matter of denying or glossing over dangerous things: it could be seen as helping the child to carry out the necessary act of splitting and idealisation which Klein (1957) felt was essential for mental health or the capacity to discriminate, and which had not previously been possible, whether for internal or external reasons. Similarly, Paul (1974) has described how a very young, non-psychotic boy first needed to establish his therapist as a separate person, after which he passed through a phase of making use of 'secondary containers' for his feelings instead of making use of her. These secondary containers were a series of vehicles that became progressively more ordinary and down-to-earth, until at last he could abandon them and feel safe enough to use his therapist as his 'primary' container.

Helen was now able to bring the material of the 'terrible' session, in which her perverse reactions to separation made her therapist feel horrified and physically sick. This was a powerful transmission of feelings, not a distanced enactment that the therapist had to fit words to. After this, Helen could make the face: her therapist writes of the importance of a changing point of view. This adoption of another point of view, seeing herself as her therapist might see her, became possible only after her therapist felt the full impact of Helen's experience. Then, as a final phase, the 'pooh-baby' could be worked over: a context had been established within which this was encompassable.

In Alexis's case, too, we see the move from experiencing himself and his object as semi-detached houses, stuck together, to a situation in which he can begin to conceive of 'empathic mental understanding between separate people.' He too went through a phase of 'infant observation', and he and his therapist had to build up a secure foundation of good experience together before aggression could be addressed and integrated. The image of the broken, black bridge, on which a fight

181

was going on, could be read as a powerful description of his motives for breaking off contact with reality and retreating into a psychotic world of idiosyncratic 'interests'. With both children, terrible and perverse constellations had to be confronted; but in large part these may be seen as a necessary communication both of actual events that no one had previously been able to face and of destructive parts of the personality that needed to be encompassed.[10] In this respect, Helen and Alexis differ markedly from other children who manifest a much stronger envious, perverse or spoiling component to their character. (Thus, Alexis's therapist writes that his sexuality was the last battleground, but that he was relieved when he could understand the reason his private masturbatory retreats were unhelpful, and could manage to give them up.) Paul gives the impression of resorting to omnipotence in order to protect himself from helplessness, and in order to make his therapist understand what it is like to feel impotent and marginalised; but one also feels that for a long time he greatly enjoyed the self-aggrandisement that went with this. Some of the children described in the last section of this book show this to an even greater extent. The degree of a child's enjoyment of perversity is an extremely important prognostic criterion in cases of autism (Reid, 1989).

Anthony's therapy illustrates the way in which a child of high academic intelligence may appear completely ineducable because of autistic withdrawal. The readiness with which he responded to treatment indicates that he was one of those autistic children who withdraw for reasons of self-protection rather than a perverse turning away from the world (Reid, 1990). His parents were able to be delighted by his improvement, which implies that any internal positions of their own that might have contributed to his difficulties were not deeply entrenched. His residual problems were not to do with intellectual incapacity, but with an uncreative relationship to knowledge which he still approached with the aim of mastery. Hoxter (1975) has described the nature of such residual autistic problems in an academically very able child.

Paul, as his therapist points out, experienced the triad of himself, breast and nipple as one in which the nipple provocatively flaunted its powers. This is a most important point in relation to the capacity to generate symbols, a capacity which depends on the working through of loving and hostile feelings towards a separate object (Segal 1957), and thus on an ordered experience of space (Rey 1986). Britton (1989) has described the importance of the oedipal triangle, on the level of both whole and part-objects, for the capacity to symbolise and to develop

182

verbal thought. Helen and Alexis, in whom the ordered differentiation of self and other had been most interfered with by impingement of various kinds, show how important aspects of their experience had become agglomerated, much in the manner of Bion's bizarre objects. Articulations of meaning were lost, as was the possibility of locating the self vis-à-vis any given aspect of experience. It was as though a potentially meaningful structure had collapsed upon itself. Thus, Alexis's quasi-symbolic objects may be thought of as 'containing' references to many different facets of experience – terror, panic, physical excitement, the possible perception of a nipple-like bump on a nurse's arm appearing in his incubator – in much the same way that a dream image 'contains' the associations to it. The point about Alexis's quasi-symbols is that the associations, and indeed the mental equipment necessary for generating them or relating them to the image, are absent or in abeyance. The hints remain locked and preserved in the image.[11] To add to the distortion, one element of experience (in the case of the arousing arm, sexualised excitement) is then overemphasised at the expense of the other elements.

Helen did not generate this kind of quasi-symbol, but similar processes may be seen in the sequences she enacted in her sessions. Thus, the material in which she choked on a toy suggested with immediate urgency to her therapist that Helen was being subjected to oral sexual abuse. It is equally plausible, though less urgently related to the projection of an immediate need to act, to read the material as an echo of Helen's post-natal distress when she choked, unable to breathe; or as an enactment of 'choking' on projections that were thrust into her. Again, it is as though all these layers of possible meaning had collapsed into each other. Interestingly, once Helen had begun to speak, her teachers commented that they could never be sure whether she was talking about the present or about the remote past; about an actual occurrence or a fantasy event.

The Father Element: theory and technique

This kind of collapse upon itself of the spatial structure of experience may be conceptualised in terms of a failure to achieve what Britton (1989) has called the triangular space in which thought can occur. This triangular space is defined by the three parties to the Oedipus relationship, at the level of both whole objects and part objects. If the paternal element, the third party which defines the Oedipal triangle, is inadequately established, the child can feel confused with the mother and properly articulated thought cannot occur.

On the other hand, projections into the child may be understood, rightly or wrongly, as being caused by an intrusive father element. For example, Daniel, discussed in Section III of this book, covered his ears with his hands whenever he saw a man approaching. At the same time, he did possess the concept of a helpful father. He would play with sellotape, first using it as a plaster, then pulling it tighter and tighter around his fingers cutting off the blood circulation. When he used scissors to free himself, he said 'Daddy': he realised the need for a father to prevent constricting entanglement with a mother figure.

The way in which each child experiences the father element will be crucial for his ability to achieve the triangular space, and therefore an orderly structure to his experience and the capacity for verbal thought. Anthony articulated his awareness of this very clearly in his story about the disastrous consequences of living alone with his 'little mummy.'[12] Paul, who experienced the nipple as flaunting its superiority, attempted to deal with this by omnipotently usurping its capacities. Improvements coincided with the emergence of the therapist as a good Daddy.

The father-element, or nipple, cannot be experienced by the child as an essential link that lends firmness and order to his universe unless at the same time he experiences mental receptivity. To put it in other terms, if mental space is made available for the child, the father element will be a source of strength that permits him to grow as a separate human being. If the child cannot be recognised as himself and provided with an experience of mental space, then he may well (mis)interpret any father element as the agent of impingement.[13]

This formulation provides a way of thinking about technical modifications in work with such children, of which Helen's therapy provides a particularly good example. Tustin (1981) and Meltzer (1975) have described some technical changes they found necessary with autistic children. Alvarez (1992), as already mentioned, has written at length about the importance of phrasing interpretations in a way that validates the needs of the autistic, borderline or traumatised child – and indeed the fact of his existence. Reid (1997) has differentiated between those autistic children who have suffered trauma and must be approached very gently, and those who have become addicted to perverse behaviour. For example, therapists will respond differently to sexualised behaviour if it comes from an abused child who might need to communicate a terrible experience, than if it comes from a child who had not been abused and whose motivation might be very different. The abused child might need extreme receptivity; the wilfully perverse child might need a robust response demonstrating a strong paternal element in the therapist.

Ultimately, of course, each child will need both; but the timing and balance will be crucial. The children described in this section lacked the experience of being perceived as human beings capable of meaningful interchange. To a large extent the experience of this in therapy was a new one for them, and had to be firmly established before they could experience a strong paternal element as a source of strength for themselves.

Notes

[1] Britton (1995) has described the way in which the infant may ascribe the mother's imperviousness to the influence of the father, with consequent complications to the Oedipus situation.

[2] The importance of emotional support for parents of premature babies is well documented. See Negri (1994) and Cohen (1995).

[3] This truth may be the recognition of unalterable impairment. Sinason (1991) has described how verbalising the almost unbearable extent of a patient's incapacity made it possible for the patient to show her intelligence and to establish a therapeutic relationship. Sellars (1994) could observe marked improvements in physical co-ordination and verbal capacity in children with cerebral palsy with whom her work had focused on recognising the immense frustrations and envy of non-impaired people which arose out of their condition.

[4] Alvarez (1995) has described similarities between children's characteristic gait and their characteristic patterns of speech.

[5] Williams (1995) calls this omega-function.

[6] As an example of this, McDougall's analysis of a nine-year-old psychotic boy, Sammy, revealed similar phantasies in his conscious productions as could be seen in his mother's unconscious material (McDougall and Lebovici, 1969).

[7] Lussier (1980) has suggested that a congenitally physically handicapped patient suffered more through his mother's lack of pride in him, which interfered with identificatory processes, than from the handicap itself.

[8] Contributions by Alvarez (1992) and Mannoni (1973) on the limiting effect of low parental expectations have already been mentioned. Brazelton et al. (1974) pinpoint the crucial role of the care-giver in assuming meaning on the basis of slender indications. Similarly, Papousek (1992) suggests that the recipient's 'readiness and capacity to decode and integrate the transmitted information' may be more important than the intention of the communicator in making communication possible. This underlines the great importance of the parents' ability to believe that their child is capable of communication: as Tischler (1979) has pointed out, many factors, internal as well as external, can come together to undermine this belief in parents of psychotic children.

[9] Thus, it is crucial to balance recognition of actual abuse (Ferenczi, 1933) and of the way in which it may dovetail with the child's phantasy life (Abraham 1907).

[10] S. Klein, 1974, stresses the need to differentiate between different motives for aggressive behaviour.

[11] Since writing this discussion, I have come across the following formulation by Erikson concerning psychotic children's speech: 'Their sayings, like dream images, indicate what they want to talk about, but do not indicate what causal connection is to be communicated'. (Erikson, 1950; pp.194-5).

[12] See S. Klein (1980) on the need for the supportive father element, which chronologically precedes the experience of the father as intrusive.

[13] Compare Britton (1995).

Part III

The Complexity of
Psychotic States

8

Psychosis and Autism

Schizophrenic, Perverse and Manic-Depressive States during Psychotherapy

Dr Geneviève Haag
Translation: Daphne Briggs

This chapter addresses the risk of schizophrenic, perverse, and manic-depressive developments during the treatment of psychotic and autistic children. I shall begin with remarks about three cases: one psychotic, two others autistic. All of them had background anxieties of falling and liquefying, which were followed by overwhelming massive projective identification once relationships had been resumed (especially relating by means of eye contact). This produced swings between dangerous schizophrenic-type outbursts and more organised relatedness in which projective identification was confined to an attempt to induce manic mutual excitement,[1] something that could clearly lead into perversion.

I would particularly like to explore and attempt to clarify a paradoxical state. This occurs when a child's constant search for confusion of identities (either by means of massive destructive projective identification in a symbiotic psychosis, or else by adhesive identification, in autistic fashion) coincides with a fear of the normal fusion (normal projective and adhesive identification) that is in fact the only way to establish the feeling that a solid base and boundaries exist. A discussion follows of differences in the origins and history of these two clinically morbid situations (autism and symbiotic psychosis), and of their interplay. In particular, I shall examine the problems of achieving relatedness by means of eye contact, and the process of establishing a sense of body boundaries and internal connectedness. This goes together with a secure sense of self and the construction of spatial relationships.

In my own experience, children who are emerging from shell-type

189

autism seem to pass through a series of more or less protracted transitional stages in one of two main directions, something that has been noted by most analysts working with such children. In one direction lies post-autistic obsessionality (Meltzer, 1975), while in the other there is a more disturbed phase, often described as psychotic or schizophrenic, characterised by hyperintrusive and more or less destructive symbiosis. Recently, I have been trying to distinguish within the latter stage those elements that are in the strict sense of the term actually schizophrenic, calling to mind the explosive 'minute splitting' that Bion (1967) drew attention to, from those elements that belong to the phenomena of manic-depressive states. The latter are, of course, based upon abnormal projective identification – intrusive rather than explosive – which exploits a range of different bodily compartments in the quest to achieve re-entry in a state of sexualised mutual excitement (Meltzer, 1988a). For some children, this is a danger-point at which there is a risk of turning to perversion, and extreme vigilance is required on the therapist's part.

I. Symbiotic States in Secondary Autism: Pauline

When Pauline began treatment at three years of age, she presented all the main signs of what Margaret Mahler (Mahler and Furer, 1968) would have described as a symbiotic psychosis. This is also called secondary autism in the United States and regressive secondary autism by Frances Tustin in England.[2]

Whenever she left familiar surroundings, Pauline would spend most of her time absolutely immobile, in a state of paralysed panic. Her large, somewhat startled blue eyes often had a staring, blank look. She had a precise and relentless memory, especially for details of decoration and for objects, as well as for certain verbal exchanges, notably any promises that might have been made to her. Her failure to individuate was patently obvious at every turn: she functioned on the basis of almost permanent massive projective identification. Thus, for instance, during the first months of treatment, she would stare at me, make a violent spiral gesture, and declare in cavernous tones 'Mme Haag is frightened.' Autistic manoeuvres sometimes put in an appearance, notably compulsive masturbation and a need to hold a little pencil in her hand (as an autistic object), but what soon emerged as belonging to the autistic level were intense anxieties about falling and spilling out, which she worked through during the first phase of treatment.

Her lack of a sense of body boundaries was impressive. Pauline was very frightened of water pouring though drainage holes (in the sink or

190

W.C.), and even of the sound of downpipes, but she was more frightened still of noises like emergency sirens or the louder sort of car horn. Whenever she heard one of these sounds far away in the street she needed to take refuge on the couch, and when she was able to begin speaking, she once let me know that these noises were 'a man', and were getting into her *zizi* (vagina) through the window. In one series of sessions she showed me how afraid she was of falling through the window, whose edge did not seem to be well defined, or else was expected to give way, since she stood panic-stricken a metre or two inside the balcony. Later on she told her teacher that she sometimes felt that the ground, which we see as horizontal, was turning into a slope and sweeping her away.

When she was between three and five years of age, Pauline's immense bodily and spatial anxieties increasingly abated, and she began to give more psychic expression to the instability in her sense of reality and sense of self, although she most frequently did this by means of intense projective identification. For several months around the age of five she repeatedly put me through situations fraught with paradoxical injunctions – allocating roles that were immediately reversed or cancelled out or starting 'games' in which the very fragile space available for play was immediately wiped out by reflex-like concretisation, while she also seemed terrified of what she had just tried to put into play. In this process I actually experienced a relationship in which the other person threatened to drive one mad (Searles, 1959). I experienced much irritation and a great sense of despair, especially since Pauline would silence even the slightest attempt at interpretation with manic and often rather sexualised excitement.

In scenes of omnipotent and tormenting control, playing for instance at being a school teacher, Pauline would order me to do exactly the same as herself, and if I began, for instance, to make a model, would immediately snatch it away, saying 'No, that's not it ...', only to give me a new task to perform, and interrupt it again straight away. In attempts to play shop, which I was at first delighted to see (at last we were into exchanges!), I was soon floored by the way in which shopkeeper and customer were immediately conflated, exchange was cancelled out, and she herself took possession both of the goods and the money. The shop was simultaneously open and shut, the shopkeeper was there and not there ... and she spoke with so many invented expressions that I could not always understand her.

Gradually the grip of this 'paradoxical' transference relationship (Racamier, 1980, p. 19) began to loosen a little. Amidst this dramatic action I was occasionally able to slip in some interpretation of her intense projection of the feeling of going mad, or of not being a person any more, when faced with situations that changed every second – but also of how, in her almost instantaneous swapping of roles, she wanted us to be separate and not separate at the same time.

I shall now present a rather more detailed account of part of a key session, aspects of which I will take up again in the theoretical discussion. Pauline was then five and a half years old.

One day, when the role-play games were very slightly more stable, she embarked upon a mealtime scene. She said that it was night, and whispered that there were caresses in the dishes – then immediately said they were 'coraces', then 'corages' (*caresse* and *orage*: storm cuddles)[3] having first taken refuge in the fireplace, which she made into a cave sealed off with two chairs. She went on to talk about storms. It was at first impossible to tell which of the two of us was the little girl and which was the mother, inside or outside of the cave, but then she stabilised the roles: I had clearly to be the little girl who was all alone at the door and had to cry, while she was the mother in a state of agitation, talking about storms .... I then talked to her about the meal-storm, Daddy's cuddles, and the Mummy who makes a noise that frightens the little girl who is all alone at the door; but also about the little girl's fury when she is alone, that changes Mummy and Daddy's cuddles into storm-cuddles. She then mimed little cries of pleasure in the cave, and I described storm-cuddles that were not smashing everything but could also be nice cuddles.

This was the first time that such a coherent sequence was able to occur, and also that a relatively coherent interpretation could 'get through'.

Very soon afterwards Pauline came over to put the end of a piece of string in my hand, and then threaded it through the handle of a double-lidded basket that had previously been used in attempts at playing shop, and she took the other end to a distance of about a metre and a half from me. She asked me if we could swing the basket in a synchronised rhythm, which I did without at the time fully understanding it, although I was encouraged by the serious, calm, studious, but also relaxed nature of the activity. She went on doing this for several minutes. I simply said that we fitted well together. There was no atmosphere of excitement, erotisation, or madness. The session ended more easily than usual, and those that followed were increasingly coherent, while the roles were progressively more stable.

With hindsight, it seems to me that Pauline had an important

192

experience during that session, represented by a rhythmical link in a context of mutual fit. After that, she alternated between states of seeking for a twinned relationship and a tyrannical, controlling one. She still frequently insisted that we do exactly the same thing, but this aroused an anxiety-laden excitement that drove her once again into adopting an intensely controlling position in which she was always a sister who snatches everything. She very seldom entered into a relationship of introjective dependency. She therefore very seldom let interpretations get through, employing two sorts of defensive manoeuvres: she either shouted to drown out my voice or stopped up her ears, or else resorted to superficiality – echoing what I had just said in a vacuous and apparently mocking way, and in effect coming out with 'ready-made' bits and pieces that she had scavenged as much from her mother's opinions as from transference interpretations.

Between these sequences, once she had made herself a somewhat better 'skin', she worked in her sessions on the experience of having a sort of 'fluff-bag' body construction, making use in the process of 'Monsieur Peureux' (Mr Fearful), a character from a popular series of children's stories who was of great interest to her. This gave expression to an experience of having a defective skin that was constantly in danger of bursting (Bick, 1968).

Despite the difficulties, some increasingly stable role play developed, and I was able to get across a few more interpretations in the midst of the drama. Pauline worked through a lot of primitive sadism in games about ophthalmologists (expressing fears of eye contact) and dentists. She also worked through the pain of feeling an outsider, rejected, incompetent, and inadequate. (Her scholastic performance was in fact very 'limited'; she was especially behind in arithmetic, and had to repeat certain classes, something her mother made an enormous fuss about.)

I myself had to cope with a lot of hatred and despair in the counter-transference. Some sessions became unbearable because of the repetition of the sort of empty nonsense described above which also had adhesive autistic features. Pauline's eye contact was rarely an exchange of looks, but was staring, and at times almost hypnotic. Indeed, she succeeded in inducing drowsiness in me, and an overwhelming urge to sleep. She herself talked about hypnotising, and later portrayed this relationship in terms of the Gorgon Medusa. Other moments were more poignant: she developed a certain talent for poetry, and took to singing in the style of Music Hall or popular songs of the Edith Piaf variety. At such times she expressed sentiments of love and hate that were so intermingled, they could only engender despair at the confu-

193

sion, and yet, at the same time, an authentic sense of shared aesthetic appreciation opened up a chink ...

Later still, when roles were more securely stabilised, she made me play for a long time at staying close to the table where she was stretched out. She pretended to be asleep, and I had to believe she was dead. She then pretended to have fits of blind rage in which she wanted to smash everything, and I had to believe she was mad. These play sequences were conducted without role confusion, though we then had to swap roles and repeat the whole sequence, and this struck me as marking a big step forward. All the same, it seemed clear to me that her pathological symbiosis was being fuelled to some extent within her family, in spite of her mother's own long-term psychotherapy, which was running in parallel.

As Pauline entered the pre-pubertal stage, things became rather complicated again, and there were new manic outbursts in her sessions. Within her family she was also having unruly episodes and saying that she did not want to grow up. Family holidays were unbearable. Her mother voiced her awareness that the members of their family group 'were destroying one another.' In France we recommend group analytic work for families with destructive interactions, an approach that employs interpretation of shared themes and the group's transference to two therapists (Caillot and Decherf, 1982, 1989). An experienced consultant confirmed that this type of therapy was indicated for Pauline's family. This seemed very quickly to calm her down, and I myself was able to benefit, in individual sessions, from moments that were even steadier and more introjective than before. All the same, we were still two sisters whose names were almost identical: Corinne and Carine: the novelty was that she now stayed all the time in the role of Corinne, while I was Carine. I shall now describe in detail a session in which there was play that seemed to me to mark an important step on the way towards introjective activity, although there were still a few envious elements within it.

After a period during which she – Corinne – was the one with all the abilities, we became colleagues with similar skills who were preparing to open a new restaurant. We were pastry-cooks, practising making cakes. The restaurant was not yet open. Pauline made a chocolate cake and I had to make a strawberry one. She gave us each containers – she took a white metal saucepan whose handle was broken, and gave me a little pan with orange decorations and two black handles. She said in rather false tones that we would have almost identical cake-tins ... and she began to line the base of her tin. I made strawberries and also put a well-packed-down pastry base into my tin. In fact it seemed 'in the air' that a solid base had somehow been stabilised, that some introjection had taken place, and that we had separate identities that were 'not completely the same'. In my own mind, I recalled how one boy had used this method of pressing a pastry base into a mould to illustrate the idea of 'being stuck to the other person's foundation', and vice versa. From it, he had made a cake roll that he later shared out as though to express a number of things – a bodily zone that we had in common, mutual eye contact, and projective identification that remained massive, but was nonetheless in the realm of the 'similar but not the same'.

Meanwhile, Pauline evoked the future customers at our restaurant by means of a dialogue between Corinne and Carine. There would be fat women. 'You know how fat women eat whole cakes: they only leave a tiny bit, a few crumbs for their poor little husbands ...' I said 'Aren't those fat women awful' She said 'Yes, they are gorgons. You know, Bernard and Bianca!' She fixed me at this point with rather staring eyes. I said 'Oh yes! They hypnotise, like in the old stories that used to be told here ...' The time came to share out the cakes. Mine was better finished than hers, and she appropriated it, adding a little bit to it, rather as she used to do. It was cut. 'I made it.' I corrected her, saying that we had made it together; otherwise it would be rather like the fat women who want to take everything, and I would be the poor little husband who got almost nothing. In fact, she made two very equal shares, and gave me the one that looked rather nicer. She ended without any manic activity and seemed very pleased with our session. All the same, she said goodbye on a slightly artificial note, and checked that she hadn't forgotten anything.

In the play sequences that followed, she used wooden animals from her box for the first time to organise a game of football. The following excerpt from the third session in which she developed this theme gives an interesting glimpse of the arrangement of the game, to compare with her old habitual defences.

She arranged the animals in two teams (in the previous session, the line-ups constantly disintegrated and had to be obsessionally control-led). She tried to match opponents to give them equal chances. The stag and giraffe were appointed goalkeepers. The hedgehog, the only one of its type and species (and the only animal given meaning right at the beginning of treatment, and held in her hand partly as an autistic object), was declared umpire. There was a brief attempt to merge the umpire into one of the teams, but she responded immediately to my protest and upheld the original setup of the game. I arranged my players in an appropriate way, verbalising 'my two forwards, my two backs, my centres.' I felt she was interested in this arrangement, but could not manage it herself: her players were either split up or stuck together. All the same, we could begin to play. I scored a goal, she took the setback well, she scored one, and then erupted in pleasure, so that her team stopped playing for a moment – the animals congratulated one another and embraced in a disproportionate display. Play resumed. I scored two goals, then she scored one. While the game was in progress – I cannot remember whether it was after her success – she suddenly became able to arrange her players in three columns, no longer exactly in the same way as mine. Her team made a few attacks on mine.

Here one can see very clearly how this new game brought out the theme of separation between our two competing teams and provoked her to some extent into resorting to adhesion (the stuckness of her arrangement) or else to aggressive, penetrating assaults (what I call hyperpenetration, as opposed to the gentle penetration of harmonious relationships). However, there was no longer any confusion between or reshuffling of the teams as there had been in previous attempts. Maintaining this with difficulty but with the support of the third-party umpire, brought triangulation into play – one consequence of preserving the separate identity of the two teams. Where feelings are concerned, Pauline's hypersensitivity to the setback led on to her manic reaction to her first success.

I shall stop there with description of this case in order to consider the symbiotic phases several other children went through as they emerged from their autistic shells.

II. Symbiotic Moments in Previously Shell-Type Autistic Children: Pierre

Pierre only started treatment at the age of five. He had a very rigid muscular shell, no language, and a hovering gaze – staring but without undue avoidance of eye contact. He began to speak around 6-7 years of age and expressed intense bodily anxieties about falling, liquefying, and, later on, of exploding and of his skin ripping – in a phantasy analogous to Monsieur Peureux's fluff-bag. (Pierre had a compulsion to possess, tear apart, and scatter the stuffing of soft fluffy toys.) At this stage he also had an intense phobia of insects, followed by an equally intense fear of contamination by germs.

A little later, when he had managed more or less to reconstruct a sense of containing 'envelopes' and to sort out his bodily compartments,

196

he went through a long manic phase in which there was intense projection into his therapist of feelings of despair, helplessness, littleness, and being crushed, that were interpreted to him. Hyper-penetration in the anal sphere (what he called his Castle of Darkness) went hand-in-hand with very perverse phantasies of torture, to which firm limits had to be set; at the same time he was invited to join his therapist 'upstairs', to leave the claustrum that Meltzer (1992) has described as resulting from aggressive projective identification into the mother's body.

At this stage, other elements of secondary autism could be seen: there was weakness in his ego boundaries, often equated with architectural boundaries, as in the previous patient. But this child had never organised such densely enmeshed states of paradoxical possession as had Pauline. I shall describe two moments of emergence in his therapy, after about ten years of work. Something reminiscent of his old defences can still be seen in them, but they also illustrate his pursuit and development of a slow process of re-transformation and reintegration of split-off and projected elements that was taking place alongside an ever-increasing investment in symbolisation and the riches of language. Here is a fragment from a session when Pierre was fourteen years old, and I had had to prepare him for an unusual absence on my part.

> He snapped at me 'You're a pain', and then an instant later became excited and said 'Can I go under the bed?' I could then picture the return of the entire anal masturbation phantasy (Meltzer, 1965) that had imprisoned him for so long, but which had disappeared for a while. I said he was expecting me to say 'No', because we both knew perfectly well why he had that idea – to get back into my bottom-Castle of Darkness when he thought I was about to leave and would no longer hear him. 'No, that wouldn't be of any use to us.' He then said 'Good.' Then, seeming to feel a rather intense bodily discomfort, he asked if he could slip between the mattress and the bedspread. I allowed this, while reminding him that much earlier on, whenever he felt unsafe in his own skin, this had helped him feel well held in my arms and my head, and not feel obliged to force his way into my bottom. Then he said 'One has to put oneself some-where!' He wrapped himself up, first of all completely, then put his head out and began to talk to me and made up a very sweet story that summed up various aspects of his history. In the story, an abandoned child is gathered up onto the back of a succession of animals (elephant, gazelle, etc.), and then finally onto the back of a sea turtle. He lingered awhile over this image in a tender and touching way: it was a very old turtle that walked slowly and from time to time lifted and turned its head towards him while asking, very gently 'Are you all right, little one?'

I understood that he was expressing his rediscovery of background security (Grotstein 1981) by means of a variety of images – some more maternal, others more paternal, while perhaps, in the image of the turtle, there was projection of his old autistic shell and the slow and patient work he had had to do to 'derigidify' it.

The other moment came a year later. For several months he had been riding the Metro alone to come from a long distance to one of his sessions. I knew he had for a long time invested a lot of meaning in the Metro, and he had begun talking to me about different types of Metro, with a good/bad split that was beginning to stabilise. He liked the old Metros which accelerated and braked gradually, made creaking noises, and moved rhythmically. Paradoxically, he loathed the 'new' Metros on rubber tyres, that everyone in Paris seemed to prefer, because they accelerated and braked sharply, their doors closed with a flushing noise, and their motion was definitely less rhythmical. At this point I suspected that his persistent lateness was caused by his spending part of his sessions acting-out in the Metro, which would also provide him with pleasurable stimulation of the senses of hearing and balance. I wondered to what extent this was autistic and defensive and to what extent he was seeking to reinforce the transference relationship. But something else troubled me, connected with the Castle of Darkness, and this was the thought that he might be putting himself at risk of attack by thugs – be kidnapped or raped. Homosexuality now came into the picture fairly often. It should be noted that at this time Pierre was becoming increasingly aware of his state, and was trying to understand why he was behind at school (although he had succeeded to a remarkable extent in finding meaning in school work, albeit only at the age of eleven, and had managed to acquire a sound basic primary education), and why he was mad ... Recently, his gross lateness had begun to diminish, after I had interpreted that his quest in the Metro had to do with our relationship.

He was only a quarter of an hour late and seemed in inner turmoil, guilty and annoyed at having lost the quarter of an hour. He asked me to make it up for him, which of course I refused to do. He then beat the mattress violently with his fist and said he was stuffed full of dust that could explode and fill the room. I linked this with his very long-standing problematic of fluffy toys that burst, and with the image of the atomic bomb that had also sometimes cropped up.

He lay down and began to talk to me about his backwardness at school, and about other people's foibles. After a while, during which he tested out how well I was in control of myself (asking me questions to

198

which he knew the answer), and whether I understood his fear of exploding, he told me that 'One RER[4] became a Metro when it leaned over going round a bend. This one had a sort of canopy (he did not know the word, but mimed it as a helmet's visor on his head). This made it like a lowered head.' I did not immediately understand 'the RER became a Metro', and asked him for clarification. He told me that he only meant the sound (so that the Metro and RER were distinguished by the particular noises they made). He said that when going round bends where it leaned over, this RER-Metro with lowered head made a sound like 'm-m-m-tagada'. In contrast, he detested another RER that runs at high speed (by this I understood him to mean running straight ahead, without looking at anyone), making a very unpleasant noise. The old crate of a Metro that he liked braked very gently, while the other one started and braked violently (he mimed with his whole body being thrown backwards and forwards).

I then asked him – and he did in fact listen to my question, put slowly and in rather gentle tones – what this old Metro made him think of, lowering its head, leaning over, and making m-m-m sounds. His face lit up and he said 'A Mummy ...' There was a short meditative silence, and then he said that the same Metro also made a shrill sound that he mimicked, like a high-pitched song. He said he also found that very attractive. I added 'Perhaps like a singing Mummy.' He smiled in a way that was both radiant and reserved, like a pang of nostalgia.

Here one can perceive reintegration of a sensory pleasure into the emotionality of relationship via personification of an object. This was an introjective moment. Pierre stopped spending part of his sessions in the Metro.

III. Baptiste

Another autistic child, whom I shall call Baptiste, had also constructed a sensory shell, especially with sound, and clung visually to abstract graphic shapes like television aerials. He started treatment at three and a half and entered main-stream schooling at the usual age, although allowances were made for some time for serious difficulties that he had in socialising. These did not improve until he was eight or nine years old. His post-autistic state was more of the obsessional sort, and was of some use in learning at school. He had, however, for a long time to do particular work on terrors connected with eye contact, and his manic projective identification took place largely 'into the head' once a three-dimensional symbiotic relationship was reasonably well established. He invested hugely in writing and drawing (in contrast with the previous child who for a long time fell apart catastrophically whenever he tried to put pen to paper), and developed a skill in drawing strip cartoons. But while he was drawing fairly elaborate phantasy scenes, his pencil-to-paper contact seemed to perform rather an important protective function for him, since as soon as he stopped drawing, he became very agitated and made a lot of sounds, especially Metro and train noises, but also singing songs in mimicking identification with singers on television.

For a long time he did not dare to look at me except through a rhythmical windscreen-wiper activity conducted with his pencil. He did this alternately in front of my face and in front of his own reflection in the mirror. We understood that at best he was inside of a weeping mother's head that seemed like a car in a downpour. When he was ready to leave this situation, he still did windscreen-wipers a little, saying that now it was the sun that was messing up the windscreen – alluding, perhaps, to the aesthetic dazzle of a gaze that he was at last beginning to face (Meltzer, 1980, 1988). Shortly afterwards he asked for brushes to do water-colour painting, and performed a brief rhythmical action with the paintbrush between his eyes and the direction of mine, in a plane perpendicular to the old windscreen-wipers activity, thereby indicating the potential penetration of eye contact, while declaring that he was going to paint a masterpiece.

The main phantasies that he went on to elaborate in better-connected cartoon strips were as follows. A first story set him up with a sister 'Niania', a sort of double who did all sorts of silly things with him, and especially turned on a tap on a pavement that began to make a flood in the town, then spread to the whole planet and gushed out into space ... or else made explosives that created a volcano that destroyed everything in an eruption of ash and burning lava. He was representing 'explosive' projective identification into a poorly differentiated object, neither containing nor able to transform an explosive emotionality.

In another more subtle strip cartoon, set in an abandoned house whose windows were veritable black holes, two friends were trying to survive. One, Yves, was trapped in the black thickness of the wall, and initially made himself known to the other figure, Julien, by making terrifying sounds, whereupon Julien immediately flung away the bottle from which he was drinking. They were hungry. Yves suggested going into a painting hanging on the wall to see if they could find a picture of food. This painting showed a house whose windows were more wide open. The jump into the painting was accompanied by a little noise, and there was a moment during which the painting was obscured. Then Yves was shown facing on the painting, 'returning', and jumped out of it again with a little sound, carrying a picture of food under his arm. The two friends, who were still hungry, went off to try to find real food, but when they found it, little mounds of cheese were glittering like diamonds (probably conflating food for the mouth and food for the eyes). Yves became confused, 'lost', and found himself in a wood, then in a narrow no-entry dustbin alley, but eventually he ended up finding his friend again and could eat the cheeses. But no sooner were they satisfied than the idea of musical entertainment, probably rather sexualised (playing the cello), caused a cello-smasher to appear, who changed the instrument into a hellish car that then became a stream of cars rushing at great speed along a motorway. Yves was thrown to the ground, as though 'blown' – he was quite literally grounded – and in the end was catapulted away by being butted in the rear on the horns of a ram that emerged from the stream of traffic ...

In this second story one sees a sort of double who is first imprisoned within a thick black wall that is probably connected with adhesive identity, and who has then to embark on a search in the picture for representations of the eyes of an object whose three-dimensionality is rather better established. In this context the little explosive noise is played down, since the emotional shock is probably quite well controlled, but it reappears at the rediscovery of the diamond-cheeses. Here, the projective identification described is no longer an aquatic or volcanic eruption into space, but a sexualised manic act of repenetration into the genital forest or the anal dustbin alley. Once again, there is the possibility of turning towards perversion (as was the case with Pierre), but here, as in other places in Baptiste's material, it appears in a much less conspicuous way than it did with Pierre.

IV. Discussion

There are many similarities in these different children's material: a constant feature is the lack of body boundaries, equated with a limiting skin. Their boundaries therefore seem to float or are projected onto architecture. Another is the extreme penetrability of their bodies by sound. We saw in Pauline a terror of bodily penetration by noises, and projection onto architecture of body-boundaries that seemed to get lost when, in the treatment room, she became unsure of the edge of the window. By contrast, later on, when she had established more internal security, it was on leaving the room that she experienced tremendous dizziness.

In Pauline's case what seemed specific to me were moments of 'paradoxical' confusion of identity, in which I myself felt so tied up in a state of helplessness and despair, faced with the threat of annihilation, that I could not help thinking that only a terrible explosion could put a stop to the immobilising process. This process could sometimes take the form of an almost hypnotic phenomenon that led to the drowsiness to which I will return below.

These phenomena did not occur in the cases of shell-type autism that I have treated or heard about; with cases of shell-type autism there may perhaps be a link instead between the risk of perversion and the more muscular character of the autistic shell. Pierre sometimes asked a lot of questions about the solidity of walls and ceilings, and when the room was redecorated he was no longer sure whether there was a solid wall behind the new wallpaper. For a very long time he also asked questions about his own bodily dimensions. We also saw how at other times he needed to feel very well held in a covering.

At a time when they were rediscovering eye contact combined with back-support (a 'solid base'), several primary (shell-type) autistic children showed me that nestling into a corner gave them a feeling of connectedness between the two halves of their body either side of the spine, and that this sense of being joined up was equated with architectural corners. They would fit themselves very snugly into a corner in the wall, spine facing the intersection (Haag, 1988), as though both to demonstrate and, perhaps, consolidate the experience itself.

Where eye contact is concerned, Pierre went through a particular stage when he was making major efforts to socialise. He became greatly preoccupied with what staring could do, which became an issue when he came too close to people who interested or intrigued him. During the same period he did a lot of mimed actions, getting me to confirm their meaning.

Pauline and Pierre had specific fears about eye contact that were clearly connected with destructive penetration and a sense of piercing and grabbing. Pauline demonstrated this especially clearly in games of 'ophthalmologist' that were conducted in an atmosphere of barely contained and very extreme sadism (needles stabbed into dolls' eyes). Baptiste, and other shell-type children, never played these sadistic games. Instead, they conveyed their intense fear of excessively sharp penetration and showed their longing for gently penetrating eye-contact. (Other shell-type autistic children displayed a fear of falling down behind eyes with no solid foundation behind them.)

Once or twice Pauline took pleasure in demonstrating her sixth sense to me, being able to detect or 'sense', her father's arrival well before hearing the sounds of his approach.

Finally, it could be said that both Pauline and, to a certain extent,

8. Psychosis and Autism

Baptiste exhibited a double personality, on one side capable of superficial adaptation, and on the other liable to become volcanic and get into a manic state; Pauline's tendency for violence was much greater than that of shell-type children. In her case perhaps we could hypothesise that the instinctual upsurge of puberty together with the demands of adult social adaptation reinforced the split between the false-self part of the personality and the tempestuous, explosive, and ultimately mad part. These aspects may have been more intermingled in childhood, although one side of Pauline had always been very well behaved in class: her explosions mainly occurred at home or in psychotherapy sessions.

V. Theoretical Hypotheses

These clinical experiences pose many theoretical problems, hinted at above. I shall now come back to the first question: why this fear of normal fusion? Although I cannot give a definitive or exhaustive answer to this question, it seems to me that a number of recent studies converge to shed some light on the situation. I shall present this material under three different headings.

1. Fear of falling; a solid base; boundaries

For these children, it seems that casting or plunging a look into another person is not accompanied by a sense of its being returned 'enriched' with psychic substance, both in terms of containment (a feeling of envelopment, a skin), and of content (emotional tones, perceptual shapes, figurative representations, personifications, and symbolic links that produce increasingly rich dramatised representations). Autistic children who do resume their development give careful descriptions of what they are feeling as they either construct for the first time or reconstruct a sense of themselves inside their own skin (Haag 1988, 1990, 1991). To summarise: the sensation of back-support must coincide with penetration by eye contact, so long as the latter is gentle and meets an elastic or springy 'base' that is able to send something back. This base must also be able to take impressions, and let itself be marked. This takes place initially without figurative representation, as though the first things sent into the depths to reach this base are simply qualities in themselves (perhaps the notion of colour in itself, equated with affects). In these children, daring to penetrate is often accompanied by noises that range from vocal modulation to piercing shrieks when there is a sense of breaking in or failure to find a 'base'. The first spatial representation of success in finding it, before it becomes a circular or spherical envelope, is a surface with broad undulations. Here are two short examples.

A child, Laurent, in a special unit with two therapists, gave us the following illustration.[5] He approached us with a brief but cold and piercing glance, and came for a moment to sit on the knees of one of us, pressing his back well into her while looking at the other. Then he stood up, turned around, and dived into her eyes very close to her face, producing the 'Cyclops effect' for a moment. Then he moved away, making a modulated, swooping sound, while at the same time reaching out his arm and holding it to his ear.

This sequence was repeated several times, with variations in which the intensity of sound seemed to relate to the quality of the base that he had found. One day, after an interruption in the rhythm of his sessions, he began by leading both of us towards the washroom with running water, dislodging us from our own support in our chairs. He drank, and spat a long distance, and then, when we had sat down again, he came, for the first time since the series of examples above, to dive into my gaze, going through it as though there were no longer any base to it. He truly gave the impression of having fallen out the other side, and sprang back with a violent arm movement accompanied by a piercing shriek. After our interpretation of having lost the base, having fallen, and making a noise that pierced the ears, he went back to enacting a situation comprising back-support, eye-contact, and modulated sound, and then went calmly to feel with his finger the grooves of the draining-board by the sink, then the wide folds of a partition curtain.

After these sessions, we had the feeling that this 'base' was more solidly established and that he was much more able in encounters outside sessions and with people who took care of him to give a steady look in which there was a mutual exchange.

I shall now give a brief summary of a sequence described in detail in several previous papers, as it is so exemplary.

Paul, after several years of work between the ages of eighteen months and four years, on the brink of perfecting his use of language by using complete sentences, produced the following display in preverbal language. The sight of two almost identical little purple containers, one of which was slightly more oval in shape than the other, more rounded one, prompted a mimed activity of pouring milk into the two containers with a third. This third came from the two tap-like projections that stuck out either side of a radiator.

One of these was nearly flat; the other was longer, with a bend in it and pointed, and the point itself had a little hole in its end. Paul mimed that this 'pipe-beak' penetrated his eye, while at the same time looking straight into my eyes in jubilation, and went quickly to find a very soft fluffy toy bird to put its felt beak over the metal beak of the radiator, replaying the penetration. Then he went round the walls of the room miming 'pressing in' with the soft toy's body. He then enacted in sequence on the couch: first back-support combined with eye contact; then rising up vertically, bouncing back, and putting the two sides of his body into the corner of a wall, spine facing where the walls met.

Several authors in France have emphasised the importance of combining touch and sight. Apart from D. Anzieu in his work on the skin ego (1985), Francis Pasche (1988, p. 50) notes how gazing at the mother makes contact with her psychic reality in the midst of longing for mutual incorporation, and that the latter is limited by pressure against the breast, which represents the limits of mutual absorption. P.C. Racamier (1989, p. 22) speaks of the absolutely necessary narcissistic seduction conducted by 'eye and skin contact'. I myself would add, in keeping with Kleinian and post-Kleinian formulations, that the 'base' or 'foundation' cannot be experienced in a way that is at once sensory and psychic, indissolubly united in the body-ego, unless maternal reverie (Bion) can return the primitive emotional states 'projected' by the baby with the added 'little difference' of transformation.

Throughout my own work on the integrative links between the back and the gaze I have referred to James Grotstein's work on an object that is now called the 'Background Presence of Primary Identification' (Grotstein, 1981, 1990). Grotstein identified the 'Background Presence' in sensations of depersonalisation specifically connected with back-support and therefore with the back as localised in the body image, and also perceived as a psychic entity:

'The Background Object of Primary Identification is the guardian of inchoate object constancy from the very beginning of life until representation of objects can replace the presentation of objects (self-objects, internal objects), allowing for transformation of the Background Object into a deity-like concept associated with a superego and ego-ideal.' (Grotstein, 1981, pp. 80-1)

I would like at this point to refer to Baptiste's strip cartoon about the figure shut up in the black wall who springs out with a loud noise. What are we to make of this fear and of the terrifying noise of brutal emergence and 'appearance'? Does the black wall take us back to the adhesiveness of the Background Presence? Does this link with Grotstein's more recent formulations (1990) about primary non-sense in the

205

sense of non-investment, a context out of which meaning is created, but was perhaps too harshly illuminated for Baptiste, as though he were brought into the light of day with a big bang or even amidst the non-sense of pathological disinvestment that Green relates to the death instinct?

In a beautiful paper read to the 50th Congress of French-speaking Psychoanalysts, Sylvie and Georges Pragier (1990), referring to Freud's 'Project' (1895), explored new metaphors from the biological sciences, notably the concept of self-organisation. They came across the observation that sound is disorganising if it is too intense, organising if it becomes a source of information, and is always the sign of change in a system. On many occasions autistic children who are developing well have drawn my attention to noise very clearly, and this recurred whenever they experienced changes that were difficult to assimilate. Baptiste highlighted the excessively loud noise associated with leaving the wall, and also much more bearable sounds connected with 'returning to' and 'leaving' eye contact and the sort of communication that leads towards representation.

It is worth noting in this context that for some months Baptiste performed a ritual on entry and exit from the room that served both to dramatise and master this theme. As he left, he would say 'Walk like you were paralysed.' I had then to stop moving, and he would turn off the light while banging the door. On his return, he would run ahead of me to shut himself in the playroom. I had to wait a moment at the door. He would open it for me suddenly, making loud noises. One day, in the midst of a session, after he had returned from nature class, I said something that showed interest in the reality of the experience he had just had. He did not reply, but exclaimed a moment later 'That made a terrifying noise!' With my question I had departed a little from my usual technique, and therefore from my normal 'setting'.

After this brief digression into noise, is Baptiste's story not essentially about the brutality with which an object that has left the background suddenly appears? About psychic trauma due to premature awareness of bodily separation (Tustin) and of an excessively fragile self, yielding a sense of skin torn off and prompting a ceaseless search for a single skin for two people? Joyce McDougall (1989) describes very well the problem of one skin between two, and also suggests that this could derive from memories of precocious autonomy connected with a premature objectification of the baby's first objects. There is therefore truly a very pressing need to go in search of pictures of food!

As for primitive superego aspects of the Background Presence, it is worth noting that in Baptiste's strip cartoon the figure who comes out of the wall is at first like a terrible God – but of course also bears the projection of the child's very weak ego, since, although he is able to go looking for representations, he becomes confused when he actually finds the external object (the glittering cheeses). Was there a shock at that point, at the moment of rediscovery – when he perceived the externality of his object, making all the agonies of bodily separation surge up again? As for the rush of sexual drive represented by a cello player who might introduce a dance or masturbation, probably accompanied by a primal scene phantasy – this prompted a phantasy of being swept off, 'blown', and cast to the ground by a stream of cars passing in a rush in front of our hero, who ends up getting butted in the bottom and tossed in the air by a ram who emerges, goodness knows how, from the torrent of traffic. Is it possible that these children experience instinctual excitement as a sort of cosmic attraction – which may be brought to a halt by persecutory and sado masochistic themes? (Baptiste once elaborated magnificently upon the theme of 'a child is being beaten' (Haag 1989), in connection with a dream of a rather rough return from a space ship!)

2. *The importance of rhythmical structuring in the first exchanges; the return of the projected; representations of creases and folds – or otherwise of black holes and annihilating space; learning to fly*

Here I refer to Frances Tustin's beautiful formulations on primitive emotionality as an eruption of bodily matter that produces flow and counter-flow to create the first sense of continuity (Tustin 1981). As I myself put it (Haag 1991), 'There is a need for these "eruptions" to be returned within something that approximates the sensation of folds. This is experienced initially in terms of bodily articulations whose suppleness is a function of there being links that mediate interchange.' Apart from bouncing and demonstrating elasticity with objects or with their bodies as a whole, autistic children also 'tell' us about the state of their bodily articulations. As soon as they have established a minimal sense of bodily separateness (which happens fairly soon in a one-to-one situation), eye contact deepens, having previously been rather tactile and two-dimensional. At the same time they perceive a 'space' between themselves and the other, which they usually bridge by a 'jump of joy' that shows their delight in this difference.

The autistic child who cannot achieve this step faces the terror of being sucked in, and of a whirling departure for outer space (Houzel,

1988). He then has a compelling need to resort to peripheral vision (Bullinger 1984). The child I have called Pierre illustrated such problems over eye contact by means of images of outer space that crop up fairly often with autistic children. While he was still in the throes of anxiety, he fantasised that he was a cosmonaut who had left his space vessel and had his connecting cord cut off. He would spin and get lost in endless space. Better, then, to go rigid as he used to do in his old autistic state, or else to get back into his object's body in a manic sweep.

After a definite improvement, he might be described as having learnt to fly: while making me listen to his favourite music (synthetic music), he would mime that he felt he was flying pleasantly in space. He could not conceive of space as infinite: he imagined that there were railings at the end of the universe and that behind the railings was a planet with people one could talk to. Along the way, certain musical tracks dived off towards a possible Hell (his manic perverse state), but luckily a good God had 'pulled' him out of that! After this he organised a good-bad split between two planets representing different qualities of human contact. One planet was like a paradise, with gentle inhabitants, while in the other lived nasty people containing Pierre's projected sadism. Pierre's pleasure in 'flying off' into shared aesthetic emotion, which never reached the heights of the more sexualised symbolisation of intimacy described by Freud, seemed to be connected initially with the sensation of a thrill of delight in the emotional sharing of eye contact.

Baptiste put this very prettily when, in the midst of imagining a double who was the same or not the same as himself, he looked in the mirror and mimed shooting an arrow into his reflection. I said this would be a funny look that would destroy the double image. He then stood facing the window and said he had wings, and would jump out and fly away. I asked him where he would land. He thought for a while, hesitated, then looked at me with a laugh and said in a loud voice 'In a reflection.' We both laughed together and I related this idea to jumping into my eyes, and to the old terrors he used to have of falling en route or even of being dazzled, which had then stopped him from looking at me and other people. In his autistic state he had had at times to cling to the shapes of standing lamps, and for a long time could not bear me to switch on the real lamp stand by my chair – probably connected with the theme of dazzling eyes.[6]

3. Reflections on the paradoxical position, and especially the risk of schizophrenia, in secondary autism related to autistic withdrawal; hypnotic manoeuvres and the phenomenon of drowsiness; more on eye contact: Medusa or Pegasus?; and hypotheses about predisposition in the choice of morbid pathways

The study of paradoxical phenomena has been especially developed in

France by P.C. Racamier (1978, 1989) in his work on families with psychotic interactions. Racamier (1978) defined the paradox as follows, 'a psychic formation that inseparably connects and interrelates two propositions or injunctions that can neither be reconciled nor opposed to one another.' Paradoxicality is 'at one and the same time a mode of mental functioning, a psychic régime, and a mode of relationship, which structures a negative and interminable narcissistic relationship.' Later on, Racamier (1989, p. 24) formulated it succinctly as 'irreversible unison'. For a long time, Pauline exerted this sort of literally petri-fied/petrifying control upon me. It was as though the Gorgon Medusa had materialised, and succeeded at times in inducing drowsiness in me. It is worth noting that she herself later elaborated the greedy and envious component of this phenomenon in the scene of the Fat Ladies.

Cléopatre Athanassiou (1989) distinguishes drowsiness from sleep and has studied in detail a similar situation in two patients whose hypnotic manoeuvre involved the repetition of isolated events with a slowness that drained her of all vitality. She sees in this a sort of paralysing attack on thought, reducing links to a state of suspended animation. She also encountered the same paradoxical configurations as the ones I found in Pauline – for example in the shopping games which started out as an interchange, only for this to be immediately cancelled out by the disappearance of one of the protagonists, by the confusion of identities, or by the paradoxical declaration that the shop was 'open-closed'. Athanassiou suggests that this can be understood in terms of a pathological part of the self controlling the ego, which it paralyses by simultaneously mimicking the needy self and the permis-sive superego – so that one is left with emptiness! I agree to some extent with this analysis. However, I would also see the situation in terms of the sufferings of a weak and embryonic self, communicated by projec-tive identification. The self, prevented from developing by a deficiency in the object's attention, is therefore perpetually on the brink of an abyss created by the engulfing effect of projections that are not returned, and by expectations that are repeatedly disappointed. The alternative to this is an eruption of destructive rage, the threat of which is keenly felt in the countertransference. Might these manoeuvres perhaps be one of the last lines of defence against the patently schizophrenic minute splitting associated with bizarre objects (Bion, 1957), or the delusional forma-tions of the 'fifth space' (Meltzer, 1975)?

The child may feel that there is no alternative to these autistic manoeuvres found in both primary and secondary autism. However, if autistic aspects of the personality are to be reintegrated, it is absolutely essential for them to be tackled with a transference object capable of receiving and transforming moments of appalling rage. These occur at points that mark a sort of parting of the ways, where at worst there is a danger of encountering schizophrenic phenomena (delusions), and at best we meet manic-depressive swings, with frequent hypochondriac anxieties, somatisation, and the risk of perversion.

In children, the outcome seems to depend upon how early treatment begins, how far the family are caught up in the morbid process, and the nature of the child's predisposition. On the latter point, many authors agree that children with primary autism tend more towards detachment (emotional non-investment or disinvestment), while in secondary autism, aggressive components of the personality are either literally explosive (causing the child to take refuge in delusion) or else necessitate perverse erotisation of hatred and destructiveness.

In all cases, fear of normal fusion has ultimately caused a sense of 'falling' due to loss of, or failure to establish, a rhythmically structured 'base' (Haag 1985). This 'base' relates to the Background Presence, is part and parcel of adhesiveness, and supports useful projective identification. It is enacted by children when they 'go to stick to the base of ' an object, but only in order to bounce back very quickly, enriched by the experience. This 'base' is reminiscent of the 'something ready to take the overflow' that Frances Tustin (1981) thought so essential. Only such an experience can offer hope of making the transition from Medusa-like looking to Pegasus-like looking (learning to fly). In Greek mythology, Pegasus brought the spring Hippocrene into existence, a flowing source of the symbolic capacity that emerges from our poetic function.

A much shortened version of this paper was published as 'Fear of Fusion and Projective Identification in Autistic Children' in Psychoanalytic Inquiry 13 (1993) pp. 63-84, in a translation by Theodore Mitrani.

Notes

[1] We would especially like to thank D. Meltzer for identifying the specific bodily zones involved in projective identification in manic states, which is so useful clinically (presentation to a professional clinical group (GERPEN), and published in their private bulletin: Meltzer, 1988a).

[2] Tustin (1990, 1992) later preferred the term 'confusional entangled children'. It should be remembered that Tustin (1972) also described the Kanner picture as secondary autism, reserving the term primary abnormal autism for the very earliest autistic states that are continuous with the post-natal

non-integrated states that she originally described as normal primary autism, but later regarded as not being autistic at all (Tustin, 1992).

[3] 'Coraces' and 'corages' were condensations of *caresse* (cuddle) and *orage* (storm). Storms terrified her.

[4] RER: (Réseau étendu de métropolitain): suburban underground network around Paris.

[5] I would like to thank Mme Nada Tannous for her valuable collaboration with this case.

[6] This is the point to mention more particularly the work of André Green on negatives and limits (1976, 1982). Green postulates that between the act of representation and the birth of a thought properly so called, a negative hallucination of the representation of the object must be formed in order for there to arise a representation of relationships within a representation, and amongst different representations (Green, 1990, p. 308). Could it be that in 'dazzling' there is too great a negative hallucination? Where limits are concerned, Green regards them as mobile and fluctuating frontiers, both in normal and pathological states. He also suggests that we should formulate the concept of boundaries not in terms of figurative representations but in terms of a process of transformation of energy and symbolisation (Green, 1990, p. 126). Whilst I agree in not equating boundaries with figurative representations, is it not possible all the same that, at the levels addressed here, certain representations of containment do support perception and underlie emotional investment in the geometric, undulating, circular, spherical, and angular spatial shapes that are then subsumed into the first pre-figurative drawings of young children and probably also into the first geometric decorative designs of all cultures (Haag, 1990)?

9

Jeremy and the Bitten Roof

Hélène Dubinsky

I have been seeing Jeremy in individual therapy for three years, twice a week. He is now eleven years old. When he was seven, he was diagnosed as autistic, but after a few months of therapy, he began slowly and hesitantly to communicate in whole sentences.

Jeremy often puts across a deep fear of falling and disintegrating. He recounted mental experiences which we took to be dreams. Although his thinking remained essentially concrete, these dreams were the first representations of his battered internal world which was depicted as a house without a roof, open to the rain and to noise from outside which drove him mad.

Jeremy's parents are very religious and are active members of their church. Mother had a breakdown during the first year of his life. She says it is the church which has helped and supported her in coming out of her depression. Mrs S is now a loving mother, attentive to her children. Jeremy has a sister, two years younger, with whom he gets on well. Mrs S tends, like her husband, to explain everything to Jeremy in scientific terms, to avoid his becoming anxious. She supports the therapy unconditionally, and is very grateful for it.

When I first met Jeremy, he would talk in odd disjointed sentences, without meaning or apparent links, and not using the first person. He avoided looking in my eyes, and walked in a jerky sort of way, very stiffly, a bit like an automaton. For a long time, except for brief moments of contact, he ignored my presence in the room. Indeed, he seemed very confused, not knowing where he was, who he was, not even feeling that he was a person, and I had great difficulties in concentrating and staying in touch with him during sessions.

Jeremy is small and looks younger than his age. His hair is fair, he has fine features, a delicate and intelligent face. He now feels very much at home in the clinic, and settles down in the waiting room with his thermos flask and his sandwiches, but shouts loudly if interrupted. He talks to the secretaries and to other people in the waiting room, telling them of his present worries and preoccupations. He also talks frequently about me. He reminds me of Saint-Exupery's Little Prince, down from his planet, a very lost Little Prince, trying to communicate at the level of his deepest feelings, yet remaining completely alone. The secretaries laugh when they listen to him, but are fond of him. Other children say 'There is a mad child in the waiting room.'

During the sessions, Jeremy gradually started talking, partly to himself, partly to me. He developed a succession of obsessional interests in our room, first with the door, and its spring, this after our first long holiday separation; after that, with the pipe work underneath the basin. For many weeks last year, he tried to grow flowers in plasticine.

He would spurt out incoherent pseudo-scientific theories, using twisted words, with the voice of a little professor talking to a very young or retarded child. He rarely speaks in his own voice. Yet his therapy has become very important to him as a place where his feelings have a space.

Emergence of Dreams: the beginnings of symbolic thought

I would like to describe an important new development during recent months, when Jeremy started remembering dreams. The feel of the sessions changed, and Jeremy now often sits very close to me, on the desk, talking to me and questioning the functioning of his mind. I shall focus on three dreams Jeremy brought to me, and the sessions linked to these dreams.

The very first dream Jeremy told me was:

> I was outside and it was raining. I ran inside the house, but it was also raining there.

This is an extract from a session, the last before Easter, when Jeremy told me his second dream. He always talks very slowly, and stops very frequently for a long time in the middle of his sentences, as if lost, and as if he needs to cling very hard to what he wants to say. Often, he has to start his sentence again and again, because the first few versions are very confused; eventually, painstakingly, he manages to say what he wants.

> When he came into the room, he noticed my new telephone, much more modern than the previous one. He sat on my desk. He started talking in his 'interpretation' voice. (He often imitates my voice and the shape of

an interpretation when he talks of his feelings.) He told me 'You feel worried to tell people your dreams, my dream is a secret. You feel so uptight that you mustn't tell your dreams. If you don't have any secrets, poor Jeremy won't get psychotherapised.' I asked him to tell me his dream, which he did:

'It was raining outside and inside. I was in the dining room, and it rained there. Rebecca looked outside the window, and she saw Bobby the Banana. I went to the bathroom, and on the landing, and it was raining. And then my mummy said "Oh no it's the slake, it's raining everywhere." I rushed down to Mummy, and I asked what slake was. She said it is a metal, stronger than all the iron in the world put together. The slake had bitten off the roof.'

I told Jeremy he seemed very worried in the dream. I suggested he felt there is a horrible daddy outside and inside the house. This horrible snake-slake daddy bites the roof and makes a big hole in the house, making it unsafe. Now it rains everywhere, and the children and mummy are left without protection. Jeremy argues, tells me he is not worried, and that he knows it doesn't rain inside. He then asks 'Tell me, if you had a dream, would it also rain inside and outside?'. I tell him that he would like to know if we share similar worries. Do I also have inside me a mummy-house where it rains. Jeremy starts again, in his interpretation tone 'You know that it rains everywhere in Jeremy's house, through the roof and the walls, and poor old Mummy lets the roof leak. Jeremy is not protected, and Daddy can drill a hole in Jeremy's mind.'

I talked about this dangerous father who drills holes in Mummy's head and in Jeremy's head – Jeremy then finds it very difficult to think for himself. I linked this with his fear of the holidays, which makes him want to go inside the house, but he finds it has a broken roof, and it rains inside. I suggested he is scared of losing me, his strong mummy therapist with a safe daddy, who helps Jeremy to think and to have a strong mind, without holes in it. Jeremy asked 'And the baby?' I told him that maybe, Jeremy would like to know if the daddy would protect the baby, rather than make him feel unsafe.

Later in the session, Jeremy asked me questions about the keys on the new telephone, and asked me how it was that I didn't know about them. I told him he was worried my mind had holes in it, like Jeremy's. He told me 'Yes, that you do not have a good mind.' I carried on talking to him about the telephone, and his desire I phone him, and he phones me, during the holiday. I also spoke about his worry that the bad daddy might come and cut this link between us. He said 'Yes.'

When Jeremy returned from the holiday, the telephone theme was still present in his mind. I was told by the secretaries that Jeremy had come to their office asking them for telephone numbers, because he felt lonely in the waiting room, and that the noise of the typewriters prevented him from hearing the ticking of the clock. Jeremy told me in the corridor 'Give me the Telephone Company.' He also told me that sometimes, one hears on the phone 'The other person has cleared.' I told him that he felt

214

that I too, had cleared. He asked me 'Who is British Telecom.' I asked him who he thought it was. He replied 'The one who keeps all the change', and I talked to him about this telephone-daddy, who keeps all the change during the holidays, all the food, but also all the words, all Mummy's words for himself. Jeremy answered, in his interpretation voice, 'Oh, poor Jeremy didn't get any food over Easter.'

Later he talked to me about those people who break telephone boxes to steal money. I spoke about the part of Jeremy who would like to steal, to take back the money which he felt had been stolen from him. He told me 'Poor Mrs Dubinsky, no food, no drinks, not even oxygen to breathe, she will have to live in a vacuum and she will die. And very very rich Jeremy has everything, all the riches in the world, and poor old Mrs Dubinsky has nothing – except the light', he added after a short pause. I told him that he feels he can't take away my light from me, my ability to help him to think and to grow. Jeremy answered, crossly, that he could think about his feelings by himself. Later he asked me 'Why is it important, to think about one's feelings?', and still later 'What do computers do, instead of thinking?'

Now here is the session of the third dream. (When he came to the previous session, the toilet had been blocked. He had told me then that it was because of poisonous gases.) Jeremy said worriedly that the toilet was still broken. Why? I told him I didn't know. He answered, sounding rather cross, 'I do not ask you what you know, but what you think.' He sat on the desk near me. He asked me 'Are you a Christian, or a non-Christian?' I ask him what he means by Christian, and he explained 'If you are not a Christian, you will not go to Heaven.' Then, he told me his dream:

'My father told me "Hide", and I hid behind trees. I saw some witches on my left. I ran to Daddy, and Daddy told me we must run straight away, and I said "My God, I beg you that witches do not exist, Jesus, Amen".' I asked him to tell me his thoughts about witches. He told me 'They have horrible black magic, which comes from the mind of the devil. They can destroy your mind and ruin your thoughts. Animals sometimes go to Heaven, it depends whether they belong to Christians or not.'

I commented that his prayer to God was important to get rid of the witches. Jeremy said he had told his dream first to his mother, and then to his father, who had said 'You should indeed pray to God to protect you from the witches, because they do exist.'

He carried on telling me that witches get their black magic from the devil, and that they practise every day. He also told me he has never really seen a witch, only in his dreams. I said that the broken toilet had been worrying him a lot. I explained that when we part at the end of the session, Jeremy in his imagination wants quickly to get inside me so that there is no real separation. The blocked toilet made Jeremy feel that I was not available for him, that there was nowhere to put his worries. Jeremy tells himself that it is the daddy who's broken it, putting poisonous gases in it. I added that this makes him believe that I am a non-Christian, a witch, like a broken toilet, and the devil is my spouse. To save himself from this witch, he feels there is only one thing to do, to pray to God.

Jeremy went towards the basin, and made a flower pot from plasticine. He explained that he made it so that people can grow flowers. He added holes in the plasticine, telling me that the pot needed holes, to let the water out when the flower goes wee-wee. I commented that he was making for himself a mummy potty which grows flower babies, but I could see that the Jeremy-flower is sitting on the pot, making sure that this flowerpot-toilet is not blocked like *mine*.

The next session was cancelled, because of a train strike in London, which made it impossible for me to reach the clinic. For the following session Jeremy was slightly late, which is very unusual. I heard him shout 'Mrs Dubinsky, Mrs Dubinsky', down the corridor. When I opened the door, he ran into the room. He told me, looking very pale, 'I am a few minutes late.' Then he added 'Never mind, it's not the end of the world.' Then, after many attempts, he managed to say 'seeing a part of a session is better than no session at all.' I told him he feels now that he has a strong mummy inside him who tells him 'Don't worry, it's not the end of the world, and Mrs Dubinsky has not disappeared.' I told him it was quite difficult to lose a little bit of his session today, since I had not been to the previous session, because of the train strike. He asked me 'What happens with the wires underneath the tracks? Is there still electricity?' I explained to him what a strike was, and I added that he was worried everything was broken, the wires, the electricity, and that I might again be like a broken toilet. Jeremy said 'Why didn't you ask the driver? Next time, make him drive the train. Talk to him, insist.' I talked about his worries, that maybe I hadn't been to see Jeremy because the daddy wouldn't let me come, or maybe this daddy driver didn't want to make the effort. Jeremy ran the water on the plasticine, and some of the water splashed on the ground.

Jeremy looked worried, and said 'It's really stupid.' I talked about how worried he felt about dirtying me, and his fear that everything could break down again. Jeremy told me 'I shall be more careful next time.' He ran the water carefully, and made the scissors spin in the water. He explained to me that the molecules would rub against each other, to create heat, and the plasticine would become softer. I asked him what he wanted to do with the plasticine. He said he wanted to make a bactery-person, who has a bacterial life, but a human body. I asked a few more questions, but he was absorbed and not listening. He said 'I wish friction existed, a force that stops things going apart.' I asked him if the bactery-person had this friction, he said 'No, the pieces are simply stuck together.'

I told him he wished there was a friction that would prevent us from separating, stop strikes, holidays, and so on, but also a friction that would hold Jeremy together. I talked again about his worry at the beginning of the session, and of his wish for a sane mummy, with a strong daddy, to hold the bits of Jeremy firmly together.

Towards the end of the session, he laid on his back on the floor, his legs and feet through the back of the chair. He told me it was as if

216

everything was upside down. 'I mix up the ceiling and the floor, but the ceiling is white and the floor is brown.' Right at the end of the session, he ran the water very fast, and told me that he wanted to flood the room, watching me to see if I was getting worried.

Discussion

At the beginning of this last session Jeremy battles against his fear of falling to bits, provoked by his panic at being late and the missed session. All the pieces of Jeremy's personality are stuck together very precariously. When Jeremy talks and thinks with me, he fears that he will lose the thread of his thought. He needs an object to hold him together, through attention, thinking and looking at him. Separation is felt as a catastrophe and to avoid it, he intrudes aggressively inside an internal mother felt to be very fragile. As a result, he finds himself inside a very damaged object, where it rains all the time, and where babies are not safe. He is also identified with this mother, whose head-roof has been bitten, and his mind is leaky, like hers.

Jeremy begs the secretary 'Give me the phone numbers. The noise of the typewriters prevents me from hearing the ticking of the clock.' I think he wanted to say 'I want to remain in contact with a mummy who talks to me, who is sane, and I don't want to be inside a house where it rains, invaded by this psychotic noise that prevents me from thinking.'

Jeremy fears deeply that the chaos he projects, his psychotic confusion and rage will damage me. It is to defend himself against this deep anxiety that he reassures himself, saying 'No, it's not me who's broken Mummy, it's the bad father.' Jeremy often perceives the parental couple as a damaged mother and a bad father and he identifies with both of them. This is shown in Jeremy's various phantasies: the roof of the house bitten by the snake, the blocked toilet filled with poisonous gases left there by the father, the witch married to the devil, and the bad train driver who prevented me from coming to the session.

A year and a half has elapsed since this sequence of dreams. He has been saying, in an obsessive way, that he wishes to live for ever because he doesn't want to die and go to heaven and be far from home. His deep anxiety seems to be that when separation takes place, he is dropped far away from his objects, far away in outer space.

For months he spoke of a fantasy of wishing to steal everything from me, my thoughts, my capacity to have babies, my money, all my riches. This is how he first described this to me: 'When I'm in front of a garden full of roses, how I wish to cut them all and take them home.' He often gets very worried and tormented about his phantasies and then either denies them or says that the devil puts evil thoughts in him, instead of just nice clean thoughts.

Symbolic Expression of Depressive Conflict

I will now report a recent session where Jeremy told me another dream. I went to get Jeremy from the waiting room. As usual he was sitting at the little table on a little chair intended for very young children, eating his packed lunch with an air of intense satisfaction. He was facing a family sitting on a bench, father and mother. The mother was holding a baby against her chest and there was an older boy. He had probably been talking to them and they looked intensely embarrassed. When I opened the door he said 'Oh, this fucking Mrs Dubinsky' (this was unusual). There was shock on the faces of those in the waiting room, and while still there, he told me 'I have had a dream.' He went on talking about having to tell me this dream in the corridor. In my room I talked about his anger in the waiting room and he said 'Yes, I was very angry, because I hadn't finished my drink.' Then coming close to me in an excited way, and with a smile, he said, imitating my accent, 'What is a breast?' and he proceeded to explain to me what a breast is, that it is what the baby sucks, where he gets the milk from etc. I said that he was mocking my accent because he felt jealous of the baby and the mummy in the waiting room which made him think of me being with my other babies. He became serious again, and said urgently 'Oh, I have a dream to tell you.'

He told me the dream as follows: 'I was in the dining room, next to the door. The dining room door was open but I tried to shut it. My budgie was flying around the dining room, then flew out of the room and then in again. Mummy said "You shouldn't let the budgie fly out." I tried to close the door but it opened again and the bird flew out through the gap. It landed on the bannister in the middle, then flew off the bannister and landed at the window, at the top of the stairs. Then it flew out of the window and went flying away. I prayed to get him back, but didn't manage it.'

Jeremy said the dream made him think that his budgie was gone and that he would have to go out of the house to catch it with a butterfly net, but he might not be lucky enough to find it. I said that I thought the budgie represents baby Jeremy and myself, the mummy, being together, and that he's trying to keep me in his control – in the cage –

because he's so worried the Mrs Dubinsky budgie will fly away and that he may not be able to get me back, not even with his butterfly net.

Jeremy argued, and said no, the dream was about Arthur, his budgie. He talked about his budgie which is still alive because it is young, but then added that his sister's hamster has died – he died of cancer and they buried it. 'Now that he's dead, will he come back to life?' he asked. He talked to me at length of how in England there are no budgies flying free because they are born and bred in captivity. I spoke of the fact that I shall only be seeing him once a week next year – might he be feeling that I will disappear and that I'm flying away to be with my other babies? 'Yes', he said with a lot of feeling. 'The reason the mummy is flying away is that she had to go to her own home.' He went on, saying 'Your home is very far away from my home.' Later he added 'I told my budgie that I had a dream and he chirped and I asked him why and he said he wanted to live in the wild.'

I think Jeremy's dream, triggered off by the death of his sister's hamster, depicts his great fear of loss and of the death of his objects and of himself. He believes I shall leave him for my babies at home, never to return. In spite of Jeremy's prayers, the budgie which flew out of the open window did not come back.

In his dream Jeremy expresses a depressive conflict – is he allowed to keep this budgie, myself, imprisoned? Will he be able to grow when I am encaged and in that way unable to look after my other babies who also need me? Jeremy is worried about the impact of his possessiveness and his obsessional control over me and at the same time is terrified to allow this budgie mummy her freedom. This ambivalence is expressed in his leaving doors and windows open, and then running after the budgie. Jeremy is showing that he wants and needs this little budgie-mummy, who chirped when he related his dream to it (and in fact the budgie heard about the dream before I did), that he needs me to be with him, listening, responding and containing his anxieties. I think that he is very frightened that if the therapy ends prematurely, he would remain lost and confused.

Jeremy's growing awareness of the confusion in his mind has brought him much pain. It also brought him the torture of jealousy and envy towards the capacities of those he is close to. In the middle of fiercely contradicting me, he said 'I'm emotionally blind and deaf – I have been emotionally blind and deaf since I was born.' And then he added 'I'm not jealous that you can hear and see emotionally – where did you get your emotional equipment?'

Conclusion

The dreams that I have reported allow us to see how Jeremy's internal world is changing, how a house with a gaping hole is turning into a house with doors and windows which can be opened and closed. From a desperate need for a strong internal, house-mind, in the earlier dreams, there is the emergence in Jeremy's fourth dream of a containing internal object, which will enable him to hear and see what is happening in his mind, to be aware of his emotional experience.

As I noted, the open door of the house and the cage seem to represent a lessening of his obsessional control of his objects, spurred by depressive anxieties. This development is however exposing him to much greater psychic pain.

In the external world Jeremy's parents say he has improved considerably. His family finds him much more involved; he discusses, argues, gets upset, and has some friends now. Instead of going to a school for autistic children which had been thought of for him, he will be joining mainstream secondary education.

Yet Jeremy is still something of a 'Little Prince', odd and solitary, but now starting to be hopeful that one day he will live and develop on earth as a live person among others.

10

'The Ghost is Coming'

The Fear of Annihilation in a Nine-Year-Old Boy

S.M. Sherwin-White

History and Background

Samuel was referred for help at the age of five. His mother described his bad behaviour, unmanageable tantrums, episodes of exposing himself, and spitting. Samuel is the second, much younger child of a second marriage. The pregnancy was unplanned and unwanted. While pregnant, Samuel's mother was told that her baby's head was too small, with all the terrifying implications of a brain-damaged child that this conveys. This information may have been a medical error. We know that she was badly depressed during the pregnancy and post-natally. She went back to work one week after Samuel's birth.

Her personal history is disturbing. She was born abroad, and reports nearly being killed at birth by a relative because she was a girl. As a young teenager she experienced the first of her two marriages, which broke down. She and Samuel's father are successful, workaholic business people. The father travels frequently in connection with work and is often away from home for considerable periods of time. Samuel misses him badly during these absences, as does his mother.

Samuel was left in the care of a succession of nannies. In recent conversations with his mother, a moving picture emerged of the terror, hopelessness and dread that she understandably felt before and after his birth. She added, with horror 'He was a vegetable until he was four. He couldn't walk. His muscles were wasted because his nanny kept him in a pushchair all the time ...' Samuel's delayed development is underlined by the fact that he is reported not to have begun to talk (apart from single words) until he was three and a half, or walked until he was four.

It is possible that his mother's shock at hearing that his head was too

221

small may have exposed him, within the womb, to what Rosenfeld has called 'osmotic pressures' (Rosenfeld 1987, pp. 185-6 and pp. 276-7); or at least to the process whereby disturbing feelings and reactions in the mother can be demonstrated to impinge upon the foetus (Piontelli, 1989, 1992; Rosenfeld 1987). It is evident from his mother's effective transfer of responsibility for him, and from her way of talking about him as an infant, that she was far too disturbed and distressed to be able to begin to offer the baby the vital primary care of the 'good enough mother'. She was unable to offer him containment and the opportunity to discover a good object: he was plunged into a situation in which 'maternal sheltering' was shattered, with all the exposure to potentially psychosis-promoting states of unintegration and disintegration that ensue. Normally, the visual interchanges between mother and baby function as a primary structuring, fostering and containing 'language' (Wright 1991, Chapter 1). For baby Samuel, however, the prospect of 'reading' messages of love and care in his mother's eyes and facial expressions was limited, if not destroyed. It needs little imagination to picture the desperate, peering, suspicious glances and stares that he would have encountered ('What is he? Is he normal? Is he brain-dead? What have I given birth to?').

The impact of Samuel's suspected brain-damage has been evoked repeatedly in therapy. In turn, he is a very good caricaturist of the disabled children in his special school. At times, when I have wanted to sum up my thoughts about him, I found that my mind was, for a while, a blank; I took this to be mainly the result of projections into me of his supposed brain-damaged state. He too can be taken over by this identity, and needs to be rescued from it.

At three and a half, Samuel did begin to talk, and gradually became so active and demanded so much attention that his mother eventually sought help for him. How this came about is uncertain. I find Money-Kyrle's formulation helpful: 'If, as I suppose, there is an innate preconception of such an object (good breast), and if no mothering that keeps a child alive is so bad that it fails to provide some realisation of it, the concept of the good breast must always at least begin to form, (Money-Kyrle 1971, p. 444) – but, it might be added, with great difficulty and confusion. In addition to preconceptions of a good object which have survived adverse circumstances, constitutional factors may be important: Samuel's capacity for love and responsiveness were not destroyed by his difficult beginnings. What struck me most forcibly when I met him was the affection, concern and love that he aroused in all those involved with him, including myself. This does not of course explain why his development suddenly accelerated: not enough is known of his history for us to do more than speculate about whether one of his nannies was particularly important for him, or whether some other change in circumstances or shift in family dynamics gave him courage.

Samuel has been assessed by the special school he attends as functioning about two and a half years below his chronological age. When he was first referred, he could not read or spell his own name, and he had speech difficulties for which he received regular speech therapy. I certainly found Samuel's talk hard to understand when I first met him. It was disjointed, his pronunciation odd and the syntax of his sentences erratic. It was also evident that he lost his linguistic grip in a state of rage or confusion. It remains unclear how far these difficulties are primarily emotional in origin, and how far of biological character. Samuel goes to an excellent school, essential for his needs; but he is continually in the company of other disturbed children, open to their projections of craziness as they are to his.

Samuel's first period of therapy ended because his therapist was pregnant. He stopped on the understanding that therapy would be resumed with 'another lady'. His violence towards his pregnant therapist was enormous towards the end. In addition to the conflicts of Samuel's internal world there was another, external factor exacerbating this already difficult situation. This was that his mother, then just over forty, had recently had an abortion at her husband's wish. These tragic events were not known at the time, but with hindsight they made some sense of Samuel's repeated enactment in his sessions of the killing of babies. These primitive eruptions of violence have not recurred in his therapy with me.

Reflecting upon how Samuel first struck me, I have wondered about a diagnosis. Here was a child who had not talked until he was three-and-a-half years old, and had had very traumatic experiences as a neonate and young infant. Was I working with a previously autistic patient in a post-autistic state, or a basically paranoid-schizoid psychotic little boy? Certainly some of Samuel's behaviour in therapy is characteristically autistic. For example, his wrapping himself up sensuously in his own voice as a protective cocoon, his intolerance of gaps or of any difference between himself and me, his wish to remain in a shell, his distressing terror of falling, of dying and spilling, are well-known characteristics of autistic children as described especially in the work of Tustin (1981). I have also found particularly cogent Klein's paper (Klein, S., 1980), in which he argues that 'behind the neurotic aspect of the patient's personality there lies hidden a psychotic problem.' Perhaps the best available formulation is that Samuel uses autistic manoeuvres to protect himself from psychotic illness, in particular from his fear of dying and disintegration.

Burping and Burp Music

The period of Samuel's therapy on which I shall focus is one in which he was preoccupied with the fear of ghosts. During this period, he began to produce prolonged outbursts of burping and a burp 'voice'. Samuel is capable of burping loudly or softly up and down the scale for up to twenty minutes. He generally begins to burp at moments of anxiety or frustration. He appears to lose himself in the physical pleasure of burping: this is visible in his expression. He says 'I like it.' When I ask him what it makes him feel like, he will say, when he is able to answer, 'My tummy feels empty, so I burp. I like it.' He looks satisfied at these moments.

It is possible that his burping, as distinct from his burp voice, resembles infantile rumination 'the active bringing into the mouth of swallowed food which has already reached the stomach and which may have started to undergo the process of digestion' (Gaddini and Gaddini, 1959). 'The food may be partially re-swallowed and partially lost, with serious consequences for the infant's nutrition. Unlike regurgitation, where the food runs out of the infant's mouth without any effort, in rumination there are complex and purposeful preparatory movements, particularly of the tongue and of the additional muscles. In some cases the hard palate is stimulated by fingers in the mouth. When the efforts become successful and the milk appears in the back of the pharynx, *the child's face is pervaded by an ecstatic expression*' (p.166). At such moments of providing his own gratification, Samuel obviously cannot take in nourishment from an outside source.

The study by Gaddini and Gaddini established a linkage between rumination (which they call 'the earliest perversion') and very difficult experiences of early feeding. They write of the mothers of ruminating infants: 'the most outstanding feature of (their) personalities seemed to be their insecurity, their disturbed object relations, their profound anxiety, their death fears, their ambivalence towards their babies and, in general, their marked inadequacy when faced with the demands of the feminine role' (p.177). Rumination is deemed to be a psycho-physical defensive syndrome in which the child withdraws his interest from the environment and focuses it upon the sensations deriving from his own body.

The sensuous satisfaction that Samuel has discovered in burping is, I think, analogous to that of the needy ruminating baby: it is a refuge particularly from his persecutory fears of ghosts, about whom I gradually came to hear. He has said explicitly that it protects him from feelings of emptiness. In addition, as with the nonsense talk he sometimes produces, the non-stop character of his burping can block communication with me. Outside the sessions, he finds in it an evidently erotic pleasure: he describes feeling happy when he burps into the ear of a little girl at school ('She likes it') and she burps into his ('I like it'). But the primary purpose of the burping seems to be the psychophysical feeling of satisfaction independent of anyone else; he can feel full through his repeated re-processing of his in-drawn breath (see Rhode 1994). It is uncertain how far he also burps to evacuate unpleasant things.

His burp 'voice', on the other hand, is deployed to talk about the ghosts who terrify him. This seems intended to deflect the murderous ghost away from Samuel, whose own recognisable voice would present him as a sitting target. He can also twist his capacity for burp talk to perverse ends, as when he gives virtuoso burp-song imitations of Michael Jackson, which increases the obscene impact of his caricatures.

Ghosts

The ghosts in Samuel's inner world function in a complex way. I shall give extracts from six sessions, including those in which the ghosts first appeared, before discussing their meaning. For some time it was obvious that the clinic was felt literally and tangibly to be haunted by extremely virulent ghosts, in which he had a quite delusional and hallucinatory belief.

> I. Samuel drew a face, with lots of legs coming from it and several eyes in the centre. He said 'It's an octopus.' He paused and looked at it. I said, as I looked at the eyes, 'I wonder, is it a ghost?' Samuel retorted, rather angrily 'No it is *not* a ghost. It's rubbish. Nothing'. He scratched it out. He added 'I must fold it up', and did so. I said that perhaps he was trying to hide the ghost and trick me (or the ghost?), and spoke also of how very frightening the ghost seemed to be. Samuel got angrier: 'Don't talk about ghosts. I don't want you to. Shut up.' I thought of how angry he gets when I talk about baby Samuel, and asked why he didn't like me talking about ghosts? Did he feel I was treating him like a baby? 'Yes', he

answered. I said, in the face of much resistance, 'Lots of children find ghosts very frightening, and I think you do.' Samuel was swearing. I asked if he had heard what I had said. 'No', he said: 'what?' I repeated that children were often very frightened about ghosts and what they thought ghosts could do. Samuel said, in a very heartfelt tone 'How do you know?' This allowed me to ask him more about what the ghosts wanted to do to him that was so frightening. He said 'They want to come and eat me up.' He stood up, holding his hand in front of him and said 'Woooo'; it sounded very ghostly, and he scrabbled with his hands trying to grab me. I said he had shown me how very frightening these ghosts were. He went on to say that they might have one eye – or four, six or ten. 'They say, "I'll catch you and kill you." '

II. Samuel began to cut his name from a picture and to sellotape the surface over his name. I said that I remembered his doing this last Thursday, and that I remembered what he had told me. Samuel said 'Yes: so the ghost can't see it and get it.' I was struck by how concretely he identified his written name with himself. Samuel said 'It's ten a.m.: the ghost is coming'. He was still sellotaping; possibly so that there should be no gap for the ghost to get through. I asked what the ghost would do. He answered 'Eat it up'. I said that he sounded worried about what the ghost would do to *him*, not to his name. He agreed 'Yes, it might like my inside and eat it.' I talked about what a very greedy, absolutely dreadful ghost it seemed to be. He said 'Yes. It eats lots of children.' He then put his sellotaped name in his box where the ghost, he said, couldn't get it. I interpreted this as an attempt to divert the ghost; he said 'Shut up. Idiot.' Towards the end of the session he drew a picture of what he said was himself, then scribbled it out, so the ghost wouldn't see.

He put his things away, and said 'The ghost is coming.' He then knocked out the ghost, and said 'I've killed him.' It was time to stop. Samuel asked if he could say just one swearword: he said 'Motherfucker, arsehole, shit, bullshit.' I felt as though these words were intended to attack the ghost. He then said 'He can't come after me', and added 'I come Wednesday, at 4:30.'

III. Some way into the session, Samuel said, sounding surprised 'I haven't brought my cars today. Perhaps on Thursday. I forgot them.' When I commented on his forgetting, Samuel said 'I don't know why'. I said 'Perhaps you felt you didn't need them?' He said 'I do.' When I asked why, he said 'To keep me safe from the ghost.'

He then began drawing, saying 'It's an ice-cream cone. A chocolate ice-cream.' He coloured it brown. We looked at his drawing. I asked Samuel about the ice-cream (a little round ice, poised on the edge of the cone), saying that it looked as though it might fall off. Samuel said 'Don't worry.' He then began to colour it all black 'so that the ghost can't see.' I talked about how there seemed to be ghosts everywhere to spoil things, how dangerous it felt, how unsure he was that I could stop them, and how

226

frightening it was. Later in the session Samuel struggled to spell his name, eventually succeeding when he copied it from the name-tape inside his school cap. Then he asked how much longer we had: it was fifteen minutes. Samuel said 'I'm going to make a camp. What's the time? Ten p.m.'

He made his camp. This involved draping the table with his rug and putting the sofa cushions and his pillow under the table. He crawled in and pretended to go to sleep. Then he looked alarmed: his feet were protruding from one end. He asked me to help him move the little table. When I asked why, was it perhaps to protect his feet from the ghost? he answered 'Yes. The ghost might get them.'

He pretended to go to sleep. Then he said, 'I've eaten the pig and bacon, and I feel sick.' This sounded quite hallucinatory. He went on 'It's eating a cow (he now seemed to have switched from an identification with the ghost) and it's still hungry.' I commented on what a very frightening, and very, very greedy ghost he felt it was – always hungry. Samuel was pretending to sleep.

He said 'It's come'. There was a scuffle; then he said 'It's dead.' He sounded relieved. When I asked how it happened, Samuel replied 'The dog bit it and killed it.'

IV. About twenty minutes before the end of the session, Samuel packed up his things and made his camp. He got under the table, saying 'What time is it? It's two a.m., three a.m. (etc.). The ghost is coming.' Samuel told me the ghost was going to get him and eat him. The atmosphere was frightening. I talked about his conviction that there really was something that he called a ghost, that wanted to kill him. He was very anxious that no part of his body should protrude from under the table (which, as usual, was covered by his blanket).

Then he became the ghost. He said, in blood-thirsty tones 'I want to eat up Samuel and get him.' He lay down, pretending to go to sleep: he seemed to feel safe and said 'The ghost has gone.'

V. Samuel had again made a camp in the therapy room. He crawled in, curled up, and said 'It's two o'clock; three o'clock; the ghost is coming.' Then, in a lower voice, he said 'Where is that boy Samuel? I want that boy. I'm going to eat him.' He snapped his teeth and made munching sounds. Samuel cried out 'Help! Help!.' Then, in tones of relief he said, looking up at me 'I punched him on the nose.' He was unable to answer any of my questions about what had happened, simply repeating 'I punched him on the nose.'

He then burped loudly several times. I asked him what he felt the burps did to the ghost, and he replied 'They frighten him.' As Samuel was lying curled up, I asked him about his dreams at night. He looked puzzled and asked 'What's a dream?' I said we had talked about them before, and wondered why he didn't remember. He asked again 'What's a dream? I don't know.' I said 'It's at night, when you're asleep. You see pictures in a dream'. Samuel seemed to understand. 'Yes, sometimes. Yesterday I was in a forest. There were ghosts.' He gave a shiver of fear. 'I ran away.'

VI. Samuel had drawn a 'picture' consisting of much green colouring, and a small, black, filled-in circle. He said the green was a garden. 'That's all.' He could add no more. When I asked about the black bit and what he thought it was, he said, after some thought 'A baby.' When I asked him about the baby, he said 'It's dead. I don't like babies. They go mmmmm (a grizzling sound).' He wrote his name on the picture.

Discussion

There is no doubt about the malignity of Samuel's ghosts and the enormity of his terror. His ghost is not a disembodied spectre, or a cartoon ghost (though that does appear in some of his drawings). It is either a cannibalistic boy, with face, hands, legs, and body and a weapon; or a devouring animal (a dog or lion) intent on 'getting' Samuel, to kill and eat him. One feature for some time was that Samuel could defeat this ghost, or even kill it. But while he might kill a ghost in one session, another would inevitably appear for him to face in a later session. There was no end to the persecution.

Freud's discussion of the supernatural (*The Uncanny*, 1919) posited a direct link between the fear of the supernatural and the projection of inner feelings: 'The dread of something terrifying, mysterious and malevolent proceeding from a demonic or supernatural agency, such as the appearance of a ghost at midnight, is always the result of the projection into the outer world of unconscious (and terrifying) repressed wishes.'

Rivière (1936) gives a moving and disturbing description of these phenomena. She writes of the 'magic power of the undying persecutors who can never be exterminated – the ghosts ... As analysis proceeds, the persecutory projective defences (i.e. the ghosts), which are always interwoven with omnipotent control, weaken along with the latter, the analyst beginning to see the phantasies approximating to this nightmare of desolation assuming shape.'

Samuel's ghosts seem in part to function in the vengeful, persecutory mode of the paranoid-schizoid position, primarily representing the dead babies that he has killed off in fantasy and whose avenging return he fears. However, when he speaks of how many children the ghost has eaten (Extract II), we get a hint that the ghost is also his own baby self that is felt to have killed his mother's babies. (In Extract VI, he says that he 'dislikes' babies: he feels guilty and persecuted when they grizzle).

228

He attempts to deal with this murderousness by killing off the baby self that should be the basis of his developing personality (Klein 1946). The black dead baby in the green garden (Extract VI) is reminiscent of Tustin's black hole (Tustin 1966); it also illustrates the way Samuel escapes attack by hiding the part of him that could grow. Altamirano (1988) has described a ghost containing projections identified with a lost primary object.

Whatever position he occupies, Samuel clearly feels threatened with annihilation. Sometimes he fights the ghost; sometimes he attempts to deal with the terror it engenders by becoming it (Extract IV). Any symbolic, 'pretend' quality easily gets lost, as in the hallucinatory quality (Extract III); and the toy cars that protect Samuel from the ghost have the asymbolic status of autistic objects (Tustin 1981).

One might think of the ghosts as a personification of the 'deadly but hidden force which keeps the patient away from living and occasionally causes severe anxieties' of which Rosenfeld has written (1987, p. 107). This deathly force might be located in himself or elsewhere. At some level, he is indeed aware that the ghost is a murderous part of himself, and we have developed a shared language to enable us to talk about this. Although he is opposed to the ghost, and thus on the side of life, this can be difficult to maintain in the face of the suicidal despair which his mother has poignantly expressed in the last two years. I did not learn until late in his therapy that his mother is herself haunted by a terrifying ghost, so terrifying that she keeps the light on at night if she is alone. This is the ghost of the relative who she says tried to kill her at birth. In a sense, the shared terror of the ghost has been a powerful, though deathly, bond between mother and child, one which therapy has helped to loosen.

Concluding Remarks

Samuel's very considerable progress in the course of therapy, both educationally and socially, was emphasised by his mother and his teacher. Samuel's mother said, with warm pleasure and understandable relief 'He talks to me now. We have real conversations.'

I was initially impressed by the affection, concern and love that Samuel evoked in all those concerned with his care. As psychotherapy proceeded it emerged clearly that a healthily loving, creative core is fundamental to his personality. He is eager for help. As he put it, in his very first words to me after a Christmas break 'I am hungry. Why were the holidays so long?' He could increasingly wake up from his ghostly nightmares and enter into life.

11

Going to Pieces

Autistic and Schizoid Solutions

Maria Rhode

In this chapter, I shall consider material from three children who experienced separateness as catastrophic fragmentation. Daniel exhibited marked autistic features, including echolalia, to which he turned for protection from a witch felt to be causing his psychotic terrors. Miguel reacted to similar experiences of fragmentation by attacking the outside world; the survival of firm boundaries encouraged him to produce articulate speech. Jonathan attacked the world like Miguel, but then retreated to autistic rituals to protect himself from the consequences. I shall discuss their material in terms of the interaction of differing experiences of fragmentation and of sensation-dominated autistic processes.

Daniel: autism as a protection against psychosis

This ten-year-old boy made very rapid progress in a year of once-weekly psychotherapy. I have few details of his early life, except that he was reported not to be developing normally at the age of two. He was hospitalised with a life-threatening illness at three, but recovered completely. Later, investigations for fragile X-chromosome proved negative. He was the middle of three children. His mother was herself from a deprived background. She rejected contact with professionals, by whom she felt criticised. Looking after herself and the children sounded like a desperate struggle. She had no supportive partner and she was said to suffer from recurrent episodes of rage and despair in which she could become violent. Daniel was taken into care at the age of six, and placed at a school for children with severe learning difficulties. His mother tried to keep in touch with him, but often failed to turn up as

231

arranged. Contact with her during his hospitalisation is likely to have been unpredictable.

Daniel was referred for an assessment by his teachers, who had recognised that he displayed all the symptoms on the *Is This Autism?* checklist. He avoided eye contact; his speech was echolalic; any change or interference provoked a tantrum in which he would tear his clothes or the wallpaper and bite his hand, which was badly scarred. Toilet-training was incomplete, though this had greatly improved since his residential placement. He was interested in shapes and lego construction, and obsessively drew houses, though he could not draw a person. He inspired enormous affection in his teachers, as he has in me, and they brought him to therapy reliably, often in their own time.

Assessment: the missing half

His assessment sessions with me meant moving from the clinical psychologist's room where we had all met together with his teacher and respite worker. He made a point of referring to 'New Room', and showing that he remembered where the old room was. Among the doll's house furniture was a dresser with a mirror, and he held it up against the left side of his face. He then sucked his left thumb and looked over his right shoulder with a haunted expression. This was to become a familiar sequence, and I spoke to him about needing his thumb in his mouth to be sure that he had a right cheek and a left cheek, a right eye and a left eye. Theoretically, this links with Frances Tustin's description of autistic children's catastrophic experience of a hole in the mouth (Tustin 1966). She and Geneviève Haag (Tustin 1981; Haag 1985) have described the experience of feeling split down the middle of the body when the child realises his separateness from the mother.

At the end of each session, Daniel said in a lifeless voice 'New Room next week.' Each week the session would start with an inventory of New Room, in a voice that was increasingly lively and hopeful: he could make 'green curtains' and 'three grey radiators' sound like a celebration. He was obviously remembering from week to week, and he would pause after linking back to previous material to give me a chance to show that I remembered too. The theme of a missing half was developed in terms of the letters W and V. In the very first session when we were all together, he had arranged pencils in a W shape. He often referred to 'Two Ladies in London': now that he was with only one lady, he made V shapes – half-Ws – instead.

232

11. Going to Pieces

He remained haunted by something in the corner; after the second session, he looked into a recess in the passage and said 'Monster'. If things became too frightening in the room, he would say suddenly, 'Go Toilet.' This might happen three or four times in a session. I would have to guess from minimal indications what was bothering him, and often I did not know. However, if I could guess, he became much more explicit. In the second session, he half muttered, half sang something that was largely incomprehensible, but out of which emerged the name, Cruella deVille. I picked up on the horrible, cruel lady who tried to kill puppies to steal their skins for herself, and how hard it was to believe that I would not be like that. His speech became much clearer, and he sang 'Cruella deVille, Cruella deVille' quite distinctly – with one 'Daniella deVille' half hidden amongst the Cruellas.

This illustrates the psychotic terror from which Daniel was protecting himself by his autistic cutting of links with real, separate people. The juxtaposition of Cruella deVille and Daniella deVille shows his fear that his own destructive feelings had invaded the outside world, and were the cause of a separation which he experienced as a flaying. (Before the Christmas break, he was to say 'Poor mouth. Poor skin.') When he felt that I could understand some of this, his words emerged more clearly out of an undifferentiated humming; when I failed to understand, his autistic withdrawal intensified. Veleda Cecchi (1990) has described how a healthy, bossy two-and-a-half-year-old girl, very possessive of her father and jealous of her mother's pregnancy, reacted with a total autistic shutdown to the experience of seeing her parents 'disappeared' by South American secret police in the middle of the night. Cecchi proposed the formulation that the traumatic event in external reality was felt to confirm the omnipotence of the child's worst phantasies.[1] This formulation would fit the situation which I suspect was true of Daniel, in which a core of good experience was unpredictably invaded by terror.

An Early Session: the monster in the corner

Daniel's third treatment session will serve to illustrate the degree to which he felt threatened by the emergence of the monster.[2]

> Daniel arrived twenty minutes late: the taxi had failed to turn up. He held my hand going along the corridor, and said 'Two ladies.' I said, yes, two ladies had brought him, (a teacher was introducing a new escort) and

233

there were two ladies here: Mrs Rhode and Dr S (the clinical psychologist). He said the usual things on the way to the room and inside it: 'Up the stairs – New Room – green curtains – three grey radiators.' I said, 'Daniel's pleased to be back – pleased to find the room the way it was last week.' He went to the sink, ran water over his sponge and sucked it for some time, with an atmosphere of happy absorption; then looked sideways over his shoulder with a look of terror. I said he was frightened of the nasty thing, and straightaway thought that this was true but unhelpfully put.[3] My misgivings were justified: he immediately said 'Toilet.' He spent a long time in the toilet, and shrank away from my hand when he came out: I thought he felt the nasty thing was in me. Back in the room, he sniffed, and I said the room was not to have any bad smells in it; how important it was for the toilet to be there – important for keeping things safe.

He calmed down, and again named parts of the room, with me repeating the words after him. Then he lay on the couch with his left thumb in his mouth and the fingers pressing on his eyeball, and carried on looking round the room and naming things. I said he felt safe with his thumb in his mouth, that things were the same, the way they were last time. He said 'Two ladies in London', and I said he held tight to the thought of the two ladies in London in the week between sessions, or when the taxi was late. He got up, went back to the sink and drank from the cup; the cup trembled and he looked over his shoulder. I spoke about needing to take great care not to be surprised, to keep safe.

There was a noise as though something were knocking against the window, and he startled. (For a long time, if someone came towards him through a doorway, he would hold his hands over his ears – compare Chapter 8.) I talked again about holding onto the Two Ladies in London when he wasn't with me, and introduced the idea of a holiday chart that he could refer to over the Christmas break. At first he appeared to take no notice, but presently came over to the box and said 'Fence – F for Farm Fence'. He fitted the fences together to make an open oblong enclosure. I said he was putting things together, and that the very first time he came there were not enough fences to close a space, so Mrs Rhode used the ruler and Daniel did too – but now there were more fences. He responded by slotting the last bit of fencing into place to make an enclosure, but then looked over his shoulder and everything came apart. I said 'Something happens to break things up.'

He said 'Two ladies', and held two bits of fence together as though they were mirror images. I said 'Two bits of fence, like two ladies. When we're together like this, Daniel feels he's all together, no gaps.' He pulled the bits of fence apart; I talked about him and me not together. He made a long L-shaped structure of two parallel lines of fencing, open at the top. Then he stretched over it on the floor, head down, hands up above his head on either side, bottom a bit in the air. It looked as though the fences were coming from his mouth, so I said it was something to do with Daniel's body, it looked a bit like a tongue. He re-arranged it so that there

234

were two open ends furthest away from him, one on either side. I said the two ends looked like his two extended hands; that he did have two hands, and two arms, but maybe when he and I were not together it was hard to believe that all his bits were there, that things wouldn't come apart or fall out.

He got out his pencil sharpener and scissors, and began to sharpen pencils. I gave him the bin, and said that was the right place to put the bits so that they wouldn't get scattered and lost. He then spontaneously looked at the holiday chart, and I was amazed to see that he was sharpening a pencil that was blue, like the blue crosses I had used to indicate missed sessions, and that he was also holding a pencil that was red like the circles with which I had marked sessions when he came. He said 'Crosses; circles; noughts and crosses!'. I talked about the two Fridays when we would not be together, and how the sessions would start again after that. He took out the scissors, and said 'V for violin.' I agreed the scissors looked like a V. He snipped at his left sleeve, then carefully approached his right thumb with the scissors, and I said when we were not together, he needed to be sure the scissors wouldn't come out and snip something, like his sleeve or his thumb or his tongue, which was poking out slightly. Though I had taken care about phrasing this, he threw the scissors away quickly, and I said 'Back in the box.' He then used the ruler to span the open box, poking his tongue out. He had once talked about a bridge while poking his tongue out, so I said, 'Yes, that was what we used for joining up the fence, and it does make a bridge.' He walked his fingers across the 'bridge', which slipped and fell into the box. The first time he took this in his stride; the next time he panicked and bit his hand, and I said, 'You needed something to hold onto.' We tried again with the bridge, with me providing a vocal accompaniment for the falling: 'Oooohh, down into the box' (compare Stern, 1985, p. 140). This was better, but he was still very anxious, so I said I would hold the ruler. He walked his fingers over it, and I said 'Over the bridge.' He put his hand beneath the ruler, saying 'Under the bridge': this felt calm and exploratory. He opened the dolls' house and tried to put in the dresser with the mirror, but it did not fit and he put it in the garage. It was the end of the time, and he said 'New Room next week'.

This early session points up the parallel between the experience of losing half of his body along with one of the Two Ladies, and the great gulf between good and bad, which Daniel is still desperate to keep apart. I could understand the degree of his urgency when I witnessed what happened when the monster did take over. We once returned to the waiting room 15 seconds before Daniel's teacher, whom he was expecting to find there. He tore himself away from me, shouting 'let go' as though I might rip his arm off. In his third term, the taxi was late again. He arrived completely beside himself, crying and shaking and screaming 'I want a sweet', and refused to come with me. I asked his teacher to bring him, and he settled once he saw the familiar room. After half an hour's work, he suddenly looked up at me and said 'Mrs Rhode', as though recognising me after a bad dream.

The Survival of the Setting

With the repeated demonstration that I came back after holidays breaks, Daniel's dependence on the toilet lessened. He became able to express hostility directly, and I could take this up in ways that were not possible in the early session I have described.

> Before his second holiday, he made a lady doll fall off the ruler bridge. I said that I was supposed to know what it felt like. He made the toy crocodile bite his finger, then sellotaped the lady doll and two little girl dolls to the ruler, and made the crocodile bite their feet. Again, I said that they were supposed to see what it felt like (and I could suddenly understand why he had once said 'crocodile' when he took his shoes and socks off).

He came back from this holiday very withdrawn, but he did not ask for the lavatory during the sessions. With some encouragement he has been able to maintain this achievement. My return despite the explicit expression of Daniel's resentment had demonstrated that he did not need to protect me or the room by using the lavatory as the place to put dangerous feelings.

A Sense of Identity

Early in treatment, Daniel showed that he possessed the concept of a father's helpful role in preventing an entangled relationship between mother and child. He had got his hand tightly tied up in sellotape, and as he cut it away, he said 'Daddy.' Similarly, it strengthened him when adults came together cooperatively. On his birthday, his key worker in the home were he lived during holidays organised a party attended by his schoolteacher. I had not known that it was his birthday, but I was struck in the session by how ordinary and sane he looked. Afterwards, in the waiting room, he excitedly asked his key worker, 'When is Mrs S (his teacher) coming?' and I realised with a shock that he was speaking in sentences. The following week, when I made a point of talking about his birthday, he said proudly 'Ten years old'. He then suddenly realised that his name was written on his box, and he read it over and over: 'Daniel Mackay. New Box. Daniel Mackay.'

This realisation of his identity ushered in a term's spurt in development. At first he related to an external figure in terms of a baby's mouth competing for the nipple with the breast or bottle. This model was rapidly superseded by that of two separate people who could move apart and come together, and finally by the concept of a three-party relationship.

Mouth and Breast in Competition

Daniel brought along to his session a packet of crisps and a little bottle of lemonade that his escort had bought him. He tapped on the closed lid of the bottle, emphasising its shutness. When he unscrewed the lid and drank, a plastic ring remained on the neck of the bottle. He passed this back and forth between the bottle and his mouth. When it was on the neck of the bottle, he showed me that his empty mouth was open in the shape of a hole. When the ring was in his mouth, he looked at the bottle fearfully, as though expecting attack. Once all the lemonade was gone, he threw the bottle in the bin and shrank away from it.

I felt that he was persecuted by a Cruella deVille-bottle with whom his mouth was competing for the nipple-skin that he felt shut him out. This links with Tustin's patient David, who built up his 'identity' by snipping bits off his father (Tustin 1972). Tustin emphasises the autistic child's life-and-death struggle with the parental figure over who shall possess the 'hard extra bit' that is felt to permit survival. Daniel's material shows how anything he gained was felt to be at the expense of someone who would then attack him. The validation of his separate identity by adults who worked together was vital in disproving this fear.

Twos and Threes

Not long after, Daniel experimented with making the two window blinds come and go, together and separately, by pulling on the cords. This was accompanied by tapping on many different surfaces to make different kinds of noises. I imitated the tapping, and talked about sounds that were different, and people who were different, and how important it was to feel he could make me come back though we were not the same. He tapped on the window sill, then on the outside ledge. I said that these sounds were different, that inside and outside the window were different. He held one arm outside the window, and tried to touch it through the glass with his other hand. I said that the glass of the window got in the way so that he could not touch his arm; but that he could see and feel it,

237

so it was not lost. He responded with emphatic biting, which it was now possible to take up as intended for me when a barrier (the glass) came between us.

Following this he moved on to three-part relationships, tapping and clicking his tongue in threes, emphasising the three syllables of 'Ta-vi-stock', cutting out triangles. He showed his preoccupation with the hidden insides of things, the third dimension (Meltzer et al. 1975), as well as with the strength of links – links between his box and the lid, between the back and the seat of chairs. In keeping with this, the monster became increasingly identified with my husband (Britton, 1989). Daniel pointedly called me *Miss* Rhode, and surveyed the room 'looking for clues', as he called it.

From the beginning of Daniel's treatment, I heard encouraging reports of his social and academic progress. First his obsessive need for control diminished: he could join in a wider range of activities without going to pieces or fearing that other children would attack him. Instead of obsessively drawing houses, he began to draw a complete person lying on a bed, as he himself often did in his sessions. After some two terms, I heard that, for the first time in his life, he was making friends with other children; also that he had learned to read and had finished his first book.[4]

Anyone who had not known him previously would at this stage have described his behaviour during sessions as psychotic rather than autistic. He still needed to control me to stop me from coming too close ('Sit in the chair please'); but when I talked about this in terms of his fear that I might have become a bad person, he could allow me to move without having a panic attack. However, he still responded echolalically to my greeting at the beginning of a session, before he had had a chance to test out whether I had become the monster. Echolalia sometimes reappeared when he left, as well, if the session had been frightening, but he could say goodbye in his own voice if some of his anxiety has been resolved. In other words, the times when he still resorted to the autistic device of equating himself with me were those times when he was frightened that I had become the monster.

Discussion

Each step of Daniel's rapid progress had to be underpinned by work on the bodily level of the early session I have presented. I would suggest that his experience of separateness as meaning the loss of half of his body fed into the width of the emotional split between good and bad as well as constituting the fate threatened by Cruella deVille. His own experience of being cut in half mirrored the condition of the Two Ladies when one of them was gone, when a W (double-you) was bisected to form a V. The moment in the third session when he put the two fences together, saying 'Two Ladies', illustrates his ability to allow the Two Ladies to enjoy bodily completeness together even when he felt deprived of it. This links with his having the concept of a good Daddy who prevents entanglement. (Unlike Alex Dubinsky's Paul, who needed years of work first, Daniel had this concept from the beginning of treatment.) The related affection he inspired in adults is a good prognostic indication, as Boston and Szur (1983) have pointed out with regard to deprived children. In the necessary split (Klein 1946) between idealised and persecutory objects, it was the ideal object that Daniel saw in the outside world, though at the beginning of treatment he could maintain it only by means of rigid control. When this broke down, he was faced with the monster – the amalgam of a bad external figure and a bad part of himself. I have suggested that he experienced frightening events as proof that his omnipotent destructiveness was uncontainable (Klein 1952; Cecchi 1990). In this he resembled those autistic children described by Meltzer et al. (1975) who are overwhelmed by premature depressive concerns. This was gradually modified by the survival of the therapist and the setting: he could then acknowledge his impulse to bite. I have described his attempts to protect himself by an autistic severing of the link with external reality: for instance by reverting to echolalia when a bad figure threatened, or by seeking refuge, in his third session, in the sensations provided by his thumb in his mouth and the pressure of his fingers on his eye.

Miguel: the assertion of mastery

Not all children react to the experience of bodily fragmentation by attempting to preserve an ideal figure. Miguel was referred at the age of eight for complete ineducability, the absence of communicative language and the habit of attacking other children. He also attacked his mother at any separation or reunion, kicking, biting, spitting and pulling her hair. He had a phobia of dogs which severely limited him. His developmental age was assessed at three and a half years.

Miguel had an older sister who was doing well, but he was born after his mother suffered a series of miscarriages which themselves followed her father's death. When Miguel was a baby, she could hardly pick him up for fear of damaging him. Her worst fears were realised when all his milestones were noticeably delayed, particularly his speech. It was not clear to me how far he spoke properly in his mother-tongue. When I saw him, he accompanied his play by indistinct jumbles of 'words' in an American accent, giving the impression that he was quoting from a video.

He related to me in three distinct ways. Mostly he shut me out by means of his stream of 'words', ignoring anything I said about his play. This consisted of repetitive sequences in which a mother and father tried in vain to protect a baby, who was thrown up into the air, dropped through vast distances, and threatened with being devoured by various wild animals. The worst was the crocodile, who attacked the parents as well as the baby. The only recognisable words consisted of the various family members reassuring each other – 'I'm OK – I'm OK – You OK?' – immediately followed by further disastrous attacks – a poignant echo perhaps of his mother's early fears (cf. Sherwin-White, this volume). Miguel derived obvious satisfaction when the parents suffered the same terrible experiences as the baby. His despair about there being any adult who could curb the dangerous animals – with which his bad self was identified – was equally obvious.

When he was not obliterating me, he began to attack me physically in the ways he attacked his mother: this became more focused around breaks in the treatment. It was often difficult to restrain him physically, though clearly it was vital that I should be able to do so. At the same time, I talked about the despair behind these attacks: they felt like a desperate bid to make an impression, and I said how important it was that I should understand how angry he felt. The third mode of relating was one in which he seemed overcome by grief and the fear of loss, and would bury his head in my lap muttering 'sorry, sorry'. When I spoke about increasing his sessions, he looked at me with amazement, as though he could not believe that I would want to see him more frequently.

Miguel was a passionate and wilful child who resented and attacked any limits. Like the boy described by Klein (1932 p. 127), he felt his good baby self (and his good parents) to be endangered by his oral sadism represented by the crocodile. He responded with relief when I could restrain him physically, and when it became clear that the room was strong enough to withstand him. On one occasion, when he saw he could not force me to open a cupboard, he produced a complete, clear sentence: 'I want you to open it.'

Like another patient, who once said 'I used to use anger as a kind of petrol', Miguel sometimes reacted destructively as an alternative to enduring extreme distress and helplessness (compare Alex Dubinsky's Paul, who reacted with delusions of omnipotence). During a session when I introduced a holiday chart, he responded at first by tearing it in half, with every appearance of distress. However, he quickly moved on from the experience of feeling ripped in two: eyes flashing with anger, he tore each half of the sheet of paper into minute bits. This schizoid fragmentation seemed a way of mastering being torn in half.

Thus, Miguel suffered many of the same terrors as Daniel – of falling as well as being torn in two – but he attempted to cope by very different means. Instead of seeking to preserve an ideal object that was under his control, he asserted his mastery: anyone who made him feel torn in two would be torn into tiny fragments. Like Daniel, he feared that no good person could contain him or survive his attacks, but this fear often drove him to re-double them (Klein 1961).[5] Evidence of an enduring, though frustrating, boundary elicited articulate speech. However, he gave the impression of being unwilling, as well as unable, to tolerate such a boundary. This perverse twist of the quality of assertiveness had serious consequences for his development.[6]

Jonathan: fragmentation, persecution and mindlessness

This seven-year-old boy came to treatment with many autistic features, including instances of echolalia interspersing jumbled-up 'words'. He communicated vividly terrors of falling and of losing his head, limbs, or body contents. After some time in therapy, when his language had improved, he pointed to different parts of the room and said 'There is my head ... there is my penis'. On one occasion he quietly fingered his tongue and cheeks with an absent expression, and I said that perhaps he was feeling bits of his face to make sure they were still there. 'You wake up in the night', he answered, 'and bits of you are gone, you can't see them. Then you go to the mirror and you see they're all there, but the mirror tricks you.'

I understood this tricky mirror as meaning that he felt tricked by me: that I was not adequately taking in and reflecting his experience of fragmentation. Jonathan often attributed any such failings on my part to my supposed preoccupation with other children. For some time he had a grievance against a television character whom he associated with his elder brother. He hated this character for being 'inside' the television; just as he sometimes imagined that privileged children literally lived inside me and looked out through my eyes. Like Miguel who visited the baby doll's sufferings on the parents, Jonathan felt that the television character should have a taste of his own fears:

> He told me how he tried to get inside the television to cut this other boy's head off. The boy retaliated, and came out of the television and attacked Jonathan, who in self-defence cut him into ever smaller pieces. These tiny pieces continued to pursue him: finally they united around his throat and choked him (Jonathan had in fact suffered from early breathing difficulties).

One solution to this problem was to watch television in a mindless way, thus evading any frustrating limits that might lead to aggression and its frightening consequences. His brother, he said enviously, watched so much television that he 'got square eyes' – that is, he was allowed to feel that his eyes were the same as the square television screen he was watching.

In a similar incident from the same period of therapy,

> Jonathan threatened to pull hairs out of my face; next reminded me of a story about a witch pulling out a little boy's hair. He then turned away from me, stared blankly ahead and twiddled his own hair.

If I had not known the context, I might have seen this as a typical, meaningless autistic mannerism. As it was, I felt he was retreating from a relationship with me that felt like a vicious circle of projection and attack. Twiddling provided him with a physical sensation in which he could lose himself, and at the same time reassured him that the threatened hair – his and mine at the same time – was still in place.[7]

Conclusions

Autistic modes and more complex mental structures are currently a topic of debate. Elsewhere in this volume, Geneviève Haag describes the 'choice' between obsessional, perverse and schizophrenic pathways facing children emerging from autistic withdrawal. Meltzer (1975), discussing an autistic patient treated by Isca Wittenberg (1975), has suggested that the emergence of a narcissistic organisation after some time in therapy was a function of the improvement and strengthening brought about by the treatment.

Tustin (1990, 1994) has referred to some children who employ autistic processes to protect themselves against a schizophrenic state, which is revealed in therapy after the autism has been ameliorated. She

11. Going to Pieces

thought of the 'autistic features' encountered to a greater or lesser degree in many children who do not have Kanner's Syndrome as being residues of an autistic mode of being that had been modified or interfered with, and that had not been integrated into the rest of the personality (Tustin 1994).

Of the children I have discussed, Miguel was not autistic, but showed anxieties characteristic of autistic spectrum disorders. His despair about loss and the way he wrapped himself up in repetitive 'stories' that shut me out were also typical of such conditions (Tustin, 1981; Meltzer et al., 1975). His third mode of relating, with its determined, masterful attacks, is more characteristic of schizoid states.[8] As well as being more obviously destructive, it implied the possible existence of a person who might contain him.[9] Jonathan's material illustrated a similar reaction when he attacked the boy in the television. When attack and counter-attack led to an unbearably threatening world, he sought refuge in autistic rituals. Daniel, who showed all the symptoms on the *Is this Autism?* checklist, and who was developing abnormally at the age of two,[10] turned to autistic coping mechanisms when he feared that his own bad self uncontainably invaded the outside world, leaving him vulnerable to psychotic terrors. When he felt understood, which implied the existence of a person who would not be swamped by his anxieties, he could communicate directly. This capacity came and went depending on his experience of me.

Such observations illustrating the oscillation and interplay between autistic and schizoid modes raise issues of reliable diagnosis and organically based symptomatology. While these are beyond the scope of this discussion, it is important to stress that the present theoretical framework in no way contradicts the possibility of organic predisposition, particularly since recent research indicates that brain functions can be modified by psychological interventions (e.g. Perry 1995). At this very detailed level of work, and in considering prognosis, it may be more useful to think in terms of the feeling response elicited by the child and the balance between various ways of coping than in terms of immutable descriptive categories.

Notes

[1] This links back to Freud's statement (1926) that, in trauma, 'external and internal, real and instinctual dangers converge', a point elaborated by Garland (1991) and by Pynoos (1996).

[2] This material was presented at the Autism Conference held at the Tavistock Clinic, 10-13 July 1996.

[3] Alvarez (1992) has emphasised the need for extremely careful phrasing: a child like Daniel could mistakenly feel that I was summoning the nasty thing, rather than helping him with his fear by naming it.

[4] Daniel's material illustrates the emotional foundations of his cognitive development. IQ tests administered to children functioning at this level rely heavily on such skills as being able to draw a person: it is clear why Daniel could not do this, and how this changed in therapy. The conceptual opposites of 'over' and 'under' the bridge became available in the third session, when work on the fear of falling made it possible to think about differences; Daniel's acquisition of arithmetical skills paralleled the work during his third term on ones, twos and threes.

[5] S. Klein (1974) points out that a manic patient retained 'sufficient vitality to be in touch with reality and hence to be able to attack it, whenever it aroused painful feelings.' He contrasts this with the 'withdrawn, autistic type of personality which gives up in apathy and despair and denies psychic and external reality completely.'

[6] Miguel's parents moved away when I had seen him for only three months, so I do not know how he developed in the long term.

[7] Alvarez (1992) has shown how seemingly meaningless autistic rituals often turn out to have meaning when they are carefully analysed. See also Briggs, this volume.

[8] Spensley (1995) has suggested that schizoid reactions can serve to ward off the fear of the autistic 'hole'. This would link with Freud's suggestion (1911) that Schreber's florid psychotic symptoms were his attempt to rebuild his shattered world.

[9] Interestingly, when Miguel was placed on Ritalin for a while, his aggression disappeared and he was left in a state of despair which his school found so intolerable that the medication was discontinued. It is regrettable that this occurred before I saw him, so that there was no opportunity for psychotherapy and Ritalin to work together.

[10] This is necessary if a child is to be considered autistic according to the criteria of DSM-IV.

12

Rigidity and Stability in a Psychotic Patient

Some Thoughts about Obstacles to Facing Reality in Psychotherapy

Margaret Rustin

This chapter is an attempt to think about a particular kind of rigidity in a post-autistic patient who lives simultaneously in a psychotic private world and in the world of relationships and shared meanings. I worked with her for nine years and shall discuss the material of a session some months prior to the end of her therapy. In considering the meaning of our interchange I wish to distinguish between the changes that have been achieved and the ongoing obsessional ruminative power of the psychotic process. I shall try to consider these from two perspectives: the patient's continuing partial addiction to delusional defensive structures, which she experiences as protective, and the analyst's countertransference difficulties in facing the limitations of the work. Both of us needed to struggle with anxieties about facing reality; the reality of the approaching end of the treatment brought these into clearer focus.

I shall begin with some details of the patient's history. She is the first child of a middle-class couple and is now twenty two years old. She has a sister three years younger than herself. When I met her parents to explore the possibility of Holly beginning psychotherapy, they told me with the most intense outpouring of feelings about her early life. The pregnancy had gone well, and Mother was waiting with happy anticipation for the arrival of a much-wanted baby. This mood was massively disrupted by what seems to have been a traumatic experience of labour and child birth, when Mother felt overwhelmed by pain, and unsupported and criticised by medical and nursing staff.

After a very long labour, Holly was delivered by forceps and said to be at risk; the parents felt this was due to oxygen deficiency, but the details are not clear.

The baby was not given to Mother to hold but nursed initially in intensive care. Subsequently breast-feeding was established and continued for three months. The outstanding memories of the early months which Mother communicated were two – firstly, the sense that whatever she did for Holly, the baby cried. She could not satisfy or calm her and felt persecuted by the baby's distress. As in the hospital at the birth, she felt criticised and found wanting as a mother. The baby's misery was not something she could take in and bear, but something she felt hounded by. She told me, with startling and moving honesty, that there was something I needed to know from the start: 'You will never understand Holly unless you bear in mind that I hated her. I feel guilty about this, but I really did hate her'. She went on to describe a second crucial event which occurred when she showed the new baby to her own mother. Here I need to include some of the history of Mother's family of origin; she herself is the younger of two sisters. Her older sister, Jane, was a severely autistic child who began to deteriorate markedly at age twelve and has been institutionalised since then. Grandmother looked at the new baby and said 'Good heavens! It's Jane.' I do not know whether Holly did resemble Jane, but what this remark heralded was a difficult struggle between Mother and Grandmother over how to treat Holly, and it aroused acute terror in Mother that this baby would indeed have a similar history.

Holly cried less after breast-feeding was abandoned and found solace in playing on her own for hours at a time. She showed very little interest in her parents or anyone else. Mother's sense of rejection and uselessness increased. At an early developmental check, deafness was suggested, but this turned out to be a false trail. Mother was terribly worried about Holly and tried to get her anxieties taken seriously. It is hard retrospectively to understand the absence of professional concern about Holly, but what probably played a part was that Mother's own intense anxiety, guilt and upset was so palpable. She seems to have felt trapped between a kind husband who tried to reassure her by dwelling on all positive signs in Holly's development and her own mother, who was committed to the notion that history was repeating itself.

When Holly was two the family consulted a child psychiatrist because of her peculiar language development – instead of responding or replying, she would repeat what was said to her. He advised treatment

246

for Mother, and this was arranged. Nearly two years later, on seeing Holly for review, he was very alarmed and said help for Holly was now urgently required. The family was referred to a hospital for psychotic children quite some distance from their home. Holly, Mother and her younger sister Caroline, aged one, were admitted together. After a brief time, Mother and Caroline returned home and Holly remained an in-patient for a further seven months with weekends at home. She was diagnosed at this time as autistic. I heard many terrifying memories of her time in hospital during her therapy. My overall impression was that there may have been chronic emotional abuse by the staff. Certainly Holly was driven mad with terror. For years this revived when approaching any break in therapy which she would experience as my sending her back to the hospital.

When she returned home, she was placed in a small school for autistic children. Holly herself gained a good deal from this school, and she progressed to be able to manage three and a half days a week in main-stream primary school, with children one year younger than herself by the time she was eleven years old. However, Mother was extremely upset by the attitude of the school staff, who, she felt, viewed mothers as responsible for their children's autistic condition. The active involvement demanded of the parents was thus a torture to her. When the school had to close down, there was a crisis about Holly's future education since main-stream secondary school full-time was clearly not an option. Eventually she was placed in a school for children with moderate learning difficulties, and when I became involved this placement was at risk, since Holly was very difficult to manage in a class of low I.Q. but otherwise fairly ordinary children. As I came to realise, Holly was being subjected to verbal and sexual abuse by the other children and had retreated behind a non-stop flow of psychotic talk which was driving the teachers mad with frustration.

A Brief Account of the Therapy

When I began to see Holly, I encountered a completely mad child. She never stopped speaking, but it was possible to detect in the flow of crazy talk that she had hopes of me. She communicated a desperate wish that I might be able to bear her projections and an intense fear that she would be too much for me as she felt she had been for everyone else. I was shocked at the bizarre discrepancy between what she herself memorably described as 'verbal diarrhoea', a flood of words with frequent

247

bodily references and confusion of body parts, and her actual physical presence. She looked uncannily like her mother, with the same hair style, and even shared a similar ultra middle-class tone of voice though with added decibels and absence of range. She had a sophisticated vocabulary and an additional private language to refer to her 'autistic objects' (Tustin, 1981). She always carried with her a bag full of small items to which she gave idiosyncratic meanings. For example, the empty boxes in which camera films arrive. These she called 'cylinders' a correct description of their shape, but to her the reference was to faecal stool. For years she held in each hand throughout her sessions one or other of these precious objects, which she said were her protectors. Her awareness of the need for protection of the vulnerable parts of the self seemed an indication of her preconception (Bion, 1962b) of the protective function of a good object and her need to locate such an object. Much later, when she discovered she had bones and thus an internal structure which did not melt when she was flooded with emotion, she was able to leave her bag closed on the table, and eventually to lie on the couch for her sessions.

She lived a life of terror – of falling to pieces, fragmenting in body or mind, and desperately trying to protect herself from a cruelly invasive object which was intent on wounding her. She always wore trousers because she needs the reassurance of layers of clothing over her vagina and anus to prevent hostile assault. For a long time, she insisted that she possessed a penis (she constructed hundreds of phallic models, e.g. of lighthouses or windmills, to represent this). Eventually, she could talk to me about her dread of 'the hole', of being and having nothing if she gave up this delusional penis. She could not bear contact with her mother and never used female nouns or pronouns during this period. Eventually she was able to acknowledge her femininity and have a much warmer relationship with her mother.

The most important thread of her therapy was the wish to drive me mad and thus rid herself of the unbearable psychological pain and confusion of feeling mad herself, and the simultaneous hope that I would survive this onslaught. For the first year or so, I spent virtually whole sessions with no idea of what was going on. The one thing I could reliably manage was to maintain the setting of the beginning and end of the session. Sometimes I could observe and describe meaningful sequences and we could have a conversation, but at other times the bombardment of nonsense was so exhausting that I was dulled into virtual inactivity or stale repetition of interpretations which had previously meant something. I felt immured in the atmosphere of a hospital ward for severe schizophrenics without the benefit of medication.

When I realised that the point was to test my sanity, Holly became able herself to tell me with flagrant enjoyment that she was trying to drive me potty. An infinite variety of formulations appeared. 'I want to drive you crazy, up the wall, round the bend', etc. The usual method of doing this was to indulge in verbal masturbation. She quickly understood this idea, and spoke about 'rubbing with my words.' However, this initial understanding did little to abate her frantic activity when she was anxious.

Over time there was a lessening of her haunting terrors, which she had spend a lifetime avoiding through obsessional rituals and thoughts. One such manoeuvre was to 'close the doors in my ears' which she would act out when she did not want to hear what I was saying. As the conviction that I was not to be trusted and would abandon her was replaced by a growing belief in my truthfulness – I seemed not to forget her, to return after holidays as promised etc. – so the need to close her ears to reality receded. The working through of these persecutory anxieties in her therapy enabled her to reduce her interminable efforts to control the members of her family. This lessening of omnipotent control allowed a more normal family life to develop. The terror she feels at each tiny step towards relaxing her omnipotence is extreme, and for years the family felt constrained by the fear of evoking her frightening tantrums. She once tried to force me to accept a ring from her for my wedding ring finger (she felt she could thus bind me to her as if in marriage) and when I did not allow her to do this she was distraught with rage and fear.

When Holly was eighteen, plans had to be made for her future. She had attended a small school for autistic children. The only local possibility was for her to attend a work-centre for learning disabled adults and to live at home. This was unsuitable, since the family, especially her younger sister, needed some opportunity for ordinary life, and Holly needed support for further social development. Most fortunately, an unusual place was found. An ordered, humane and down-to-earth institution with good community links offered her a long-term home. It was agreed that Holly could be brought for continuing therapy once a week. Holly could attend further education classes and be part of a large community where she became liked and respected. She is on the residents' committee, and is not seen as a mad person at all. The contrast between the Holly I know and Holly 'the resident' is quite dramatic.

Introduction to the Session

This is the last session before an Easter holiday and it is planned to end the therapy in the summer. This decision was made by me and was something Holly seemed to understand. She seemed able to tolerate it as an idea as long as we could speak about her wish to keep in touch with me from time to time. She felt this link to an external Mrs Rustin would keep alive what she called 'the inside Mrs Rustin' with whom she often had conversations. Perhaps also it was felt to keep alive the importance and reality of her experience of madness which she had shared so starkly with me. In the last period of a long analysis, there is often a revisiting of old themes.

With Holly this process has had the effect of making me feel full of doubt about how much has been achieved. Sometimes it seems I have only succeeded in helping her to elaborate fundamentally narcissistic structures, which do enable her to function with less anxiety and in more socially-acceptable ways, but which also render her very difficult to reach. The energy required to go on with the struggle to draw her out of her retreat (Steiner 1993) and into more lively contact with reality is phenomenal. This is true both with reference to her internal reality, her contact with emotional experiences, and to external reality. In the session to be discussed I attempt to speak to her from outside the ongoing psychotic flow which occupies so much of her mental space.

As a preliminary, I would like to explain some references in the material. First, the people Holly speaks about. Gwen was her key worker when she first went to live away from home. When Gwen became pregnant she left her work, so she represents Holly's anxiety about being abandoned in favour of another baby. Maureen, an older woman of very calm temperament, replaced Gwen. She is extremely important to Holly, who discovered the quality of 'motherliness' in Maureen. Holly is possessive of Maureen and believes that she and Maureen will always live in the same house. Granny is a sinister figure from the point of view of her prospects for psychic change. In reality, she indulges Holly's obsessions, and tends to blame everyone else for Holly's problems. In Holly's internal world she is an ally in all her masturbatory phantasies as Granny is always in favour of the avoidance of mental pain. Sally is one of the older women who accompany Holly to the Clinic. The muffin man is a character in a children's song – 'Do you know the muffin man?' – and has become a fixture in her imagination, representing the idea of a man who would protect her against the terrifying anxieties aroused by anything female. He is a man who can feed her muffins and sweets, and help her to avoid contact with the feeding breast.

Holly uses some private words in this session. I understand the meaning of these as follows:

1. A 'shuddle' is a masturbatory phallic object which has the qualities of a shuttle (always moving), of muddle, of shit, and of shuddering, or shivering with dread.

2. A 'wally' in children's slang is someone stupid, out-of-touch – this word is used as a form of abuse of other people. For Holly there are many types of wally and she is very frightened of them, especially brown or black wallies. She has no doubt heard other children call her a wally.

3. A 'wibble' has reference to a nipple-penis confusion, to an intrusive object, and one which is wibbly-wobbly, that is, in permanent motion, unstable and excited.

4. A 'hamihocker' – these are the most frightening creatures in Holly's dreams and phantasies. Her perception of the external world used to be full of hamihockers. They now occur only in her dreams. They have a quality of ruthless machines, with an intention to hurt her. They are very complicated conceptions, somewhat like Bion's idea of 'bizarre objects' (Bion, 1967). They are conglomerates of persecutory fragments.

The Session

In the corridor on the way to my room Holly said 'The shuddle made me laugh in the toilet. I was worried he would pick me up, and poke my bottom.' When she lay on the couch she added 'Gwen was like a shuddle when she was my key-worker.' I said she wanted me to know she was frightened. This was the last session of the term and this is the last holiday before she stops coming to the Clinic to see me. She is worried that I am going to turn into a Gwen-person in her mind who is hurting her by leaving her to look after another baby. 'Mm. That's it', Holly said. 'Yesterday in the café Jane told me off. The strange man upset me. He took no notice. I said "Please may I have a cream carton" [repeats *sotto voce*] and he did not listen. I was going on and on. He was Mr Rustin. He was an ignoring Daddy.' After a brief pause she added 'I've come to talk to you.' I said that she felt that the Daddy aspect of Mrs Rustin was not listening and understanding how hard it was for her not to go on having therapy every week, like more and more cream cartons, but that she hoped that she could talk to me about this problem of not feeling understood. Holly said 'He told me not to ask silly questions. The strange man mocked me.' I said that she felt mocked instead of understood, but that she hoped to find in me a Daddy who could think about her endless desire for milk. 'That's right.'

Holly went on 'Maureen (present key-worker) told me to pack it in. The man made me miserable.' I said she was miserable that this was the last session this term. 'Maureen made remarks about me.' I said she was letting me know that even Maureen gets fed up with her sometimes, and she is worried that I do too. 'It was at MacDonalds. Maureen made me feel offended. She made me blush. She made me feel pink. She made me red in the face ... I love Maureen O'Dowd. In the restaurant I laughed about the yellow potty-boat. The Granny-boat.' Holly giggled and imitated a sickly-sweet old lady cooing over a baby. 'The black man reminds me of a shuddle.' I said she was preferring to be mad now instead of sad. Holly replied 'Yesterday I was kissing the skeleton spoon.' I said she was agreeing with me: she wanted to pretend that frightening ideas about dying, and specially about the Mrs Rustin inside her turning into a skeleton, could be turned into an exciting joke. Holly responded 'I like the bottom of a yoghurt carton and saying I'm not a magician.' I said that she often tried to believe she was a magician.

Holly then told me she was going home on Sunday. 'Tomorrow it will be two nights until I go home, then it will be one night, then it will be Sunday.' I said she liked to be clear, it helped her to wait. I explained that she was also thinking about the three sessions she will miss during the holidays, and that she has quite a clear picture of this in her mind, and knows that she will then be returning to see me. Holly said 'Yes, I have a clear picture.' Pause. 'Sally told me to wait.' I said she feels everyone is expecting her to be able to wait. Holly said 'I find it very difficult. I had to talk to Maureen'. I said she was thinking about two different ideas she has about me. Sometimes she feels I am asking her to manage something that is so difficult for her, to learn how to wait, but she is also pleased to be able to tell me about this and feel understood. Holly said 'I've come to talk to you.' I said she was finding it helpful, and Holly replied with real feeling 'Yes, I'm finding it very helpful'.

She went on 'The strange man made me sad.' I said she was feeling jealous of the Daddy who she felt I would be with during the holiday. 'He mocked me.' I said she was afraid of an idea of a Daddy who would laugh at her sadness. 'He had black eyes. A white nose. He was pale. I was homesick.' I said 'You felt you had lost the friendly understanding Daddy inside you.' 'Sally told me to stop demanding. I don't like you taking away my blue spoon. I'm afraid you will throw it away.' I asked her to tell me about this spoon. 'Maureen gave it to

12. Rigidity and Stability in a Psychotic Patient

me from Disneyland. It goes purple in the water.' I said she felt I would be jealous of something special that she had as a present from Maureen, so jealous that I would want to take it away from her. Holly explained 'Sometimes I bang the spoon on my mouth ... I've come to talk to you.' I talked more about her hope that I could bear her having something that she liked that was nothing to do with me, and how important it was to her to remember that Maureen is fond of her when she knows she made Maureen feel irritated with her in MacDonalds.

'I'm going shopping tomorrow. I shall buy nivea, shampoo, bubble bath. Then next time I shall buy spoons, white ones to play with. I play with them in my hospital. I give myself a tonic. I'm going to buy toothpaste on Saturday.' I said she had lots of ideas about how to look after herself during the holiday. 'I shall be nice and clean and look pretty.'

'I dreamt about the yellow potty in the passage way. The music made me laugh. It reminded me about the muffin man who I held onto when I was little.' I said there were different ways of holding on: old ways, like in her dream, and new ways like the plans to take care of herself and think about the part of her that wanted to get better and stronger. Holly said 'like holding on to the melamine round the thermos that I got from Mummy.' I said she was thinking about her different ways of holding on. Holly continued: 'Going back to square one. Using the base of a yoghurt carton as a shuddle. The red pointer I was scared of, digging into me. It was wibble shaped.'

I said she understands that her old ways of holding on hurt her, were not good for her. The new ways make her feel better. 'In my dream I held the pointer to stop it digging into me. The bird was in my dream. I want to kiss the black bird that flies, I use the yoghurt carton as a pet, a bird, and I kiss it. I think that kissing the yoghurt carton is a joke.' I said she was getting into a muddle now. Holly went on 'I use it as a nipple. I kiss it and say "you said the creed". It's perfectly natural.' This last phrase was uttered in a different voice and I asked whose voice it was. Holly replied 'I want to trick you.' I said the trick was to get things in a muddle. Holly continued 'I use it as food ... as a hamihocker, as a foot.' I said she was showing me that the trick is that a bit of plastic can be made into anything she fancies in her mind, there is then no difference between anything at all. Holly said 'The noise in the distance reminds me of a creamy white wally. I want to rub on the white wally. But the grey wally scares me.' I said she knew that all these imaginary things changed quickly in her mind, that she could not get hold of anything solid to keep herself feeling safe. 'They turn into shuddles that frighten me. When Maureen is my key worker I rub on the shuddle. I want you to do that and be the same as me and get excited.' I said she wanted me to be lonely like her, not to have a Daddy to be with, so that I would really understand why she tries to rub away her unhappiness. Holly

253

added 'I want to comfort in my bottom. I kiss the shuddle in my dream. Then it smells of my bottom.'

I said we were near the end of the session now and that Holly was trying to distract herself from her sad feelings, and that we both knew that when she filled up her mind with these bottom-thoughts it was hard for her to think of anything else. I wondered if there was anything she could do about it. 'Clear it up', she said. I wondered if she wanted to. 'I want a window catch to let the fresh air in. It will take the stale smells away.' I said she was tired of the old stuff. Holly said 'I am. I am tired of shit as well. I want fresh air instead of shit. Shit makes me sick. The man of shit kicks me inside me and makes me feel sick. The bottom man. The chocolate man.' I said she was telling me that her faeces in her bottom have sometimes felt to her to be just like a penis and this idea made her feel very muddled. 'Black men and children remind me of shit.' I said she was afraid that I was sick of her and would only remember the messy, muddled Holly. She replied 'I've come to talk to you.' I said she now believes I could also keep the other aspects of Holly alive in my mind. 'I don't like going back to the shuddle.' I said she was afraid of the part of her that creates muddle and terror. 'I've got the base of a yoghurt carton at the convent. I find it unbelievable! (shouted). I want it to be a bosom, I shove it on my mouth.'

I said she did not believe it actually was. It was very painful for her when at the end of the session she felt that I was the mother she needed who had good things that could feed her in my mind. Now it was time for us to stop. Holly said goodbye as she left. This is not a very frequent occurrence.

Discussion

This session reveals forces in conflict in Holly's mind. There are moments of contact with creative potential but also evident is the power of the undertow of her autistic thinking. Keeping her feet on the ground, being grounded in reality, is extremely difficult for her to sustain because it involves so much pain, but in this session there are a number of moments in which she moves towards reality. The many references to colours in Holly's associations might be considered an indication of her growing interest in distinctions and potential transformations, and her growing awareness of ambivalence in contrast to extreme splitting between good and bad. Images of hope in her material have been sustaining to me and her attacks on her own and my being able to see something good or beautiful have been the counterpart. She has a recurrent phantasy of taking my eyes out of their sockets so that all

I would see would be dark emptiness. This is a terrible but clear description of her attempts to destroy my hope.

At the beginning of the session we are on familiar territory. She resorts to the shuddle to deaden feeling and projects disgust and despair into me, which is intended to obscure from herself and me her anxieties about loss. When this situation is contained, she goes on to speak about her possessiveness and greed. I have a vivid image of a bowlful of little cartons of cream, and of Holly's desire for the whole lot. Also implicit is the problem she has of getting stuck on one particular thing, the need for sameness and repetition. This is a continuing difficulty for her parents, who try to introduce her to new experiences, while Holly demands always to have the same food (scrambled eggs, chocolate pudding, etc.) and the same treats (going for a bus ride to a place where she can go shopping, for smooth round objects of some kind) and the same conversation (she bullies her mother to speak the script she provides and Mother needs a lot of courage to deviate from this). Important in contrast to this passion for repeating something comfortingly familiar is the reference to the strange man. This is the strangeness of the unknown, which stimulates in Holly not curiosity and interest, but panic. She projects her harshly critical superego into the man. On this occasion I did not enquire about the reality of what had happened, but sometimes I have done, and it has become quite clear that Holly knows she is talking to me about what is going on in her mind, and can distinguish quite well between that and actual events.

The first shift in the direction of tolerating reality is when she tells me that Maureen got fed up. She has previously maintained an unpunctured idealisation of Maureen, and I registered a shock of excitement and hope as she dared to acknowledge a change. A second surprise is when I heard she was in MacDonalds. I do not think I have ever before been allowed to know that she has been in a particular public place, a place I too could know. We are always stuck together in a world lacking specificity of time or place; I am rarely allowed to share Holly's real life activities, and I felt a thrill to catch this glimpse.

As she struggles with the mixed emotions evoked by Maureen who has shamed her, but whom she loves, an intolerable situation develops. If she were to bring together the shame and the love, she would experience guilt which she cannot bear, so there is a defensive retreat from this threshold.

But with some support from me, she rejects the magic solution and

255

emerges to locate herself very firmly in time. The clarity of her thinking is impressive, and there is a further development when she describes seeking help from Maureen with the problem of waiting instead of resorting to magic. This is a firm choice for dependence on an external object, which is a real and non-idealised object, and against the narcissistic evasion. This is followed by a real gift to me when she tells me I have been very helpful. Holly has felt that she has been given something good, and experiences and expresses gratitude. This is linked with being able to stay, for a few moments, in a sad rather than mad state. She is 'homesick', in touch with missing something essential to feeling that she has a psychic home. This home is both a place in my mind and her internalised capacity to think about herself, which so often gets destroyed. The problem of mourning all that has been lost in the years of her deluded existence is frequently too much to bear, even briefly.

At this point she is more able to feel her own desire for something outside herself, and can acknowledge her demandingness. This experience is terrible for her, both because she fears overwhelming a weak object and because she has so little capacity to bear the frustration of not possessing all that she desires. So the insupportable need is projected into me, and Holly investigates, as so often before, whether I can stand such emotion.

When I made the link back to Maureen, I think this revived her hope of having the capacity to sustain her loving feelings for Maureen, but at this moment there is an explosion of envy at the creative work we have been doing together. The retreat to the yellow potty is a vicious attack on the part of herself that can take in caring capacities. The introjective identification has been quite fully experienced and the bitter disappointment and despair evoked in the dependent part of the self that is now being betrayed is projected wholesale into me.

In such circumstances, it is hard to believe in the reality of what has just been happening. The slough of despond (Bunyan's *Pilgrim's Progress*) sucks one in. I have found that to describe the destruction, which I have done many, many times, is not enough to bring about a shift. This is because Holly is no longer aware of any hope at all, but is entirely in the grip of the counter-system of narcissistic object relations, with all the false friends aiding and abetting this disavowal. So I have learnt to speak about the projected sane part of her.

I believe that my incipient mindless despair mirrors my patient's problem, and that it is my task not to become hopeless and confused, but to speak up for the temporarily abandoned, dependent infantile self.

12. Rigidity and Stability in a Psychotic Patient

The therapist's problem, with a psychotic patient, is often echoed by the way in which parents and teachers get stuck in very low expectations and cannot remain responsive to the possibilities for change and development. Much of my work with Holly's parents has been to try to pull them out of this state of numbed passivity in the face of her destructiveness.

The next part of the session illustrates Holly's struggles with psychic truth. In her dream, there is contact with reality: the bird flying away is a well-known image for us of my freedom to leave her, which hurts and threatens her. She substitutes for this the pet, the autistic object that can be manipulated in any way she wishes. But she is aware that a trick is being played. The trick is the claim that we are exactly the same, in which case she could not miss me, for I would have nothing to offer her. As the trick is elaborated, and everything is reduced to an anal world, depression wells up in me, depression about her vulnerability to psychotic delusion, and the tremendous limitations of my work. At this point, I think I felt that I could not do any more. She had to do something. But I could remind her of her capacity to make such a choice, as I did in quite an explicit way, by asking her if she could do anything about the overwhelming anal stink. The idea of fresh air has been an important discovery for her, as the image of opening a window involves a recognition that the inside world so impregnated with her rubbish can be improved by contact with an alive outside world if she allows it in.

The last minutes of the session are a tremendous struggle between her mad system of confusing, useless, manipulable things (an empty yoghurt carton – she used to have literally dozens of these at any one time) and the quality of contact she can have with a real person. She is fighting for her sanity when she protests about the unbelievable nature of this way of looking at the world, and the fight enables her to say goodbye to me because she has allowed my existence to continue after her departure.

Discussion

I think Holly is always battling with the painfulness of facing what Money-Kyrle describes as 'the facts of life' (Money-Kyrle 1978). These are three fundamental truths to be faced if we are to achieve mental stability. There is firstly the difference of the generations – adult and child, analyst and patient do not have the same responsibilities or

257

capacities. Secondly, the difference of the sexes – male and female can have complementarity, but they are distinct. If we have the physical attributes of one sex, we must lack those of the other. Both these distinctions are a source of mental pain because they give rise to envy and jealousy. Thirdly, there is the reality of the passage of time, and our own mortality.

Holly struggled to deny the difference between herself and her parents: she tried to blot out her mother, and create a world in which there were only Daddy and herself, no mother and no sister. Externally this has greatly changed, but in the transference it has to be confronted again and again. She also tried to maintain that a delusional penis was equivalent to a real one, and that she could be a boy if she wanted. This idea too has given way to a knowledge of her longing for a boy-friend, but as in this session, there is a frequent retreat to equating faeces and penis, and thus denying difference and lack.

But perhaps most central in this final phase of work is the issue of the termination of the treatment. Time is now of the essence. We have had a lot of time together, and its coming to an end raises for both of us problems of mourning. Most urgent for Holly is the question of whether she has enough strength in the sane part of her mind to provide a continuing bulwark against madness. In particular, will she be able to forgive me enough for leaving her to remain in touch with me internally and thus converse with herself. There is the problem of the rage and envy with me when I am not her possession, and the cruelty with which she can take revenge both on me and on the part of herself that is deeply attached to me. In so far as these destructive processes unravel our work, her stability is undermined, and she then resorts to obsessional rigidities to prevent a psychotic breakdown. These rigid structures are serviceable in a certain very limited way, but they prevent any real relationships developing, and they have their own fragilities too, since they are impervious to reality and therefore vulnerable when change forces its way into consciousness. So the question is whether she can achieve acknowledgement of the end of our work and mourn both what it has offered her, and what it cannot do. For both of us, this involves bearing my limitations. Holly has often seen me close to my wits' end. Distinguishing between what I have failed to understand or bear and what I could and did provide for her can be the basis for her continued internal contact with an imperfect but valuable object. She once told me that the inside Mrs Rustin was telling her in a horrid hissing voice that she would never come back and see her because she was 'fed up to the back teeth.' Then she acted out unlocking the doors in her ears and announced 'Now I can hear the outside Mrs Rustin.' When I asked what she could now hear she said 'You are talking sense in a kind voice.'

For the therapist of such a patient there is also a painful process to face. Therapeutic zeal or omnipotence takes a massive bashing in work of this sort although the awareness of one's dependence on one's own internal good objects to withstand the loneliness of working with a psychotic patient is both tested and deepened. My patient is still a very fragile and limited person, though she is now a human being who can give pleasure and contribute to life, and receive pleasure through relationships. She remains very vulnerable to external circumstances, which may not always be as supportive as they now are.

I think there has been a tendency for me to experience in the counter-transference a reluctance to face the facts of life. The pervasive atmosphere of being in another world, not at all the same as the everyday world, created in such therapies interferes with realistic thinking. I have certainly had the idea that I could never end Holly's treatment, but that I am needed on a life-long basis. The patient's difficulty in internalising a good object is colluded with once one starts to think that only an external analytic presence can make a difference. One is also in danger of agreeing with the patient's view that such a specially-needy baby must never be faced with the reality of there being other babies to consider.

There is a particularly seductive quality in the weird understandings achieved – no-one else can make sense of the details of her rituals, for example, and this tends to generate ideas of therapeutic self-importance. There is a pressure to go on elaborating interpretations of the autistic defences and to lose sight of the need to pull the patient out of them. There is a dulling of necessary anger at the cruel waste of her life and the potential waste of the therapist's time. She has always made it difficult for me to mobilise my justified anger with her because she experiences resistance to her manoeuvres as physical and mental assault, and because she then attempts to twist the straight talking into a sadomasochistic exchange.

The setting for psychoanalytic therapy with its emphasis on structured reliability is a double-edged matter with such patients – the regular sessions can become part of the patient's organised evasion of life unless one is very attentive. From this point of view, it is crucial that the setting of an analysis is understood to include its termination. Working towards ending has helped me to reflect more constructively on ways in which I have sometimes been co-opted to maintain a psychotic equilibrium rather than consistently challenge it.

Discussion

Margaret Rustin

The clinical cases presented in this section exemplify the complexity and fluctuations in childhood psychosis. Many of the points made in the discussions of the cases of the earlier sections apply here also and will not be reiterated, but some additional factors are worthy of exploration. Some of the children have a history of diverse diagnosis, others, studied over long periods, demonstrate that emergence from autism can usher in a profound risk of a more manic-depressive or schizophrenic type of illness. Clearly, autistic phenomena may serve as a defensive shield to protect the self from the more extreme fragmentation of schizophrenia. A sub-group of patients diagnosed as autistic seem to be sheltered by their autism from the more extreme and life-threatening ravages of other forms of childhood psychosis.

Hypersensitivity

Traumatic early impingement is a prominent feature. The flooding of an immature mental apparatus by unmanageable stimuli appears repeatedly in the children's early history. The child's immaturity is sometimes combined with possible brain damage (Samuel), sometimes with severely disturbed states of mind in the mother, ranging from anxiety and fragility (Holly) to delusional attacks on the baby (Jonathan). There is some evidence of inter-generational transmission of unmourned and unmetabolised earlier catastrophes in the family histories. Mary, a young child similar to Holly, provided a graphic example of this when she drew a wild picture with a red pen, spoke of the babies burning in the furnace, and muttered 'Auschwitz' under her breath. She was the daughter of a man who had in his adolescence lost all his family in the Holocaust and escaped through a degree of collaboration of which he was deeply ashamed. This child perpetually assaulted herself, in a

261

desperate effort to punish the bad internal objects by whom she felt dominated. The relationship between Samuel's ghost and the ghost haunting his mother is another instance of this link (Sherwin-White).

The children convey some of the ways in which such overwhelming and unmodulated psychological intrusions influence their ways of seeing the world. It is striking that sensory over-stimulation and hypersensitivity is marked. Distressed responses to sounds which would be acceptable to an ordinary child are noted – Mary, for instance, heard unexpected noises as 'thunder', and was recognised by her family as being able to hear things going on in a next-door room with uncanny clarity. She tried to protect herself from the persecution of this, perhaps felt as something like 'white' noise, by stuffing up her ears with bits of cotton wool or tissue, and repeated ear infections were a painful consequence, intensifying her terror of what could get into her ears and cause hurt. A similar intolerance to bright light leads to children seeking shelter in various ways – drawing curtains, going under rugs, shutting their eyes or hiding behind hair or hands. This difficulty is related to the panic about encountering a direct gaze – the eyes of the other are felt as suffused with brilliant penetrative power. Holly's intense preoccupation with eyes was expressed in a long-standing fantasy that she would take out her therapist's eyes. Not surprisingly this attempt to diminish persecution was accompanied by nightmares of monsters with blazing red eyes, as the emptied eye-sockets became suffused with retaliation.

The other senses are similarly over-sensitised. The children's tendency to shrink from physical contact, related to 'tactile defensiveness' as theorised by Ayres, in her creative research in physiotherapy (Ayres 1979) are often reminiscent of the responses of children who have been physically or sexually abused. Differential diagnosis can be a subtle matter in this respect, particularly as the psychotic child's capacity for clear communication about the external world is so damaged by poor differentiation between internal and external reality. There is often an acute sense of smell, partly understandable as related to their bodily confusions, in which top and bottom are frequently reversed. Confusion between head, maternal breast and bottom, and between mouth and anus are endemic, as described by Tustin (1981) and Meltzer (1967). The widespread observation of eating difficulties in psychotic children, particularly extreme faddiness, is linked to the way in which the sense of taste is suffused with paranoid anxieties. One way of trying to control the panicky confusion about whether food that is offered is really good and wholesome or dangerous and poisonous is to eat as little as possible, as few different foods as possible and also food which is easily recognised, not mixed up. Intolerance of 'lumps' is another common difficulty, as the smoother textures seem to relieve the child's anxiety that indigestible hard stuff is being forced into them. Eating scrambled egg, chocolate pudding, yoghurt etc. feels safe.

The desperate need for sameness of experience and terror of anything unknown may be rooted in these over-intense sensory experiences. The children remind one continually of tiny infants for whom it feels natural to provide a simplified protective environment in which light, noise and temperature are modulated, and new experiences, like the baby's first tastes of solid food, are provided in tiny doses.

These hypersensitive bodily experiences run parallel to and are entangled with overflowing, disordered and frightening experiences of mind. The difficulty in creating meaningful patterns leads to a sense of an overcrowded mind, perpetually spilling out the too-muchness of experience. The children's incapacity to forget anything, perhaps born of a desperate anxiety that only holding on to all the bits and pieces of experience safeguards any continuity of being, faces us with a startling absence of normal childhood amnesia. Two of the children described in these pages spoke of remembering their birth. These 'memories' of being squashed in the birth canal, poked with forceps, trying to stay inside are very difficult to assess. Perhaps they are usefully considered as an amalgam of bodily persecutory experiences (for instance Holly's very clear account of her terror during a brain scan at age 4 being connected with a traumatic birth) but the difficulty for the children in letting go of any of the details of their torments, however much this is fuelled by rage and unforgiving resentment, does raise the question of whether they are forced to remember what most of us are free to forget. In writing about birth memories revealed in analysis, Winnicott wrote 'In the analytic setting we find that carefully collected primary persecutions can be remembered. Then, at long last, the patient can afford to forget them' (Winnicott 1949). How one longs for these children to have the relief afforded by the capacity to forget and to repress. They seem doomed to a Kafkaesque infinite reliving of moments which become progressively denuded of emotion and meaning. Their not-quite-human quality of being is related to this. The important and the insignificant are not differentiated in their overloaded memory systems. Events are not clearly located in present or past because these categories have not developed – we are in the world of a continuous present, which often seems to create an atmosphere of suspended animation. The obsessional perseveration and holding on to apparently meaningless detail, have a paradoxical effect, although as the cases will demonstrate amply, it is sometimes possible to reconstruct the original significance, and of great importance to keep in mind that meaning is often buried somewhere in the jumble of bizarre language and behaviour. While repetitive activities serve to hold together a fragile personality in however primitive or uncreative a fashion, they also build a barrier of torturing incomprehensibility which frustrates those trying to reach the child behind the barricades. It thus renders the child less likely to receive the understanding of his plight which could ameliorate the situation.

Overlapping Psychological Factors

The most difficult cases with which to make progress are those in which there is a complex mixture of forces at work. Factors in the family (for example, mental illness in a parent, the impact of catastrophic political and social events) interact with those in the child, which may be constitutional (for example, the balance of loving and destructive impulses, the natural endowment both mental and physical) or a consequence of experience (Rosenfeld 1987). Particularly crucial aspects of experience are the intra-uterine environment, the nature of the birth and the early contact with mother. In the cases under discussion there is frequently a very disturbed early start in life which seems to undermine both the child's predisposition to seek contact with the external world and the mother's belief that she can understand and care for her baby effectively. The absence of early benign interactions is a predominant feature.

The therapist thus encounters a child in whom there are elements which seem the consequence of introjected damage, for example, deficits which follow early deprivation, and elements which lie in the child's contribution. These include both the adverse aspects of the innate endowment and the defensive measures which the child has turned to for psychic survival but which in turn prove anti-developmental. This is a very primitive version of the 'double deprivation' thesis developed by Henry (1974). A very important feature of the therapeutic process is the gradual elucidation of which of the maladaptive defences the child is able to let go, once supportive contact with the fragile baby-self has been established, and which are perversely clung to. The danger is that the mad 'games' which replace the ordinary child's developing relationships with the external world take such a hold of the child's mind that it becomes very difficult to unstick his attachment to these false gods. It is quite a mind-numbing experience to see just how convincing a pseudo-

Discussion

life can be lived by a child in manic flight from psychotic terrors. The complexity of private languages of gobbledegook (Holly and Samuel) the infinite taste for repetitive chuntering (Joseph 1982), the weirdly perverse variations of a world-turned-upside-down (Meltzer 1992) can hold the personality to ransom, when excitement effectively replaces meaningful links. Progress is slow because the elements of trauma, abuse and perverse defences have solidified into a defensive system which is the only thing the child trusts. It is an extreme version of the pathological organisation described as characteristic of adult borderline states (Steiner 1993). Added to this can be the refusal to give up grievances, the unwillingness to forgive, also described by Steiner.

Indications for Treatment

The cases described in this section have usually required very long periods of treatment. When this is possible, outcomes have proved worthwhile from a number of perspectives. Improving the quality of life for the children and their families is a crucial aim. Some children, especially when treatment begins in early childhood, have made enormously impressive recoveries, been able to benefit from relatively normal schooling and achieve rewarding relationships with families and peers (Jonathan, Samuel, Pauline). Others have moved from being a source of active torment to other people at home and at school and profoundly distressed in themselves to becoming constructive and valued members of a community, able to enjoy and develop some of their own capacities while needing ongoing shelter (Holly). The overall picture is that these extremely ill children are able to benefit markedly from psychotherapy, and to respond with relief to the discovery of meaning and a capacity for thought.

It will be evident that the management of the countertransference feelings evoked in this work is a great challenge. At times the children seem to do all they can to numb the therapist's mind, destroy her capacity for hope and courage, and generally make themselves hateful. While the degree of hatred of reality and underlying envy are massive forces with which to contend, for both child and therapist, it is interesting to see how much commitment, interest and indeed love the children can inspire. When they do mobilise teachers, therapists and others to make efforts on their behalf, this seems to be an indication that there are lost positive resources in the child. Initially their positive capacities seem only accessible in the countertransference, that is, via the response they evoke in adults trying to help, but therapy can sometimes restore

265

these growth points to the child. The massiveness of the projective identification has the consequence that the patient may be unaware of the split-off capacity for love and reparation for a very long time. Holly's understanding of the need for 'fresh air' was an example of a beginning development of this sort. These genuine developmental sparks need to be carefully distinguished from a seductive fascination which the intricate complexity of the psychotic imagination can exert. Therapies subverted by mutual idealisation of crazy phantasy can get nowhere.

The greater understanding which has been achieved over the last twenty years or so in making use of Bion's ideas has led to important changes in technique (Spillius 1988 and Alvarez 1992). This creates a new starting point for current work and the case of Daniel is an instance of the benefits of these developments. The shift achieved in once-weekly work over a modest period with an experienced therapist indicates the potential application of what has been learnt through intensive clinical practice. Alongside this cause for hopefulness is the awareness of the massive psychological damage which these children have sustained and often then elaborated at their further expense. This raises difficult issue in determining the length of treatments, particularly in the light of the scarcity of psychotherapeutic resources. These are tackled in the discussion of Holly, one of the patients who often made her therapist feel that only a life-long presence would save her from falling into madness as the easier though deadly option. Mary, the eloquent child mentioned earlier, once explained that for her to stay sane was as difficult a task as winning an Olympic Gold Medal for a gymnast performing on the four inch beam. The terror of falling off never left her.

The final point to be emphasised is the crucial negotiation of a relationship of trust with parents. Very often the parents of psychotic children have felt blamed for their children's illness instead of finding sympathy and understanding of the family's tragic circumstances. A humility of spirit is needed when we are asked to intervene, since our efforts to help require so much persistence and endurance from the children's families, and the outcome of psychotherapy cannot be known in advance.

Postscript

'I'm not a Collapsti, I'm a Human Being'

Margaret Rustin

The statement above was made in a spirit of protest by a psychotic child, reproaching her therapist. The child had invented a race of beings called 'collapstis'; in her drawings they resembled traffic lights, and made one think of the sort of robots who feature in children's television programmes. They were an obsessional preoccupation. The hapless therapist, who was well aware that 'collapstis' were a representation of a barely-human aspect of her child patient, had lapsed into a too-concrete response to a communication about collapstis and thus failed to sustain the distinction between internal and external reality. Imagine her delight when the child asserted her capacity for clear thinking. This is an instance of a treasured moment in psychotherapy when a psychotic patient comes right out of the apparent prison of phantasy and engages directly with the therapist. A reminder that even the maddest child has the potential for everyday good sense.

This volume provides an overview of current thinking and practice among a group of child psychotherapists with special interest and experience in this field. We intend the book to be seen as a contribution to evolving understanding: much remains to be explored. The interconnections between mind and brain, psyche and soma, thought and emotion, are of enormous importance in the study of severe childhood disturbance, but also of wider relevance, just as ideas arising from research in Post-Traumatic Stress Disorder in young children have changed the way we think. Workers in both fields note the plasticity of the psycho-physical system and the consequent crucial importance of early intervention. In this postscript, we shall outline some points which need, in our view, to be emphasised in considering the work reported on in these pages and in future work.

267

First, some disclaimers. Because it is case-based, this book is not inclusive, and because we work in one tradition, the theories we have used are similarly selective. We do not for instance refer to the large body of American work (Mahler et al.) nor to the Lacanian tradition, although we hope our ideas will interest clinicians working in these traditions. The original impulse to work on this book in fact arose from a conference held in Paris which brought together Lacanian analysis and British Object Relations theory in relation to the understanding of psychosis.

We should like to note some neglected topics. There is rather little about adolescents; in particular we have not described adolescent manic breakdown or psychotic depression, hysterical symptoms, anorexia, self-cutting and other self-injurious behaviour, severe panic attacks. All of these can lead to the need for in-patient treatment. We do, however, consider that all these states have a psychotic element, although they are not necessarily classified as psychoses, and we think that ideas derived from the study of childhood psychosis are relevant to understanding these phenomena.

For instance, Mary, the child referred to in the discussion of Section 3, cut her wrists extensively because of a wish to cause tetanus: she perceived herself as tormenting others by her outpouring of distress and felt that 'lockjaw' would silence her and bring an end to their unbearable reproaches. She always refused to have either stitches or anti-tetanus injections during her frequent visits to out-patients. For very depressed patients the sensation of pain and the sight of blood also seems to be a reassurance of their aliveness, and to be an extreme instance of the head-banging, self-pinching and poking seen in psychotic young children in states of desolation and despair. (Mary had fractured her skull as a one year old, taken into hospital without her mother to be forcibly weaned onto solid foods.) Similarly, the early eating difficulties described may usefully be considered as related to later anorexias (e.g. Holly). One outcome of repressed early trauma can be a later breakdown, either due to the trigger of something too close to the traumatic experience (for example the impact of later sexual intercourse on a sexually abused child) or as a consequence of a greater sense of security, which may allow the encapsulated psychosis to emerge and be worked through.

Now for some implications of our work. We wish to underline the importance of taking seriously observations of young children which take place in the ordinary course of community child health provision when strange behaviour and patterns of relationship are noted. Children at risk of psychosis are often described as 'odd', 'in a world of their own', 'loners'. There is an understandable tendency for parents to be reassured that children will 'grow out of it.' This is often misplaced optimism; rather, schizoid children who are caught in their phantasies need intensive early investigation. Families need help in encouraging the children out of their private worlds, the children need both special educational provision ('odd' children are often not a behavioural problem in school and therefore usually overlooked in the early years) and child mental health input. Psychotherapy can be considered as an option where possible, but a much broader range of children can be helped when a psychotherapeutic contribution is sought within an overall multidisciplinary assessment. Management decisions can be influenced by an understanding of the child's phantasy life, as the range and content of phantasies is a useful adjunct to other indicators of mental state. Psychotherapeutic consultation can also be an important resource to those educating and caring for psychotic children in community contexts, as it extends their understanding of the children and of the effect the children have on them.

As our cases illuminate, long-term psychotherapy can make a tremendous difference. These detailed case studies are in a tradition of clinical description common to psychoanalysis and other clinical disciplines. Our approach to treatment and research needs to be set alongside studies from other perspectives – epidemiological, organic and sociological. Together, the research outcomes could represent an achievement in working together as researchers parallel to what is needed in the practical care of the children and their families. It cannot be overemphasised that psychotic children and young people need a high level of community care. Schools, Child Mental Health teams and Social Services are all involved and need to be cognisant of the preventive potential of early intervention. Long-term clinical follow up is an essential aspect of the care required, to prevent deterioration and to build in the support needed by families with such a vulnerable member. Child psychotherapists are sometimes teased about their tendency to think long-term, because of their developmental perspective, but there is no doubt that parents and children seen from time to time over years appreciate enormously regular opportunities for review. This is preventive mental health in action. For those children who do receive psychotherapy, termly review meetings when treatment ends represent a support for the internalised containment of the psychotic pressures and can help the patient hold on to sanity.

The theoretical implications of our work are diverse. Here we should like to highlight the unhelpfulness of simplistic dichotomies, particularly that between mind and brain. We now know that the content of phantasy life influences the development of the brain (Perry 1995). There are conditions like autism which may set a ceiling on developmental potential, but the sometimes successful treatment of these intractable states raises new questions about aetiology.

Attention to the phenomena of secondary handicap (Sinason 1992) has helped to differentiate between organically defined impairments and individual variations in the way the brain is used. Whilst the idea that intellectual under-functioning is linked to emotional factors is not new, it remains little understood. Perhaps the overall commitment in theoretical debate can be inflected towards dialogue between contrasting traditions of thought. Psychoanalytic classification does not map easily onto psychiatric categories, but the losses entailed through theoretical fragmentation are great. The children's difficulties in integrating elements of experience sometimes seem to be echoed in the professional discourse when communication is replaced by dogmatic assertion.

One final point: the absence of intervention is often influenced by anxieties about the unhelpfulness of diagnostic labels since labelling is perhaps rightly held to cause secondary problems. Help for these children is dependent on support for their parents and sympathetic understanding of their predicament at the point of diagnosis in particular, but also over the years that follow. This involves the wide range of agencies referred to earlier.

We look forward to ongoing dialogue and hope that our own discoveries of the meaningfulness underlying the strangeness of these children will encourage others to explore ways in which they can be helped more fully to enter a community of others.

Glossary

Maria Rhode

Adhesive identification/equation The establishment of a (precarious) sense of identity through the phantasy of sticking to the surface of the object of identification. Separation can therefore be experienced as a tearing away and spilling out. The surface adhered to may be literally the skin, or the object's superficial qualities. The impression conveyed is one of mimicry, rather than of growth arising from digested experience. (Bick 1968, 1986; Meltzer 1975, 1986.) Tustin (1994) writes of adhesive equation to emphasise the complete absence of differentiation between self and other.

Alpha function The mental function by means of which, during the process of containment, unthinkable experiences are transformed into *alpha-elements*, W.R. Bion's term for psychological units which are usable for dreaming, thinking and memory storage (Bion 1962a).

Autism A condition characterised by impairments of emotional and social contact, cognitive capacities, and language development. Children are distressed by change, and engage in repetitive ritualistic behaviour as well as idiosyncratic use of their bodies such as hand-flapping and toe-walking. They typically avoid eye contact, and ignore the existence of separate people, who may feel excluded as though by a barrier. Kanner's Syndrome children are often mute or echolalic; Asperger's Syndrome children have language but tend to use it in unusual ways.

Autistic objects Hard objects that many autistic children carry about with them. They are not used symbolically as playthings, but for the sake of the sharp sensations they generate and which reassure the child of his continued existence (Tustin 1980).

Beta elements The raw material of experience, consisting of unmentalised sense impressions, and suitable only for evacuation (Bion 1962a). When beta elements have been subjected to alpha-function, they are transformed into alpha elements, which are usable as the units of mental functions (dreaming, thinking, memory storage, and so on).

Bizarre Object Objects in the external world into which bits of the self or ego-functions have been expelled. This model, advanced by Bion (1956), powerfully illuminates puzzling aspects of psychotic experience. For example, a person who has expelled his visual equipment into a gramophone may

271

feel that the gramophone is watching him. Bizarre objects, unlike elements that have undergone *alpha function* (q.v.), are unsuitable as building-blocks for thought or dreaming: they can be agglomerated, but not articulated in an orderly way.

Claustrum See projective identification.

Concrete thinking A failure in the symbolic, 'pretend' dimension of thought, inadequate alpha-function leading to the use of symbolic equations (q.v.) rather than symbols. As phantasies are not distinguished from actions, the state of the inner world (see Internal objects) and of external reality are equated with each other, and a feeling may be experienced as something tangible.

Confusional state A state in which the self or parts of it cannot be properly distinguished from objects in external or internal reality. Concomitantly symbols cannot be distinguished from the thing symbolised. Thought processes become confused, one of the most important confusions being that between good and bad objects and parts of the self.

Containment The process, described in *Learning from Experience* by W.R. Bion (1962a), by which the baby's emotions are received by the mother who 'digests' them by means of her capacity for unconscious reverie, and returns them to the baby in manageable form. This serves as a model for therapeutic interaction.

Countertransference This term has been used in various ways to refer to conscious and unconscious aspects of the therapist's emotional response to the patient. Some writers have seen it as an interference that arises when the patient touches on unresolved areas in the therapist. Others have emphasised its importance as a vehicle for communication (Heimann, 1950; Brenman Pick 1985). Feelings aroused by psychotic patients can be powerful and disturbing (Bion, 1955; Winnicott, 1947); thinking about them constitutes a major part of the therapeutic work.

splits, so that the baby recognises that the idealised and hated mother are the same person. Relationships are with whole objects for whom love and concern are felt (Klein 1935). This leads to feelings of guilt for harm done in phantasy, and the wish to make reparation. In the working through of the depressive position, love mitigates hatred and hope and security increase. If this fails, manic triumph may be resorted to, or paranoid-schizoid trends may be reinforced.

Dismantling A process by which autistic children focus on information from one sensory channel, so interfering with integrated perception. This does not attack and damage the object of perception in the way that splitting processes can (Meltzer et al., 1975).

Infant observation A discipline which is part of the preparation for clinical work in many psychotherapy trainings, and is also pursued for its own sake and as a method of research. An observer visits the family of a new-born baby once a week for two years, and makes as full a record as possible of the interaction of family members while taking care to influence this as little as possible. The observer pays careful attention to his or her own feelings as well as to the details of the interaction. This is a fruitful way of learning about primitive processes, and of understanding how actions express emotion during the preverbal period.

Internal objects Figures to whom the self relates and who have become internalised, so building up the 'inner world' of object relationships (Klein 1940).

Introjective identification The process by which the qualities of the self are built up through the phantasy of introjecting (taking in) and thus containing objects with whose qualities the self can then identify.

Narcissistic (pathological) organisation A type of character structure in which strength is not derived through dependence on good parental figures with whom the self can identify. Instead, the part(s) of the self that seek good object relationships are terrorised by bad parts of the self, typically organised as a Mafia-type gang under the sway of a gang leader who dispenses false information about the world (Rosenfeld 1971; Meltzer 1973; Steiner 1982). Such a character structure may serve to ward off the fear of chaos and fragmentation or depressive pain (Steiner 1987).

Object A technical psychoanalytic term for a person with whom the self (or subject) has an emotional relationship. An *external object* is such a person in external reality, while an *internal object* (q.v.) has been introjected and thus become part of the inner world. Hence, *object relations theory*. See also *part objects*.

Oedipal Triangle In Freud's writings, erotic desires for each of the parents and rivalry with the other make up the complex system of the developing child's Oedipal constellation (Laplanche and Pontalis 1973, pp. 282-7). Freud traced the importance of these triangular relationships for the individual's character and sexual life. More recent work has focused on the relationship between the negotiation of the Oedipal triangle and the capacity for thought (Bion 1959, Britton 1989).

Obsessionality A character structure or defence in which rituals play an important part, based on the assertion of omnipotent control over objects, who are typically kept apart from each other. One of the possible outcomes after emergence from an autistic state.

Omnipotence The belief that one's phantasies are all-powerful, and therefore that internal reality is indistinguishable from external reality. Hence, for example, *omnipotent destructiveness*, in which destructive phantasies are felt to bring about any damage that takes place in external reality.

Paranoid-schizoid position A state of mind characterised by the splitting of objects into extremely good (ideal) and extremely bad ones (Klein 1946). The self relates to *part objects* (q.v.) rather than to whole, integrated ones; its prime concern is for its own survival, whereas in the depressive position the prime concern is for the good internal object.

Part objects One particular aspect or function of an object related to by the self, for example, the mother's breast as a source of nourishment. Relationships to part objects are characteristic of the paranoid-schizoid position. In the depressive position, different currents of emotion become more integrated as do different experiences of the object, so that relationships are typically with *whole objects* (for example, the mother rather than the breast).

Phantasy This spelling was adopted by Freud's translators to distinguish largely unconscious phantasy from conscious fantasy, which is more like day-dreaming. In Melanie Klein's work, unconscious phantasy had a central importance: she thought that it was present from the beginning of life, as the mental expression of instincts (Isaacs, 1948). As such, it is an essential aspect of mental functions such as feelings, dreams, and thought. Phantasy (internal reality) and external reality interact, each having an effect on the other; difficulties can arise if phantasies interfere with the perception of external reality or if they are felt to be so powerful as to determine external events (Omnipotence, q.v.). Children's play is an enactment of their phantasies, and therefore a vital communicative link. In the course of therapy, phantasies can be made conscious and modified.

Preconception W.R. Bion (1962b) suggested that the baby is born with an *innate preconception* of people, qualities, structures and functions in external reality with whom relationships can be established; for example, with the preconception of a nipple for the mouth to latch onto. When such a *preconception* meets with its *realisation* in external reality, this mating leads to the birth of a *concept*.

Projective identification The phantasy that parts of the self are lodged in an object with whom the self then identifies (as opposed to introjective identification, where the object is taken into the self). This can occur with the motivation of controlling the object or of evading painful emotions that stem from a realisation of separateness (Klein, 1946). Bion (1962a) described *benign projective identification*, by which non-verbal communication takes place between mother and baby or between patient and therapist (cf. *containment* and *alpha-function*). Meltzer (1992) suggested reserving the term projective identification for this benign process, and using the term *intrusive identification* to describe the intrusive lodging in the object of parts of the self, leading to the experience of living inside various compartments of the internal mother (the *claustrum*).

Psychosis A state of severe disturbance in areas of functioning, such as perception and thinking, into which the individual has no insight. Thus disturbances of perception (hallucinations) and thought (delusional ideas, and the fragmentation of the form of thought) are not felt to be signs of illness. Contact with external and internal reality is massively altered, and the capacity to function is grossly impaired in many areas of life, including relationships.

Psychiatrists broadly divide psychoses into those with a primary disturbance of mood (affective psychoses such as manic-depressive illness) and those with a more primary disturbance of thinking and perception (such as schizophrenia). The psychoanalytic work of W.R. Bion has demonstrated the affective roots of cognitive processes in general and of schizophrenic thought disorder in particular. He has emphasised the coexistence of psychotic and non-psychotic parts of the personality (Bion, 1957).

Childhood psychoses are much less common than those seen in adults.

274

Some resemble adult psychosis, such as *early-onset schizophrenia*; others do not (e.g. *autism*, q.v., and the *pervasive developmental disorders*).

Schizoid Characterised by the use of splitting mechanisms. People with schizoid character formation may suffer from feelings of unreality, depersonalisation and alienation from their emotions.

Schizophrenia A psychotic condition characterised by profound disturbances of thinking and perception. The form of thought may itself be disturbed, with unusual use of words, neologisms, and disruptions in finer grammatical structures. Unrealistic ideas may be held with such conviction that they are termed delusional, and are not amenable to discussion. Delusional ideas may take a number of forms, most notably persecutory, paranoid or grandiose. Disorders of perception usually take the form of hallucinations, most often auditory, but occasionally visual or tactile. These symptoms may eventually be overlaid by states of apathy and reduced motivation. Kleinian psychoanalysts working with adult schizophrenics have stressed the hypertrophy of projective identification, and of fragmentation of the self as a consequence of minute splitting (Klein, 1946; Segal, 1950, 1956; Bion, 1967; Rosenfeld, 1965).

Skin function The experience of parts of the self being passively held together through the mother's or therapist's attention in a way that corresponds to the bodily organs being held inside the skin (Bick, 1968). When this experience is lacking, *second skin* functions may be resorted to in order to hold the self together. These are qualities of the self rather than of the object: for instance, muscularity.

Splitting Freud (1927) described a splitting of consciousness that permitted contradictory views to exist side by side. Klein (1946) viewed splitting as the mechanism for dealing with anxiety characteristic of the paranoid-schizoid position, splits in the object leading to splits in the self. When this is excessive, integration is interfered with. However, the split between good and bad is a necessary developmental step, which must be adequately established if confusional states are to be avoided (Klein, 1946, 1957). Schizophrenia is characterised by minute splitting and fragmentation of self and objects (Bion, 1956; Rosenfeld, 1952).

Symbol formation The process by which one thing can be used to stand for another without being confused with it. This underlies all representational activity, linguistic as well as pictorial, and is the basis for creativity in child and adult. In psychotic states, this capacity is interfered with so that a symbol is equated with the thing symbolised, leading to what Segal (1957) has called *symbolic equations*. Thus, a child may feel that a drawing *is* the thing it depicts, rather than a representation of it.

Transference The process first described by Freud (1905) by which emotions from the past are re-experienced in the present in relation to the therapist. In Kleinian theory, the term includes the projection onto the therapist of internal objects.

References

Abraham, K. (1907) 'The experiencing of sexual traumas as a form of sexual activity', in *Selected Papers of Karl Abraham*. No. 13 of the International Psycho-Analytical Library, London: Hogarth, 7th impression (1968).
—— (1924) 'A short study of the development of the libido, viewed in the light of mental disorders', in *Selected Papers on Psycho-Analysis*, 418-501, London: Hogarth (1927); repr. (1979).
Altamirano, N. (1988) 'El fantasma', *Revista de Psicoanalisis*, 45: 815-24.
Alvarez, A. (1980) 'Two regenerative situations in autism: reclamation and becoming vertebrate', in *Journal of Child Psychotherapy*, 6: 69-80.
—— (1985) 'The problem of neutrality: some reflections on the psychoanalytic attitude in the treatment of borderline and psychotic children', *Journal of Child Psychotherapy*, 11: 87-103.
—— (1991) 'Wildest dreams: aspiration, identification, and symbol-formation in depressed children', *Psychoanalytic Psychotherapy*, 5: 177-89.
—— (1992) *Live Company*, London and New York: Tavistock/Routledge.
—— (1995) 'Fantasia inconscia, pensare e camminare: alcune riflessione preliminari', in *Richard e Piggle*, 2: 190-206.
—— (1996) 'Developmental psychotherapy for autism', *Clinical Child Psychology and Psychiatry*, 1 (4).
Anzieu, D. (1985) *The Skin Ego*, New Haven/London: Yale University Press.
Athanassiou, C. (1989) 'La somnolence', in *Journal de la Psychanalyse de l'Enfant*, 6: 197-228.
Ayres, A.J. (1979) *Sensory Integration and the Child*, Los Angeles: Western Psychological Services.
Balbernie, R. (1985) 'Psychotherapy with a mentally handicapped boy', *Journal of Child Psychotherapy*, 11: 65-76.
Balint, M. (1969) 'Trauma and object relationship', *International Journal of Psycho-Analysis*, 50: 429-35.
Baron-Cohen, S. et al. (eds) (1993) *Understanding other Minds: Perspectives from Autism*, Oxford: OUP.
Bettelheim, B. (1975) *The Uses of Enchantment: The Meaning and Importance of Fairy Tales*, Harmondsworth: Penguin Books.
Bick, E. (1968) 'The experience of the skin in early object relations', *International Journal of Psycho-Analysis*, 49: 484-6. Also in *Collected Papers of Martha Harris and Esther Bick*, Strath Tay: Clunie Press (1987).

References

—— (1986) 'Further considerations on the function of the skin in early object relations', *British Journal of Psychotherapy*, 2: 292-9.

Bion, W.R. (1956) 'Development of schizophrenic thought', *International Journal of Psycho-Analysis*, 37: 344-6. Also in *Second Thoughts*, London: Heinemann (1967); repr. London: Karnac Books (1984).

—— (1955) 'Language and the schizophrenic', in Klein, M., Heimann, P. and Money-Kyrle, R.E. (eds), *New Directions in Psycho-Analysis*, London: Tavistock.

—— (1956) 'Development of schizophrenic thought', in *International Journal of Psycho-Analysis*, 37: 244-6; also in *Second Thoughts*, London: Heinemann (1967).

—— (1957) 'Differentiation of the psychotic from the non-psychotic personalities', *International Journal of Psychoanalysis*, 38: 266-75. Also in *Second Thoughts*.

—— (1959) 'Attacks on linking', in *International Journal of Psycho-Analysis*, 40: 308-15; also in *Second Thoughts*.

—— (1959) 'Attacks on linking', *International Journal of Psycho-Analysis*, 40: 308-15. Also in *Second Thoughts*.

—— (1962a) *Learning from Experience*, London: Heinemann; repr. London: Karnac Books (1984).

—— (1962b) 'A theory of thinking', *International Journal of Psycho-Analysis*, 43: 306-10. Also in *Second Thoughts*.

—— (1963) *Elements of Psycho-Analysis*, London: Heinemann.

—— (1967) *Second Thoughts: Selected Papers on Psycho-Analysis*, London: Heinemann; repr. London: Karnac (1984).

—— (1991) *A Memoir of the Future*, London: Karnac Books, p. 447.

Bollas, C. (1987) *The Shadow of the Object. Psychoanalysis of the Unthought Known*, London: Free Association Books.

Boston, M. and Szur, R. (eds) (1983) *Psychotherapy with Severely Deprived Children*, London: Routledge; repr. London: Karnac Books (1990).

Bower, T. (1977) *The Perceptual World of the Child*, London: Fontana Paperbacks.

Brazelton, T.B., Koslowski, B. and Main, M. (1974) 'The origins of reciprocity: the early mother-infant interaction', in Lewis, M. and Rosenblum, L.A. (eds) *The Effect of the Infant on its Caregivers*, London: Wiley Interscience.

Brenman Pick, I. (1985) 'Working through in the countertransference', *International Journal of Psycho-Analysis*, 66: 157-66; also in Spillius, E.B. (ed.) *Melanie Klein Today*, Vol. 2: *Mainly Practice*, London and New York: Tavistock/Routledge, p. 34-47.

Briggs, S. (1997) *Growth and Risk in Infancy*, London: Jessica Kingsley.

Britton, R. (1983) 'Breakdown and reconstitution of the family circle', in Boston, M. and Szur, R. (eds) *Psychotherapy with Severely Deprived Children*, London: Routledge.

—— (1989) 'The missing link: parental sexuality in the Oedipus complex', in Steiner, J. (ed.) *The Oedipus Complex Today: Clinical Implications*, London: Karnac.

—— (1995) 'Second thoughts on the third position', paper read at a Clinic Scientific Meeting, Tavistock Clinic, London, October, 1995.

Bruner, J.S. and Sherwood, V. (1976) 'Peekaboo and the learning of rule structures', in Bruner, J.S. et al. (eds) *Play*, Harmondsworth: Penguin.

Bullinger, A. and Robert-Tissost, C. 'Contribution de la psychologie du développement à la compréhension de quelques aspects de l'autisme précoce', in *Colloque ARAPI.*, 12.

Caillot, J.P. and Derchef, G. (1982) *Thérapie Familiale Psychanalytique et Paradoxicalité*, Paris: Clancier-Guenaud.

—— (1989) *Psychanalyse du Couple et de la Famille*, Paris: APSYG [Association for Group Analysis].

Castets, B., Lefort, R. and Reyns, M. (1962) 'Note critique sur la notion d'arriération mentale et quelques notions connexes', in *Evolution Psychiatrique*, 27 (3), cited in Mannoni, M. (1973).

Cecchi, V. (1990) 'The analysis of a little girl with an autistic syndrome', *International Journal of Psycho-Analysis*, 71: 403-10.

Cohen, M. (1995) 'Premature twins on a neo-natal intensive care unit', *Journal of Child Psychotherapy*, 21: 253-80.

Cornwell, J. (1983) 'Crisis and survival in infancy', *Journal of Child Psychotherapy*, 9: 25-31.

Descamps, M.A. (1988) 'L'irrationnel et le merveilleux', *Etudes Psychothérapeutiques*, 19: 179-84.

Druon, C. and Bollas, C. (1988) 'Réflexions sur l'approche psychologique des problèmes dans un service de réanimation néonatale', paper presented at the London-Rome conference, Tavistock Clinic, London, August 1988.

Dubinsky, A. (1986) 'The sado-masochistic phantasies of two adolescent boys suffering from congenital physical illness', *Journal of Child Psychotherapy*, 12: 1.

Erikson, E. (1950) *Childhood and Society*, revised version, New York: Norton & Co.; repr. Penguin Books (1965).

Ferenczi, S. (1933) 'Confusion of tongues between adults and the child', in *Final Contributions to the Problems and Methods of Psycho-Analysis*. No. 48 of the International Psycho-Analytical Library, London: Hogarth (1955); repr. New York: Brunner/Mazel (1980).

Fonagy, P. (1996) 'Attachment and theory of mind: overlapping constructs', lecture to the Association of Child Psychology and Psychiatry, London.

Fordham, M. (1976) *The Self and Autism*, London: Heinemann.

Fox, N.A., Calkins, S.D. and Bell, M.A. (1994) 'Neural plasticity and development in the first two years of life: evidence from cognitive and socioemotional domains of research', in *Development and Psychopathology* 6: 677-96.

Fraiberg, S.H., Adelson, E. and Shapiro, V. (1975) 'Ghosts in the nursery: a psychoanalytic approach to the problem of impaired mother-infant relationships', *Journal of American Academy of Child Psychiatry*, 14: 387-422.

Freud, S. (1895) 'Project for a scientific psychology', *S.E.*, 1: 295-341.

—— (1905) 'Fragment of an analysis of a case of hysteria', *S.E.*, 7: 7-122.

References

—— (1911) 'Psycho-analytic notes on an autobiographical account of a case of paranoia (Dementia Paranoides)', *S.E.*, 12: 9-82.
—— (1911) 'Formulations regarding the two principles of mental functioning', *S.E.*, 12: 218-26.
—— (1918) 'From the history of an infantile neurosis', *S.E.*, 17: 7-122.
—— (1919) 'The uncanny', *S.E.*, 17: 217-52.
—— (1926) 'Inhibitions, symptoms and anxiety', *S.E.*, 20: 87-172.
—— (1927) 'Fetishism', *S.E.*, 21: 152-7.
Frith, U. (1989) *Autism: Explaining the Enigma*, Oxford: Blackwell.
Gaddini, R. and Gaddini, E. (1959) 'Rumination in infancy', in: Jessner, L. and Pavenstedt, E. (eds), *Dynamic Psychopathology in Childhood*, New York: Grune & Stratton.
Garland, C. (1991) 'External disasters and the internal world: an approach to the psychotherapeutic understanding of survivors', in Holmes, J. (ed.), *Textbook of Psychotherapy in Psychiatric Practice*, London: Churchill Livingstone.
Green, A. (1976) 'Le concept de limite', in *La Folie Privée*, Paris: Gallimard (1990) p. 103-140.
—— (1982) 'La double limite', in *La Folie Privée*, Paris: Gallimard (1990) 293-316.
—— (1990) *La Folie Privée*, Paris: Gallimard.
Grigsby, J. and Schneiders, J.L. (1991) 'Neuroscience, modularity and personality theory: conceptual foundations of a model of complex human functioning', *Psychiatry*, 54: 21-37.
Grotstein, J.S. (1981) 'Primal splitting: the background object of primary identification and other self-objects', in *Splitting and Projective Identification*, New York: Aronson p. 77-89.
—— (1990) 'Néant, non-sens, chaos et le trou noir', paper presented at the Societé Psychanalytique de Paris, 8 June.
Haag, G. (1985) 'La mère et le bébé dans les deux moitiés du corps', *Neuropsychiatrie de l'enfance*, 33: 107-14.
—— (1986) 'Hypothèses sur la structure rhythmique du premier contenant', *Gruppo*, 2: 45-53.
—— (1988) 'Reflections on body ego development through psychotherapeutic work with an infant', in *Extending Horizons*, R. Szur and S. Miller (eds), London: Karnac Books, p. 135-150.
—— (1990a) 'Le dessin préfiguratif de l'enfant, quel niveau de réprésentation?', *Journal de la Psychanalyse de l'Enfant*, 8: 91-129.
—— (1990b) 'Les troubles de l'image du corps dans la psychose infantile', *Thérapie Psychomotrice*, 86: 50-65.
—— (1991) 'Nature de quelques identifications dans l'image du corps (hypothèses)', *Journal de la psychanalyse de l'enfant*, 9: 73–92.
—— (1991a) 'Nature de quelques identifications dans l'image du corps', in *J. Psychanalyse de l'Enfant*, 10: 73–92.
—— (1991b) 'De la sensorialité aux ébauches de pensée chez les enfants autistes', *Revue Internationale de Psychopathologie*, 3: 51–63.

279

Heinmann, P. (1950) 'On counter-transference', *International Journal of Psycho-Analysis*, 31: 81-4, 1950.

Henry, G. (1974) 'Doubly deprived', in *Journal of Child Psychotherapy*, vol. 3, no. 4. Also in Daws, D. and Boston, M. (eds), *The Child Psychotherapist and Problems of Young People*, London: Wildwood House (1981).

Hobson, P.R. (1993) *Autism and the Development of Mind*, Hove: Laurence Erlbaum.

Hocking, B. (1990) *Little Boy Lost*, London: Bloomsbury.

Hopper, E. (1991) 'Encapsulation as a defence against the fear of annihilation', *International Journal of Psycho-Analysis*, 72: 607.

Houzel, D. (1988) 'Autisme et conflit esthétique', *Journal de la Psychanalyse de l'Enfant*, 5: 98-116.

Hoxter, S. (1975) 'The residual autistic condition and its effect upon learning – Piffie', in Meltzer, D., Bremner, J., Hoxter, H., Weddell, D. and Wittenberg, W., *Explorations in Autism*, Strath Tay: Clunie Press.

—— (1983) 'Some feelings aroused in working with severely deprived children', in Boston, M. and Szur, R. (eds), *Psychotherapy With Severely Deprived Children*, London: Routledge & Kegan Paul.

Isaacs, S. (1948) 'The nature and function of phantasy', *International Journal of Psycho-Analyisis*, 29: 73-97; also in Klein, M., Heimann, P., Isaacs, S. and Riviere, J. (eds) *Developments in Psycho-Analysis*, London: Hogarth (1952) p. 67-131.

Joseph, B. (1975) 'The patient who is difficult to reach', in E. Bott Spillius and M. Feldman (eds), *Psychic Equilibrium and Psychic Change: Selected Papers of Betty Joseph*, London (1989), p. 75-87.

—— (1982) 'Addiction to near-death', *Ibid.*, London and New York: Tavistock Routledge.

—— (1984) 'Projective identification: some clinical aspects', *Ibid.*, London and New York.

Kilchenstein, M.W. and Schuerholz, L. (1995) 'Autistic defenses and the impairment of cognitive development', in *Bulletin of the Menninger Clinic*, 59: 442-59.

Klauber, T. (1997) Chapter on work with parents, in Reid, S. and Alvarez, A. (eds), *Autism and Personality*, London: Routledge, in press.

Klein, M. (1923) 'The role of the school in the libidinal development of the child', in *The Writings of Melanie Klein*, Vol. I, London: Hogarth (1975).

—— (1928) 'Early stages of the oedipus complex', *Ibid.*

—— (1930) 'The importance of symbol-formation in the development of the ego', *Ibid.*

—— (1931) 'A contribution to the theory of intellectual inhibition', *Ibid.*

—— (1932) *The Psycho-Analysis of Children*, London: Hogarth; revised translation repr. in *The Writings of Melanie Klein*, Vol. II, London: Hogarth (1975).

—— (1935) 'A contribution to the psychogenesis of manic depressive states', in *The Writings of Melanie Klein*, Vol I, London: Hogarth (1975).

—— (1937) 'Love, guilt and reparation', *Ibid.*

—— (1940) 'Mourning and its relation to manic depressive states', *Ibid.*

—— (1945) 'The oedipus complex in the light of early anxieties', *Ibid.*

References

—— (1946) 'Notes on some schizoid mechanisms', in *The Writings of Melanie Klein*, Vol. III, London: Hogarth (1975).

—— (1952) 'Some theoretical conclusions regarding the emotional life of the infant', *Ibid.*

—— (1952) 'On observing the behaviour of young infants', *Ibid.*

—— (1955) 'On identification', *Ibid.*

—— (1957) *Envy and Gratitude*, London: Tavistock Publications. Also in *The Writings of Melanie Klein*, Vol. III, London: Hogarth (1975).

—— (1958) 'On the development of mental functioning', *Ibid.*

—— (1961) *Narrative of a Child Analysis*, London: Hogarth; repr. in *The Writings of Melanie Klein*, Vol. IV, London: Hogarth (1975).

Klein, S. (1965) 'Notes on a case of ulcerative colitis', *International Journal of Psycho-Analysis*, 46: 342-51.

—— (1974) 'Transference and defence in manic states', *International Journal of Psycho-Analysis*, 55: 261-8.

—— (1980) 'Autistic phenomena in neurotic patients', *International Journal of Psycho-Analysis*, 61: 395-401; repr. in Grotstein, J.S. (ed.), *Do I Dare Disturb the Universe?*, Beverly Hills: Caesura Press (1981).

Laplanche, J. and Pontalis, J.B. (1973) *The Language of Psycho-Analysis*, No. 94 of the International Psycho-Analytical Library, London: Hogarth.

Lewis, E. and Page, A. (1978) 'Failure to mourn a stillbirth: an overlooked catastrophe', *British Journal of Medical Psychology*, 51: 237-41.

Lussier, A. (1960) 'The analysis of a boy with a congenital deformity', *Psycho-analytic Study of the Child*, 15.

—— (1980) 'The physical handicap and the body ego', *International Journal of Psycho-Analysis*, 61: 179-85.

Mahler, M. and Furer, M. (1968) *On Human Symbiosis and the Vicissitudes of Individuation*, New York: International Universities Press.

Mannoni, M. (1973) *The Retarded Child and the Mother*, London: Tavistock.

McDougall, J. and Lebovici, S. (1969) *Dialogue with Sammy*, London: Hogarth,; repr. London: Free Association Books (1989).

—— (1989) *Theatres of the Body*, London: Free Association Books.

Meltzer, D. (1966) 'Anal masturbation and projective identification', *International Journal of Psychoanalysis*, 47: 335-42.

—— (1967) *The Psycho-Analytical Process*, Strath Tay: Clunie Press.

—— (1973) *Sexual States of Mind*, Strath Tay: Clunie Press.

—— (1975) 'The psychology of autistic states and of post-autistic mentality', in Meltzer, D., Bremner, J., Hoxter, S., Weddell, D. and Wittenberg, I., *Explorations in Autism*, Strath Tay: Clunie Press.

—— (1980) 'About imagination', *Quaderni di Psicoterapia Infantile*, 3: 134-44.

—— (1986) 'Discussion of Esther Bick's paper "Further considerations on the function of the skin in early object relations"', *British Journal of Psychotherapy*, 2: 300-1.

—— (1986) *Studies in Extended Metapsychology*, Strath Tay: Clunie Press.

—— (1988a) 'About projective identification', in *Bull. GERPEN*, (Group for Study and Research on the Psychoanalytic Treatment of Children and Infants) 13, 61.

—— (1988b) 'The aesthetic conflict', in *The Apprehension of Beauty*, Strath Tay: Clunie Press.

—— (1992) *The Claustrum, An Investigation of Claustrophic Phenomena*, Strath Tay: Clunie Press.

Meltzer, D., Bremner, J., Hoxter, S., Weddell, D. and Wittenberg, I. (1975) *Explorations in Autism*, Strath Tay: Clunie Press.

Meltzer, D. and Williams, M.H. (1988) *The Apprehension of Beauty*, Strath Tay: Clunie Press.

Money-Kyrle, R.E. (1968) 'Cognitive development', *International Journal of Psychoanalysis*, 49. Reprinted in *The Collected Papers of Roger Money-Kyrle*, Strath Tay: Clunie Press (1978).

—— (1971) 'The aim of psycho-analysis', *International Journal of Psychoanalysis*, 52. Reprinted in *The Collected Papers of Roger Money-Kyrle*, Strath Tay: Clunie Press (1978).

Murray, L. (1992) 'The impact of maternal depression on infant development', in *Journal of Child Psychology and Psychiatry*, 33: 543-61.

Murray, L. and Trevarthen, C. (1985) 'Emotional regulation of interactions between two-month-olds and their mothers', in Field, T. and Fox, N. (eds), *Social Perception in Infants*, Norwood: N.J.: Ablex.

Negri, R. (1994) *The Newborn in the Intensive Care Unit*, London: Karnac Books with the Clunie Press.

Ogden, T.H. (1989) *The Primitive Edge of Experience*, Northvale: Jason Aronson; repr. London: Karnac Books (1992).

O'Shaughnessy, E. (1964) 'The absent object', *Journal of Child Psychotherapy*, vol. 1. no. 2.

Papousek, M. (1992) 'Early ontogeny of vocal communication in parent-infant interactions', in Papousek, H., Jürgens, U. and Papousek, M. (eds), *Nonverbal Vocal Communication: Comparative and Developmental Approaches*, Cambridge University Press.

Pasche, F. (1975) 'Réalité psychique et réalité matérielle', in *Le Sens de la Psychanalyse*, Paris: Presses Universitaires de France, (1988) p. 43-54.

Paul, K. (1973) 'The development of containment in a three-to-five-year-old boy', *Journal of Child Psychotherapy*, 3: 31-44.

Perry, B.D., Pollard, R.A., Blakley, T.L., Baker, W.L. and Vigilante, D. (1995) 'Childhood trauma, the neurobiology of adaptation and "use-dependent" development of the brain: how "states" become "traits"', *Infant Mental Health Journal*, 16: 271-91.

Piontelli, A. (1989) 'A study on twins before and after birth', *International Review of Psycho-Analysis*, 16: 413-26.

—— (1992) *From Fetus to Child*, London and New York: Tavistock/Routledge.

Pragier, S. and Pragier, G. (1990) 'Un siècle après l'Esquisse: questions pour aujourd'hui', in *Revue Française de Psychanalyse*, 56: 1503-29.

Pynoos, R.S. (1996) 'The transgenerational repercussions of traumatic expectations', paper read to the Sixth International Psycho-Analytic Association Conference on Psycho-Analytic Research, University College London, March.

References

Racamier, P.C. (1978) 'Les paradoxes des schizophrènes', *Revue Française de Psychanalyse*, 42: 877-969.
— (1980) *Les Schizophrènes*, Paris: Payot.
— (1989) *Antoedipe et ses Destins*, Paris: Apsygée [Association for Group Psychoanalysis] Editions.
Reid, S. (1989) 'Subgroups of autism', unpublished paper.
— (1990) 'The importance of beauty in the psycho-analytic experience', *Journal of Child Psychotherapy*, 16: 29-52.
— (1997) Chapter in Reid, S. and Alvarez, A. (eds), *Autism and Personality*, London: Routledge, in press.
Rey, J.H. (1979) 'Schizoid phenomena in the borderline', in J. Le Boit and A. Capponi (eds), *Advances in the Psychotherapy of the Borderline Patient*, New York: Jason Aronson. Also in E.B. Spillius (ed.), *Melanie Klein Today, Developments and Practice*, Vol. I: *Mainly Theory*, London: Routledge (1988).
— (1986) 'The schizoid mode of being and the space-time continuum (beyond metaphor)', in *Universals of Psychoanalysis in the Treatment of Psychotic and Borderline States*, J. Magagna (ed.), London: Free Association Books.
Rhode, M. (1994) 'Autistic breathing', *Journal of Child Psychotherapy*, 20: 25-41.
Rivière, J. (1936) 'Hate, greed and aggression', in Klein, M. and Rivière, J. (eds) *Love, Hate and Reparation*, London: Hogarth; repr. New York: Norton (1964).
Robertson, J. (1965) 'Mother-infant interaction from birth to twelve months: two case studies', in Foss, B.M. (ed.), *Determinants of Infant Behaviour*, Vol. III, London: Tavistock Institute of Human Relations.
Rosenfeld, H. (1947) 'Analysis of a schizophrenic state with depersonalization', in *Psychotic States*, London: Hogarth (1965).
— (1949) 'Remarks on the relation of male homosexuality to paranoia, paranoid anxiety and narcissism', *Ibid.*
— (1950) 'Notes on the psychopathology of confusional states in chronic schizophrenias', *Ibid.*
— (1952) 'Notes on the psycho-analysis of the super-ego conflict in an acute schizophrenic patient', *Ibid.*
— (1954) 'Considerations regarding the psycho-analytic approach to acute and chronic schizophrenia', *Ibid.*
— (1964) 'The psychopathology of hypochondriasis', *Ibid.*
— (1964) 'On the psychopathology of narcissism', *Ibid.*
— (1971) 'A clinical approach to the psychoanalytic theory of the life and death instincts: an investigation into the aggressive aspects of narcissism', in *International Journal of Psycho-Analysis*, 52: 169-78. Also in E. Bott Spillius (ed.), *Melanie Klein Today*, Vol. I: *Mainly Theory*, London and New York: Routledge (1988).
— (1987) *Impasse and Interpretation*, London and New York: Tavistock Publications.
— (1987) 'Projective identification and the psychotic transference in schizo-

phrenia', in *Impasse and Interpretation*, London and New York: Tavistock Publications.

Searles, H. (1959) 'The effort to drive the other person crazy', in *Collected Papers on Schizophrenia and Related Subjects*, New York: International Universities Press.

Segal, H. (1950) 'Some aspects of the analysis of a schizophrenic', *International Journal of Psycho-Analysis*, 31: 268-78. Also in *The Work of Hanna Segal*, London and New York: Jason Aronson (1981).

—— (1956) 'Depression in the schizophrenic', in *International Journal of Psycho-Analysis*, 37: 339-43. Also in *The Work of Hanna Segal*.

—— (1957) 'Notes on symbol formation', in *International Journal of Psycho-Analysis*, 38: 391-7. Also in Spillius, E.B. (ed.), *Melanie Klein Today*, Vol. 1: *Mainly Theory*, London: Routledge (1988).

—— (1979) 'Postscript 1979: notes on symbol formation', in *The Work of Hanna Segal*, London and New York: Jason Aronson (1981) .

—— (1981) *The Work of Hanna Segal: A Kleinian Approach to Clinical Practice*, London and New York: Jason Aronson.

Sellars, D. (1994) *Broken Links: A Study of Physical Disability, Communication and Emotional Development*, unpublished M.A. Thesis in Psychoanalytic Observational Studies, The University of East London and the Tavistock Clinic.

Sinason, V. (1986) 'Secondary mental handicap and its relationship to trauma', *Psychoanalytic Psychotherapy*, 2: 131-54.

—— (1990) 'Passionate lethal attachments', *British Journal of Psychotherapy*, 7: 66-76.

—— (1991) 'Interpretations that feel horrible to make', *Journal of Child Psychotherapy*, 17: 11-24.

—— (1992) *Mental Handicap and the Human Condition*, London: Free Association Books.

Spensley, S. (1985) 'Cognitive deficit, mindlessness and psychotic depression', *Journal of Child Psychotherapy*, 11: 35-50.

—— (1985) 'Mentally ill or mentally handicapped? A longitudinal study of severe learning difficulty', *Psychoanalytical Psychotherapy*, 1: 55-70.

—— (1995) *Frances Tustin*, London and New York: Routledge.

Spillius, E.B. (ed.) (1988) *Melanie Klein Today*, Vol. I: *Mainly Theory*, London and New York: Routledge.

Steiner, J. (1979) 'The border between the paranoid-schizoid and the depressive positions in the borderline patient', *British Journal of Medical Psychology*, 52: 385-91.

—— (1982) 'Perverse relationships between parts of the self: a clinical illustration', *International Journal of Psycho-Analysis*, 63: 241-51.

—— (1987) 'The interplay between pathological organizations and the paranoid-schizoid and depressive positions', in *International Journal of Psycho-Analysis*, 68: 69-80. Also in Spillius, E.B. (ed.) *Melanie Klein Today*, Vol. I: *Mainly Theory*.

—— (1992) 'Patient-centred and analyst-centred interpretation: technical implications of "containment" and "countertransference"', paper presented at a

References

conference on The Psychoanalytic Approach to Borderline States, University College London, January 1992.
— (1993) *Psychic Retreats*, London: Routledge.
Stern, D.N. (1985) *The Interpersonal World of the Infant*, New York: Basic Books.
Summit, R.C. (1983) 'The child sexual abuse accomodation syndrome', *Child Abuse & Neglect*, 7.
Symington, N. (1981) 'The psychotherapy of a subnormal patient', *British Journal of Medical Psychology*, 5: 187-99.
Taylor, G. (1987) *Psychosomatic Medicine and Contemporary Psycho-Analysis*, New York: International Universities Press.
Tischler, S. (1979) 'Being with a psychotic child: a psychoanalytical approach to the problems of parents of psychotic children', *International Journal of Psycho-Analysis*, 60: 29-38.
Trevarthen, C. (1977) 'Descriptive analyses of infant communicative behaviour', in Schaffer, R.H. (ed.), *Studies in Mother-Infant Interaction*, London: Academic Press.
Trevarthen, C. and Marwick, H. (1986) 'Signs of motivation for speech in infants, and the nature of a mother's support for development of language', in Lindblom, B. and Zetterstrom, R. (eds), *Precursors of Early Speech*, Basingstoke (Hants): Macmillan.
Tustin, F. (1966) 'A significant element in the development of autism', *Journal of Child Psychology and Psychiatry*, 7: 53-67.
— (1972) *Autism and Childhood Psychosis*, London: Hogarth; repr. London: Karnac Books (1995).
— (1980) 'Autistic objects', *International Review of Psycho-Analysis*, 7: 27-39. Also in *Autistic States in Children*, London: Routledge (1981); revised edition (1992).
— (1980) 'Psychological birth and psychological catastrophe', in Tustin, (1981). Also in Grotstein, J.S. (ed.), *Do I Dare Disturb the Universe?*, Beverley Hills: Caesura Press (1981).
— (1986) *Autistic Barriers in Neurotic Patients*, London, Karnac.
— (1981) *Autistic States in Children*, London and Boston: Routledge & Kegan Paul; revised edition (1992).
— (1990) *The Protective Shell in Children and Adults*, London: Karnac.
— (1994) 'Autistic children who are assessed as not brain-damaged', *Journal of Child Psychotherapy*, 20: 103-31.
Urwin, C. (1993) 'Autistic Processes: theories of mind and communication by-path in autistic, borderline and non-communicating children', audiocassette, recorded at Association of Child Psychotherapists Annual Conference, London Business School, 1993.
Williams, D. (1992) *Nobody Nowhere*, London: Doubleday.
Williams, G. (1990) 'E come dover ricostruire Dresda con il secchiello e la paletta, riflessioni sulla riparazione autentica', in *Prospettive Psicoanalitiche nel Lavoro Istituzionale*, 8.
— (1992) 'Reversal of the container-contained relationship', in *Internal Landscapes and Foreign Bodies*, London: Duckworth (1997).

—— (1997) 'On different introjective processes and the hypothesis of an omega function', *Ibid.*

—— (1997) 'Foreign bodies', *Ibid.*

Winnicott, D.W. (1948) 'Paediatrics and psychiatry', in *Collected Papers: Through Paediatrics to Psychoanalysis*, London: Tavistock (1958); repr. London: Karnac Books (1992).

—— (1947) 'Hate in the countertransference', *Ibid.*

—— (1949) 'Birth memories, birth trauma and anxiety', *Ibid.*

—— (1951) 'Transitional objects and transitional phenomena', *Ibid.*

—— (1956) 'Primary Maternal Preoccupation', *Ibid.*

—— (1960) 'Ego distortion in terms of the true and false self ', in *The Maturational Process and the Facilitating Environment*, London: Hogarth, (1965); repr. London: Karnac Books (1990).

—— (1988) *Babies and their Mothers*, London: Free Association Books.

Wittenberg, I. (1975) 'Primal depression in autism – John', in Meltzer, D.R., Bremner, J., Hoxter, S., Weddell, D. and Wittenberg, I. *Explorations in Autism*, Strath Tay: Clunie Press.

Wright, K. (1991) *Vision and Separation Between Mother and Baby*, London: Free Association Books.

Index